DEMANDING DEMOCRACY

MARC STEARS

Demanding Democracy

American Radicals in Search of a New Politics

PRINCETON UNIVERSITY PRESS

Princeton and Oxford

Copyright © 2010 by Princeton University Press

Published by Princeton University Press, 41 William Street, Princeton, New Jersey 08540

In the United Kingdom: Princeton University Press, 6 Oxford Street, Woodstock, Oxfordshire OX20 1TW

Library of Congress Cataloging-in-Publication Data

Stears, Marc.
    Demanding democracy: American radicals in search of a new politics/ Marc Stears.
        p. cm.
    Includes bibliographical references and index.
    ISBN 978-0-691-13340-9 (hardcover : alk. paper)   1. Democracy—United States.   2. Radicalism—United States.   3. Political movements—United States.   4. Political activists—United States.   5. United States—Social conditions.   6. United States—Politics and government.   I. Title.
    JK1726.S74 2010
    320.530973—dc22   2009030292

British Library Cataloging-in-Publication Data is available

This book has been composed in Minion

Printed on acid-free paper. ∞

press.princeton.edu

Printed in the United States of America

10 9 8 7 6 5 4 3 2 1

The prairie-grass dividing—its special odor breathing,

I demand of it the spiritual corresponding,

Demand the most copious and close companionship of men,

Demand the blades to rise of words, acts, beings,

Those of the open atmosphere, coarse, sunlit, fresh, nutritious,

Those that go their own gait, erect, stepping with freedom and command—

    leading, not following,

Those with a never-quell'd audacity—

    those with sweet and lusty flesh, clear of taint,

Those that look carelessly in the faces of Presidents and Governors, as to say,

    Who are you?

Those of earth-born passion, simple, never-constrain'd, never obedient,

Those of inland America.

    —Walt Whitman

CONTENTS

In addition to these acts of kindness, many friends and colleagues have helped directly with the text. Terence Ball, Eldon Eisenach, Sudhir Hazareesingh, Mark Hulliung, Mathew Humphrey, Desmond King, and Adam Sandell all read the first draft in its entirety; Desmond and Adam even read bits of it twice! The trenchant criticisms and thoughtful recommendations I received from them all have immeasurably improved the final version. Many others also provided insights on individual chapters and on the book's central ideas. I am delighted to acknowledge the help of Andrew Abbott, Nancy Bermeo, Nigel Bowles, Peter Breiner, Jayant Chavda, Michael Freeden, Gary Gerstle, Eileen Gillooly, Michael Guppy, Cori Hayden, Liz Irwin, Ben Jackson, Annie Kingston, David Leopold, Robert Lieberman, Jane Mansbridge, Robert Mason, David Miller, Avia Pasternak, Dan Polin, Fiona Ross, Andrew Sabl, Quentin Skinner, Adam Swift, John A. Thompson, Mark Wickham-Jones, Stuart White, and Hughie Wong. They have all helped far more than they know.

In addition to these rich and rewarding conversations, perhaps the greatest pleasure of writing and research is the possibility it brings to work in some of the world's greatest libraries. I have had immense satisfaction in seeking knowledge in the British Library of Political and Economic Science, the Butler Library of Columbia University, the National Library of Scotland, the State Historical Society of Wisconsin, the Tamiment Institute at New York University, the Library of the University of Western Australia, and, almost as good as any library, the Brattle Bookstore in Boston, where I discovered texts that would otherwise have remained completely unknown to me.

Most of all, though, I thank Lizzy Pellicano. Lizzy is a democrat in exactly Walt Whitman's sense. She combines a restless, impatient, and independent spirit—"never constrained"—with generosity, empathy, and a passion for justice: truly "close companionship." Living and working with her has enabled me to see the world anew.

INTRODUCTION

The United States is abuzz with talk of a new democracy. For the first time for many decades, political campaigners have captured the nation's imagination by ardently condemning its prevailing order. They have denounced professional politicians for their hypocrisy, excessive partisanship, and cut-throat adversarialism; they have derided special interest groups for their corrupting influences; and they have demanded that citizens be provided more direct access to key decision-making processes. The same campaigners have also devised a host of new institutional arrangements to assist in this transformation. They have designed consultative committees and citizens' juries to encourage citizen participation in policymaking; they have devised websites to facilitate dynamic political conversation across cyberspace; and they have sought to restore municipal squares and urban parks to the safe havens for public political discussion that they once were said to be.[1] Even presidential politics appears to have been swept up in the hurly-burly of these new democratic demands. In January 2007, as Barack Obama announced his candidacy, he insisted that what the United States needed was not a new set of policy programs but a wholly "new kind of politics." It is time for American democracy to be renewed, Obama implored, time to ensure that its politics become "less bitter and partisan," less "gummed up by money and influence," and more targeted on finding commonly acceptable solutions to the immeasurable problems that confront the United States today.[2]

---

[1] For examples and overviews, see Benjamin Barber, *A Passion for Democracy: American Essays* (Princeton: Princeton University Press, 2001); Archon Fung, *Empowered Participation: Reinventing Urban Democracy* (Princeton: Princeton University Press, 2006); Archon Fung and Erik Olin Wright, eds., *Deepening Democracy: Institutional Innovations in Empowered Participatory Governance* (London: Verso, 2003); John Gastil and Peter Levine, eds., *The Deliberative Democracy Handbook: Strategies for Effective Civic Engagement in the Twenty-First Century* (San Francisco: Jossey-Bass, 2005); Arthur Lupia and John Matsusaka, "Direct Democracy: New Approaches to Old Questions," *Annual Review of Political Science* 7 (2004): 463–82; and Cass R. Sunstein, *Republic.com* (Princeton: Princeton University Press, 2001).

[2] See the editorial "Obama Jumps Into Presidential Fray," *Washington Post*, January 17, 2007, A1. See, too, Barack Obama, *The Audacity of Hope: Thoughts on Reclaiming the American Dream* (New York: Crown, 2006).

Many political philosophers, both inside and outside the United States, have been similarly swept along by this call for a "new kind of politics." One widely cited group of theorists—the deliberative democrats—even has a serious claim to have provided the intellectual inspiration for this movement for democratic renewal. Since the early 1990s, Bruce Ackerman, James Bohman, Joshua Cohen, John Dryzek, James Fishkin, Archon Fung, Amy Gutmann, Cass Sunstein, and Dennis Thompson, amongst others, have emphasized the need for wide-scale reform in American democratic life. They have insisted, in particular, that politicians and citizens should amend their political conduct and learn to approach politics in a spirit that is more inclusive and less antagonistic than at present, more focused on common advantage and less on sectional interest.[3] It is no surprise, therefore, that these thinkers see great opportunities in the current trend toward reform, emphasizing in particular the possibilities that it provides for rejecting the excessive partisanship of the politics of the 1980s and 1990s and of engendering a deeper and wider commitment to deliberative civic virtue amongst the American public as a whole.

The ideals and practices of deliberative democracy have not been welcomed by everyone, however. In recent years a second group of equally well-regarded, if rather more intellectually disparate political theorists—including William Connolly, John Dunn, William Galston, Raymond Geuss, Chantal Mouffe, David Runciman, Ian Shapiro, Michael Walzer, and Sheldon Wolin—has rejected both the philosophical principles and the political proposals that underpin this search for "a new kind of politics."[4]

---

[3] For introductions, see Bruce Ackerman and James Fishkin, *Deliberation Day* (New Haven: Yale University Press, 2004); Seyla Benhabib, ed., *Democracy and Difference: Contesting the Boundaries of the Political* (Princeton: Princeton University Press, 1996); James Bohman and William Rehg, eds., *Deliberative Democracy: Essays on Reason and Politics* (Cambridge, Mass.: The MIT Press, 1997); John Dryzek, *Deliberative Democracy and Beyond: Liberals, Critics, Contestations* (Oxford: Oxford University Press, 2000); Amy Gutmann and Dennis Thompson, *Democracy and Disagreement* (Cambridge, Mass.: Harvard University Press, 1996), and Amy Gutmann and Dennis Thompson, *Why Deliberative Democracy?* (Princeton: Princeton University Press, 2004); James Fishkin, *Democracy and Deliberation: New Directions for Democratic Reform* (New Haven: Yale University Press, 1991); Stephen Macedo, ed., *Deliberative Politics: Essays on* Democracy and Disagreement (New York: Oxford University Press, 1999); Jane Mansbridge, ed., *Beyond Self-Interest* (Chicago: University of Chicago Press, 1990); and Cass Sunstein, *The Partial Constitution* (Cambridge, Mass.: Harvard University Press, 1994). For commentary and background influences, see Simone Chambers, "Deliberative Democratic Theory," *Annual Review of Political Science* 6 (2003): 307–26; Jürgen Habermas, *Communication and the Evolution of Society* (Boston: Beacon, 1979); and John Thompson and David Held, eds., *Habermas: Critical Debates* (Cambridge, Mass.: The MIT Press, 1982).

[4] For diverse introductions, see John Dunn, *The Cunning of Unreason: Making Sense of Politics* (London: HarperCollins, 2000); Raymond Geuss, *Philosophy and Real Politics* (Princeton: Princeton University Press, 2008); Chantal Mouffe, *The Return of the Political* (London: Verso, 1993); Mark Philp, *Political Conduct* (Cambridge, Mass.: Harvard University Press, 2007); Ian Shapiro, *The State of Democratic Theory* (Princeton: Princeton University Press, 2003); David Runciman, *Political Hypocrisy: The Mask of Power, From Hobbes to Orwell and Beyond* (Princeton: Princeton

Known here as "democratic realists," these thinkers are divided in many ways but they nonetheless share an insistence that the theory of deliberative democracy is naively optimistic as to the possibilities of democratic politics in a country like the United States. "[P]olitical philosophy must be realist," Raymond Geuss has summarized, meaning that it should "be concerned in the first instance not with how people ought ideally to act"— as deliberative democrats tend to be—"but rather with the way the social, economic, political etc., institutions actually operate at some given time, and what really does move human beings to act in given circumstances."[5] When democratic politics is approached this way, the realists insist, it becomes clear that its processes must always be at least partially shaped by the manipulative strategies, devious practices, and exclusionary tactics that deliberative democrats and their fellow travellers strive to replace. Realists contend that it is only unhelpful queasiness, delusional hypocrisy, or even idle utopianism that prevents aspirational reformers from appreciating this and recognizing that the search for a "new kind of politics" will invariably lead to disappointment. More worrying still, the political consequences of such blindness could well be disastrous. When efforts at reform fail, the realists recall, they often provoke political discontents and social dislocations that far exceed those that preceded them.[6]

The intense controversy between these two groups has captivated academic attention in the last few years and it has done so in a way that very few other debates have been able to match. Yet despite this excitement, there is little new about arguments concerning a "new kind of politics" in American political thought. Controversies about both the desirability and possibility of democratic reform have been a constant in the history of America. From the very earliest years of the republic, federalists and anti-federalists, liberals and republicans, Whigs and Democrats have disputed the meaning and implications of "democracy."[7] The twentieth century was even more fecund in this regard. Throughout that turbulent age, reform

---

University Press, 2008); Michael Walzer, *Politics and Passion: Toward a More Egalitarian Liberalism* (New Haven: Yale University Press, 2004); and Sheldon Wolin, *Democracy Inc.: Managed Democracy and the Specter of Inverted Totalitarianism* (Princeton: Princeton University Press, 2008).

[5] Geuss, *Philosophy and Real Politics*, 9.

[6] See the discussions in William E. Connolly, *Pluralism* (Durham, N.C.: Duke University Press, 2005).

[7] See Joyce Appleby, *Liberalism and Republicanism in the Historical Imagination* (Cambridge, Mass.: Harvard University Press, 1992); Bernard Baylin, *The Ideological Origins of the American Revolution* (Cambridge, Mass.: Harvard University Press, 1967); Alexander Keyssar, *The Right to Vote: The Contested History of Democracy in the United States* (New York: Basic, 2000); and John G. A. Pocock, *The Machiavellian Moment: Florentine Political Thought and the Atlantic Political Tradition* (Princeton: Princeton University Press, 1975).

movements—including the Progressives of the 1910s, the trade unionists of the interwar years, the civil rights campaigners of the 1950s and 1960s, and the New Left of the early 1970s—demanded democratic political transformations on an unprecedented scale. There were agitations for specific reforms—direct election of U. S. senators, the expansion of the suffrage, and the restriction of the Supreme Court's right of judicial review of legislation—and there were demands for vast structural changes, including the democratization of industrial decision making, the abolition of the party system, and the dismantling of federalism. There were also deep and wide-ranging philosophical investigations of the nature of the democratic ideal as the movements sought to advance their programs to an often deeply skeptical American audience.

To many scholars, these movements are best understood simply as precursors to today's deliberative democrats. They are certainly seen as such by deliberative democrats themselves, who are frequently keen to celebrate their historical lineage by drawing affinities with one or other of these earlier movements, and especially with the movement for African American civil rights.[8] This is, however, a serious mistake. For even though there are some similarities between deliberative democracy and twentieth-century movements for democratic reform, there are also crucial differences. Most importantly, whilst the final *goals* of these movements often did include achieving a democratic order where deliberation and the pursuit of common agreement would shape our political lives, the practical political *methods* by which they sought to secure that order were strikingly different from those recommended by deliberative democrats today. Indeed, when it came to the question of how the campaign for democratic change should be conducted, these movements were far closer to today's democratic realists than they were to the deliberative democrats. Change would not come easily in the United States, they all argued, and the cause of democratic reform therefore required an insistent and not a deliberative politics. Reformers would need to employ a wide range of forms of political action—including many that might be rejected today as manipulative or even coercive—if they were to have a hope of securing their "new kind of politics" in the future.

This book recovers, re-evaluates and rehabilitates the arguments that these movements made in defense of this view. It contends that these movements collectively constituted an American radical democratic tradition in

---

[8] See, among others, Dryzek, *Deliberative Democracy and Beyond*, 51–52; Gutmann and Thompson, *Why Deliberative Democracy?*, 50; and John Rawls, *Political Liberalism* (New York: Columbia University Press, 1993), 247–50. For effective commentary on this trend, see John Medearis, "Social Movements and Deliberative Democratic Theory," *British Journal of Political Science* 35 (2004): 53–75.

the twentieth century: a tradition that was bound together by the central conviction that a new democracy in the United States could be built but only if American citizens cast aside many of the traditional behavioral constraints that restricted their political conduct and become willing relentlessly to campaign, protest, and to struggle for democratic reform. Reason, persuasion, and deliberation alone could not create a new democracy, all of the movements of the radical democratic tradition insisted. It would have to be forged through "buoyant, crusading, and militant" political action.[9]

Democratic Theory Today

The debate about democratic reform today is conducted largely in ignorance of the arguments of this American radical tradition.[10] The individual movements themselves are, of course, recalled both by historians and political scientists, but remarkably little has been written about the democratic ideals that they shared or about why they sought to secure democratic change in the way that they did. This absence is greatly to the detriment of our current debate. The radical democratic tradition contributed extensively to the development of American political institutions in the twentieth century and it also presented theoretical and practical arguments of impressive subtlety and potentially of great importance. It is, therefore, those arguments that this book seeks to restore. Before that work can begin, however, we need to be clear about the precise contours of the current debates so that we will be able both to identify their core concerns and striking silences.

The current argument over a "new kind of politics" began in American political theory in the early 1990s as a critique both of prevailing democratic practice in the United States and of liberal political philosophy's response to that practice. The last two decades of the twentieth century were a bleak period for American liberalism, shaped as they were by conservative dominance of both formal politics and national culture.[11] It was unsurprising, therefore, that many liberal and left political theorists had little time for American democracy. Such democratic life, they charged, had been

[9] John Dewey, "Democracy is Radical," *Common Sense* 6 (1937): 11.

[10] There are, of course, exceptions to this trend. The arguments of Bonnie Honig and James Tully, for example, bear a striking resemblance to aspects of the radical democratic tradition. See Bonnie Honig, *Political Theory and the Displacement of Politics* (Ithaca: Cornell University Press, 1993), and James Tully, "Political Philosophy as a Critical Activity," *Political Theory* 30 (2002): 533–55.

[11] See Eric Foner, *The Story of American Freedom* (New York: W. W. Norton 1998), 307–13, and Mary C. Brennan, *Turning Right: The Conservative Capture of the GOP* (Chapel Hill: University of North Carolina Press, 1995).

corrupted by unjust influences, especially by the power of money and special interests, and perverted by the unsavory political behavior of key actors, especially by established parties and pressure groups who always seemed more keen to satisfy themselves than to serve the common good. As a result, many liberal political philosophers turned their backs on democratic politics altogether in the 1970s and 1980s and sought solutions to the political ills they identified through the courts instead. If neither elected politicians nor the citizenry themselves could be entrusted with liberal concerns, the argument went, then the judiciary, and especially a reform-minded American Supreme Court, might at least be relied on to protect and enforce the extensive system of individual rights that liberals held so dear.[12]

It was this move that deeply worried the theorists who would become known as the "deliberative democrats." Even if democratic life is currently unsatisfactory in crucial respects, thinkers like Amy Gutmann and Dennis Thompson insisted, citizens of a nation like the United States cannot simply be expected to sit back and wait for their interests to be served by unelected judges. Rather, it is vital that such citizens be involved in the process of governing themselves. However unreliable such citizens currently appear, they must be given the opportunity to structure their own laws and to shape their own collective life-chances. Such democratic ideals have been fundamental to progressive politics since the founding of the republic, the deliberative democrats explained, and are simply too important to give up on, despite the ills that beset actually existing democratic practice.

It was for this reason, then, that deliberative democrats began to insist that Americans must aspire to a nobler, purer, and more socially just form of democracy. Reformers in the United States should thus seek to create forms of democratic life where real discussion could occur between citizens, so that they could be alerted to the inadequacies of the prevailing social and political order and could begin to transcend their different interests and identify shared goals once again. It was not judicial action that the crisis of American liberalism demanded, the deliberative democrats explained, but a full-blown democratic renewal.

This argument found an appreciative audience and deliberative democratic ideals quickly became commonplace in liberal philosophical circles. As the years have passed, the demands of deliberative democrats have

---

[12] For paradigmatic statements of this view, see Rawls, *Political Liberalism*, esp. 173–211, and Stephen Holmes, *Passions and Constraint: On the Theory of Liberal Democracy* (Chicago: University of Chicago Press, 1995), esp. 42–68. For early and perceptive criticism, see Michael Sandel, *Democracy's Discontent: American in Search of a Public Philosophy* (Cambridge, Mass.: Harvard University Press, 1996), and Jeremy Waldron, *Law and Disagreement* (Oxford: Oxford University Press, 1999).

become even more ambitious. Within the last decade, many have begun to contend that the very legitimacy of core American political institutions depends on the existence of such deliberation. This argument depends on two claims. First, citizens can only legitimately be required to obey the law if it that law can be justified to them in terms that they could reasonably be expected to accept. And, second, the only way of testing whether they could, in fact, be able to do so is for the law to emerge from a deliberative setting where every citizen aims reasonably to persuade others of the necessity or desirability of their preferred political outcomes. If laws emerge in any other setting then they may well just represent the dominating will of one group over another, and that, in turn, would render them illegitimate.[13]

Despite the undeniable attractions of this underlying ideal, deliberative democratic political philosophy has also become the subject of sustained criticism. Most notably, the group of otherwise quite dissimilar political theorists known here as democratic realists have dismissed the whole notion as an empty pipe-dream. To these thinkers, deliberative democrats simply fail to appreciate three fundamental facts about democratic politics.[14] First, they neglect to acknowledge that real and deep differences will always divide citizens from each other in societies such as the United States, rendering the search for any form of reasonable agreement essentially hopeless. Second, they overlook the fact that self-interest is one of—if not the most important—determinant of the political conduct of both citizens and professional politicians and it is extremely unlikely that it could ever be replaced. And, third, they refuse to accept that power imbalances are endemic to the practice of politics both because governing authority is always ultimately dependent on coercion and because we live in deeply unequal societies where some will always be able to call on greater resources and talents in their political interactions with others.[15] For these thinkers, the implication of these three facts is straightforward: democratic politics

[13] The connection between deliberation and legitimacy was first discussed in Barnard Manin, "On Legitimacy and Political Deliberation," *Political Theory* 15 (1987): 338–68 and Thomas Nagel, "Moral Conflict and Political Legitimacy," *Philosophy and Public Affairs* 16 (1987): 215–40. It reached its apogee in John Rawls, "The Idea of Public Reason Revisited," in his *The Law of Peoples* (Cambridge, Mass.: Harvard University Press, 2002), 131–80. For excellent commentary, see Gerald F. Gaus, *Contemporary Theories of Liberalism* (London: Sage, 2003), 119–47, and Eric MacGilvary, *Reconstructing Public Reason* (Cambridge, Mass.: Harvard University Press, 2004).

[14] On the similarities and disagreements between these thinkers, see William Galston, "Realism in Political Theory," available online at http://www.law.yale.edu/documents/pdf/Intellectual_Life/ltw_galston.doc.

[15] See Aryeh Botwinick and William E. Connolly, *Democracy and Vision: Sheldon Wolin and the Vicissitudes of the Political* (Princeton: Princeton University Press, 2001); Joseph M. Schwartz, *The Permanence of the Political* (Princeton: Princeton University Press, 1995); James Tully, "The Agonic Freedom of Citizens," *Economy and Society* 28 (1999): 161–82.

can never be about the pursuit of a reasonable agreement between a diverse citizenry, as deliberative democrats appear to propose. It is instead a continuous struggle for political power, usually involving the identification of "friends" and "enemies"—as Carl Schmitt once put it—where the battle for control over the coercive apparatus of the state always takes precedence over the achievement of highly moralized objectives, however hard moralists and politicians might work to persuade us to the contrary.[16]

These realists further charge that the deliberative democrats' naivete in the face of these facts is more than just misleading. It also has the potential to be exceptionally dangerous. Political efforts grounded in a position that ignores these concerns are likely to have perverse consequences. All three facts matter here. First, the deep diversity of the citizenry entails that political attempts to identify a common good are not only foolhardy but also have the potential to collapse into homogenizing, normalizing, and repressive efforts to enforce an artificial unity. Second, the inevitability of self-interest in political conduct further ensures that reform proposals based on the possibility of its eradication open the way to even worse forms of corruption and manipulation as normal political practices are forced underground. Third, and similarly, the unavoidability of inequalities of power in politics necessitates that the "high-flown language" of deliberative legitimacy will become merely a "mask for power relations," again allowing these inequalities to exert even greater influence hidden from the public gaze.[17] If there is to be any sort of democratic reform, any "new politics," the realists insist that it must be grounded on a thoroughgoing assessment of the necessary limitations on democratic politics. But it is probably better just to admit to the necessary constraints of democratic politics and to craft an alternative response to the problems of our political order instead.[18]

The deliberative democrats' response to these critics has been strident. They argue that the so-called democratic realists are really just democratic pessimists. Realists go morally awry because they arrive at their normative recommendations from a picture of the way the world of democratic politics is today rather than by attempting to identify how a democratic system ought to be. The most their approach can ever hope to offer is a relatively minor improvement on the status quo. A truly better political order, on the other hand, can only be built if theorists start by trying to identify the desired

---

[16] See Carl Schmitt, *The Concept of the Political* (Chicago: University of Chicago Press, 1995 [1932]).

[17] Runciman, *Political Hypocrisy*, 206.

[18] See Mark Lilla, *The Reckless Mind: Intellectuals in Politics* (London: Granta, 2001), and David Runciman, *The Politics of Good Intentions: History, Fear and Hypocrisy in the New World Order* (Princeton: Princeton University Press, 2006).

end-state—by offering an "ideal theory"—and then think carefully on how such a goal could be realized even in the very "non-ideal" conditions of the present. As John Rawls, a relatively late convert to deliberative democracy, explained: deliberative democracy should be understood as what he called a "realistic utopia."[19] He contended that it is always essential in political theory first to describe the long-term goal as fully as possible and only then to think about how "this long-term goal might be achieved, or worked toward usually in gradual steps."[20] If deliberative democracy seems overly optimistic it is simply because its advocates have rightly begun their work by spending most of their time in outlining, examining, and fine-tuning their democratic ideals rather than by being bogged down in descriptions of the non-ideal present. Their task has been to describe democratic life as it ought to be rather than as it is currently conducted.[21]

Crucial though this response is, it nonetheless admits that the deliberative democrats' job cannot finish with ideal theory alone, or at least it cannot if they wish their ideals to become anything other than philosophical abstractions.[22] If deliberative democrats wish to insist that their ideals could effectively be realized at some point in the political future of the United States, then they must also offer some account of how the transition from the non-ideal to the ideal might occur. They must provide an account, that is, of what the gradual steps Rawls talks about will be and explain how they can identify the ones to take. But this crucial task has been tackled extraordinarily rarely by deliberative democrats. Some of them have despaired of responding to it at all. Charles Larmore once meekly suggested that "what should be said about the less-than-ideal case is not entirely obvious."[23] Most others, though, write as if the transformation is to be achieved through a sort of behavioral mimicking, where citizens are encouraged to act "as if" they lived in an ideal democracy, even though the conditions for such a democracy properly to function have yet to be attained. The assumption behind this recommendation is presumably that the example of good citizen behavior—with its emphasis on reason-giving, mutual respect, and a concentration on the common good—will prove infectious, such that citizens and professional politicians will eventually develop bonds of trust and

---

[19] See Rawls, *Law of Peoples*, 124–26.

[20] Rawls, *Law of Peoples*, 89.

[21] For discussion, see Charles Mills, "Ideal Theory as Ideology," *Hypatia* 20 (2005): 165–84, and Adam Swift and Stuart White, "Political Theory, Social Science, and Real Politics," in David Leopold and Marc Stears, eds., *Political Theory: Methods and Approaches* (Oxford: Oxford University Press, 2008), 49–60.

[22] They might not harbor such ambitions, of course. On which, see David Estlund, *Democratic Authority: A Philosophical Framework* (Princeton: Princeton University Press, 2008), 258–76.

[23] Charles Larmore, "Political Liberalism," *Political Theory* 18 (1990): 352.

political solidarity that will allow them collectively to transcend sectionalism and adversarialism and encourage them to craft a new deliberative democracy for them all to enjoy together.[24]

Only one leading deliberative democrat, Archon Fung, has provided a consistent critique of this position. Fung accepts that it might well be self-defeating for deliberative democrats simply to approximate ideal behaviors in non-ideal settings in the hope that they will somehow "catch on." If deliberative democrats "limit themselves to communicative methods even under highly adverse conditions such as extreme inequality, pervasive disregard for deliberative norms, and systematic domination," he explains, then they would be very likely to lose all of the political contests in which they engaged. He suggests that "no sensible political ethic can require unilateral disarmament."[25] On the other hand, Fung does not break entirely from the deliberative democrats' proclivity to insist on the importance of "mimicking" deliberative behaviors in the non-ideal present. According to his account, deliberative democrats must avoid reinforcing the least desirable elements of political life. A campaign for deliberative democracy that employed negative advertising, for example, might perpetuate the least desirable elements of partisanship; a campaign that involved actively misleading, intimidating, coercing, or bribing citizens would seem even more unlikely to help in securing a more deliberative future.

In response to this difficulty, Fung proposes that citizens today should commit themselves to a "provisional set" of ethical principles as they decide upon their political conduct, principles that he calls "fidelity," "charity," "exhaustion," and "proportionality." None of these principles are fully ideal in themselves, he contends, but if citizens could limit themselves to behaving in accordance with them in the non-ideal present then they would have a better chance of crafting an ideal deliberative democracy for the future. These are citizen behaviors, then, that are said to approximate the deliberative ideal, to encapsulate its moral core, whilst at the same time making it possible to create a more ideal deliberative democratic order in the future.

There is much that is persuasive in Fung's account, and I return to it in more detail in the conclusion. It suffers, however, as a result of what Bonnie Honig has called the "paradox of politics": the problem that the creation of an ideal democracy must at least partially be dependent on the existence

---

[24] See Gutmann and Thompson, *Why Deliberative Democracy?*, esp. 1–3. For extensive discussion, see Marc Stears, "Liberalism and the Politics of Compulsion," *British Journal of Political Science* 37 (2007): 549–52.

[25] Archon Fung, "Deliberation Before the Revolution," *Political Theory* 33 (2005): 399.

of a number of "ideal democratizers" in the much less than ideal present.[26] It is entirely unclear on Fung's account where his principled citizens—his "ideal democratizers"—are going to come from. Fung is silent indeed both on the question of how citizens are to be persuaded to sign-up for the deliberative ideal itself and how they are to be persuaded to conduct their actual political lives according to his four principles. How can citizens faced with corruption, glaring inequalities, hierarchies, and power differentials in the existing political order be expected to moderate their political behavior in the search for a better future? Who are these individuals who can be expected to labor under a political self-denying ordinance when even the most thoughtful of deliberative democrats cannot tell them exactly how or when their ideal is likely to reach fruition?

The pervasive difficulty of these questions is clearly demonstrated if we simply ask how many citizens in the United States today could genuinely be considered to be supportive of the deliberative democratic ideal and how many are likely to be persuaded to conduct their political lives according to Fung's principles in the present. If the answer to these questions is "not very many," then it is extraordinarily difficult to see how the process of deliberative reform is expected to get started. As Bonnie Honig explains, "the paradox of politics catches us in a chicken-and-egg circle that presses us to begin the work of democratic politics in *medias res*."[27] Fung believes that the building of a better deliberative democratic future requires citizens who are able to behave today in ways that, if not ideally deliberative, are nevertheless infused with deliberative values. He even argues that this is the "distinctive moral challenge" of our times.[28] Yet he does not say how or why he expects people to be able to rise to it. The vital question, therefore, is where are these steely, committed, deliberative citizens to come from? And that is the challenge that no deliberative democrat has yet been able to meet.

Reflecting on all of these themes, three crucial questions emerge from the contemporary debate on democratic reform. Those questions start first with the issue of what an ideal democracy would look like. They then move, second, to concerns about the extent to which prevailing systems fail to match that ideal. They conclude, third, with the challenge of how citizens should behave in the here-and-now if they wish to transform that imperfect present into the better future. In recent political theory, remarkably few scholars have taken on all three of these questions directly. Deliberative democrats have offered very detailed answers to the first—that concerned

---

[26] See Bonnie Honig, "Between Deliberation and Decision: Political Paradox in Democratic Theory," *American Political Science Review* 101 (2007): 1–17.

[27] Honig, "Between Deliberation and Decision," 2–3.

[28] Fung, "Deliberation Before the Revolution," 416.

with the nature of the ideal democratic order—but have provided little by way of insight with regard to the second. Democratic realists have, on the other hand, provided similarly sustained examinations of the second—involving the identification of serious imperfections in the political present—but they too often paint a depressingly pessimistic picture of what might be achieved in response to the first. The third question—that of how we might persuade citizens to embrace the ideal and of how those who are committed to it should behave in the absence of a large number of fellow citizens who share their aspirations—remains effectively unanswered by either side.

The Radical Democratic Tradition

It is precisely in this way that the movements of the twentieth-century American radical democratic tradition differed from both deliberative democracy and democratic realism. Rather than either advancing an ideal of deliberation or building a theory on a pessimistic reading of existing democratic possibilities, the twentieth-century movements that constituted this tradition shared and shaped an approach that combined elements of the arguments of their more recent rivals. Like the latter-day realists, they recognized that the inadequacies of American democracy ensured that political change could not be forged through a politics of reason, consensus, and inclusion alone, but would also require "buoyant, crusading, and militant" forms of political action, including forms that might be rightfully described as adversarial, manipulative, and even coercive.[29] Like the deliberative democrats, however, they also looked forward to a time when such actions were no longer necessary, a time when democratic politics would become more open, less exclusive, more egalitarian, and perhaps even more deliberative than the politics that had existed since the founding. The promise of democracy, they argued, was unfulfilled in various ways, corrupted by ill-motivated citizens or leaders, and unsettled by the prevailing radically unequal distribution of social and political power.

The constitutive task of the radical democratic tradition was to bring these two claims together. They did so by insisting, first, that it was possible to rectify those ills and thus to secure a "new kind" of democracy but, second, that any such effort would require a full range of political strategies encompassing electoral and non-electoral politics, reasoned and passionate appeals, and noncoercive and coercive forms of protest alike. Most of all, these movements insisted that it was crucial to distinguish between the

---

[29] Dewey, "Democracy is Radical," 11.

sorts of democratic political actions that were required in the present and those that would be appropriate in some improved future democracy. It was necessary to craft a politics that would enable a better regime to be created but it was also vital not to act as if such a future had already come.

None of the movements that composed the radical democratic tradition believed that the end of democratic reform justified the use of any means of political action, though. They did not suggest that citizens should take to the streets whatever the consequences nor did they argue that it was always acceptable to impose one's view of the future order on unwilling fellow citizens whatever the cause of their objections. Rather, they strongly believed that the choice of political means had to reflect crucial democratic ideals. They thus generally resisted calls to insurrection or revolution—if not always some more minimal use of violent force—partly on immediate moral grounds and partly because they believed that such methods of regime change would generate animosity between social groups for decades to come, preventing the creation of a peaceful, open, and inclusive democratic order in the realizable future.

Despite such caution, the theorists of the twentieth-century radical democratic tradition continually insisted that it was nevertheless wrong to circumscribe too tightly the actions that might be required in the present. The selection of political means had instead to be both goal-oriented and context-sensitive. Such orientation and sensitivity further required that citizens—or at least citizen-activists—possess an astute sense of political judgment. Citizens would need to be able to assess both the efficacy of contrasting types of political action in varying contexts and to evaluate the ethical appropriateness of that action in each given instance. Assessments of democratic political action in this tradition always thus existed at the intersection of principle and action, of ideal and strategy, and citizens needed to understand the connections and disconnections between these ways of thinking. Radical democrats, then, demanded that citizens develop a kind of practical wisdom that would enable citizens to make these strategic yet principled decisions on a regular basis. They would need to know when to compromise and when to hold out, when to argue and when to concur. They would need also, of course, to be able to muster the courage required by the often desperate struggle to build a better democratic future and, equally importantly, to exhibit the patience necessary to hold back from such struggle when the occasion demanded.

The answers to these precise judgments, and political theorists' evaluations of citizens' abilities to make the right call, dramatically shifted across the twentieth century. All was not stable within the radical democratic tradition. It knew its moments of optimism and of pessimism, of clarity and opacity. At their best, however, the movements of the tradition developed a startlingly clear sense of what was required, explaining that democracy demanded that citizens develop special kinds of political virtue, kinds suited both to the immediate political contexts within which they lived and campaigned and to the demands of the cross-temporal transformation to which they were committed.

It is not surprising that this body of work has been overlooked or misunderstood in recent years, as this approach to political action sits ill with both the deliberative and the realist approaches, at least as they are usually understood. Most deliberative democrats are unwilling to accept the use of distinctly nondeliberative political action in the hope that such action will bring about an improved future.[30] Many realists, on the other hand, are deeply wary about promises relating to the future in general. They worry that such promises either mask attempts to enforce some homogenizing ideal—an ideal that might serve the interests of some but will also exclude concern for others—or promote a misguided optimism about the possibilities of politics that might lead citizens and politicians in dangerous directions. Realists thus often prefer to commit themselves to a politics that can maintain political ambiguity, uncertainty, or contestation rather than one that ties itself to a single determinate goal. They are also often worried about the temporal orientation of radical theorizing, suggesting that its focus on bringing about a better future betrays a worryingly unilinear understanding of change across time: one that neglects the possibility that the judgements about the desirability of elements of the past, present, and future partly depend on the varying perspectives of the viewer.[31]

This book seeks to demonstrate that both of these concerns are misguided, at least in their most exaggerated forms. The remainder of this introduction explains how.

Plan of the Book

This book investigates the contentions of the radical democratic tradition as it was forged across the twentieth century, revisiting the arguments of its proponents and the practices of its exponents, and outlining how its essential recommendations can be reclaimed today. It is a journey that takes in all

---

[30] See David Miller, *Citizenship and National Identity* (Cambridge: Polity, 1997), 159. For a more subtle assessment, see Andrew Sabl, "Looking Forward to Justice: Rawlsian Civil Disobedience and its Non-Rawlsian Lessons," *Journal of Political Philosophy* 9 (2001): 307–30.

[31] See Connolly, *Pluralism*, esp. 97–130.

of the major contributors to the tradition's evolution and that takes seriously both their weaknesses and their strengths. It is structured in two parts.

The first part covers the period from the beginning of the century to the end of the Second World War. It begins with the Progressive reformers of the first fifteen years of the century. These reformers initiated the twentieth-century radical democratic tradition. They did so by placing a conception of the common good firmly at the center of their democratic ideals whilst also arguing forcefully that multiple sorts of political action, including action that might have appeared sectional or even coercive to others, was needed to realize such a good in the imperfect democracy of the United States. Chapter 2 demonstrates what happened to this idea during the interwar years, and especially during the years of the Great Depression. Concentrating on the ferocious critique of prewar Progressivism provided by Reinhold Niebuhr and Walter Lippmann, and on attempts to salvage Progressive theory from that critique, the chapter illustrates that the Depression Era provided a particularly pessimistic moment in the development of the American radical democratic tradition, a moment when a "realist" assessment of prevailing political circumstances almost entirely overwhelmed prospects for a better democratic future. Chapter 3, though, demonstrates the ways in which the more optimistic parts of the radical democratic tradition were nonetheless reasserted in the later interwar years. Featuring a new evaluation of the contribution of John Dewey, this chapter suggests that the ideal of a more inclusive and harmonious democratic future re-emerged late in the Depression Era but was newly combined with support for a far more vigorous and adversarial account of the efforts that would be required to secure immediate political change. At the heart of these moves, the chapter shows, was the Congress of Industrial Organizations (CIO), whose buoyant and crusading efforts on behalf of the democratic rights of industrial labor would remain highly contentious within American democratic thinking for the remainder of the century.

The CIO's vision struggled for traction in the aftermath of the Second World War, and the second part of the book turns to dramatic changes brought about in the postwar period. It begins, in chapter 4, in the immediate aftermath of the war, when radicals were presented with an even more serious challenge than they had been in the years after the First World War. Once-strident campaigners grew tired and skeptical during the war and many came to believe that the primary role of activists was to conserve the good in the present order, rather than try to build anew. The result was a period characterized by overwhelming caution and by the sense that even if change in American politics was sought, it could only ever be expected to be achieved incrementally. Chapter 5, though, demonstrates that this moment of caution gave way as the traumas of war faded from memory and that by the mid-1950s both optimism and political drama had returned to radical democratic thought, courtesy of the civil rights movement. The chapter examines the democratic theory and practice of that movement in the 1950s, concentrating especially of the Congress of Racial Equality, the Student Non-Violent Coordinating Committee, and the Southern Christian Leadership Conference, and demonstrating how these groups reinvigorated the radical democratic tradition by responding to the critiques of the post-war pessimists in a new and distinctive way. Chapter 6 moves that story on still further, tracing the ways in which the student activists of the 1960s, especially those associated with Students for a Democratic Society, borrowed from the democratic theory of the civil rights movement and transformed it from an account of democracy as racial justice into one of the struggle for democracy as lifestyle experimentation. The conclusion draws the lessons from each of these moments together, and outlines ways in which the tradition of radical democracy is able to respond to the demands of the present.

This intellectual journey is one that takes in both philosophical and practical elements; that is, the book surveys both the ideas and the practices of the movements that shaped the radical democratic tradition. Indeed, it has to cover both. The gap we so often notice today between those who think about democracy's demands and those who follow those demands on the streets or in the corridors of power is a relatively recent phenomenon; writers about democratic action in the twentieth-century United States were generally also practitioners of a certain type of democratic action. It follows that there are indeed great texts to be examined here, including Herbert Croly's *The Promise of American Life*, John Dewey's *The Public and its Problems*, Walter Lippmann's *The Phantom Public*, Reinhold Niebuhr's *Moral Man and Immoral Society*, C. Wright Mills's *The Power Elite*, and even John Rawls's *Theory of Justice* and *Political Liberalism*. But there are also pamphlets and speeches, newspaper articles and editorials in journals of opinion, and the newsletters of activist organizations.

In addition to the various kinds of texts, there are also manifold practices discussed in this account. One of the immediately notable things about the radical democratic activism of the twentieth-century United States is the apparent continuity in political strategy, in what scholars of social movements have called "repertoires of contention."[32] The trade unionists of the 1930s thus invented the sit-down strike, a method that gave way to the sit-

---

[32] See Sidney Tarrow, *Power in Movement: Social Movements and Contentious Politics* (Cambridge: Cambridge University Press, 1998), and Doug McAdam, Sidney Tarrow, and Charles Tilly, *Dynamics of Contention* (Cambridge: Cambridge University Press, 2001).

ins at lunch counters in the southern states that initiated the civil rights movement, which in their turn inspired the university campus "occupations" of the late 1960s and 1970s. Songs of protest, too, passed from generation to generation; spirituals sung by slaves were picked up by the trade unionists of the 1930s, later adapted to the cause of civil rights, and finally found a new life once more in the folk music revival of the 1960s.[33] Even at the beginning of the twenty-first century, rock musician Bruce Springsteen could be found mobilizing against the Republican Party with the very same songs.[34]

This continuity is partly the consequence of shared personnel and joint organizational allegiance. Research into the twentieth century's trade union, civil rights, and student protest movements often throws up the same names; people like Abraham J. Muste, Reinhold Niebuhr, and Bayard Rustin moved from one movement to another, and brought new generations of colleagues with them. Such research also reveals how the organizations these activists led were institutionally interconnected: demonstrating, for instance, how the Progressive Intercollegiate Socialist Society gave way to the Depression Era's League for Industrial Democracy, which itself spawned the Students for a Democratic Society of the 1960s.

The similarities in political action between the generations are also the result of shared political ideals and shared political arguments. These shared ideals were partly the result of these movements' continual invocation of concepts derived from earlier American political traditions. All of these radical democrats thus drew heavily from both the republican and liberal traditions that had given shape to much American political argument since the founding.[35] As shall be seen, they tried constantly to reformulate core elements of those traditions in accordance with their own aspirations. They argued that the concrete structures of American governance required radical renewal if the nation was to be able to deliver upon the promise of its underlying values. But the causes of continuity extended far beyond the use of a shared national conceptual inheritance. These twentieth century movements also offered remarkably similar answers to the more precise—and more radical—question: what should American citizens actually *do* if they

---

[33] See Robert Cantwell, *When We Were Good: The Folk Revival* (Cambridge, Mass.: Harvard University Press, 1996).

[34] Bruce Springsteen, *We Shall Overcome: The Seeger Sessions* (New York: Sony Records, 2006).

[35] For an introduction to efforts to reformulate the broader traditions of American political theorizing in a more radical direction, see Foner, *Story of American Freedom*; Gary Gerstle, "The Protean Character of American Liberalism," *American Historical Review* 99 (1994): 1043–73; Carol Horton, *Race and the Making of American Liberalism* (Oxford: Oxford University Press, 2005); and Marc Stears, "The Liberal Tradition and the Politics of Exclusion," *Annual Review of Political Science* 10 (2007): 85–101.

want to overcome undemocratic injustices and exclusions and attempt to construct a better political order for the future?

In tracing those arguments, this study examines the tradition's offerings in rarefied political theory, in popular political argument, and in actual political practice. Not everything, or everyone, can be here, however. Three exceptions are of particular note. First, this study focuses exclusively on a tradition of democratic and American political thought. Movements that rejected democracy or proposed a directly revolutionary means of getting there are thus excluded from examination, and groups who self-consciously turned their back on American political traditions also only infrequently appear in the following pages. There is, therefore, little of the American Communist or anarchist traditions here. Second, it will also be noted that relatively little is said here about the inner workings of the Republican or Democratic parties. This is for the simple reason that most of the theorists and activists of the radical democratic tradition worked outside of either party, moving into closer or looser alliance with them as conditions allowed. Frequently, indeed, they were highly critical of party politics in general, seeing it as a block on democratic progress rather than as a means for securing democratic change. Finally, the thinkers and movements discussed in this book were also interested mostly in the politics of class and the politics of race; they sought to create a new democracy for the American worker and to overcome the exclusion that often faced Americans who belonged to minority racial and ethnic groups. Therefore, the analysis rarely addresses the "identity politics" of cultural allegiance that emerged in the United States after the 1970s. Movements in this regard could be included too, and their contributions to the theory of radical democracy added to the account, of course, and I hope such work will follow.

Despite these exceptions, the book's ambitions remain expansive. It aims to recuperate a tradition of thinking about democracy and democratic reform that stretched across the twentieth century but has been neglected by political theory today and to ask whether it still has anything to say to us. It will argue that in the last few decades American democratic political theory has been trapped between a deliberative democratic ideal that can often seem naively optimistic and a democratic realist one that can just as frequently appear excessively pessimistic. And it aims to show that it has not always been thus. Most of all, I hope that this study of the radical democratic tradition will show those who go in search of a "new kind of politics" in the twenty-first century that they might still find twentieth-century predecessors who can help to show the way.

PART ONE

1900–1945

CHAPTER ONE

Making the Nation a Neighborhood

The twentieth century began in the United States, just as the twenty-first has, with demands for a new democracy. The call for democratic renewal was at the very heart of aspirations for reform during the dramatic years that stretched from the century's opening to America's entry into the First World War, a period that has come to be known as "the Progressive Era." American democracy, reformers insisted at this time, had been built for a different age: both its institutions and its citizen practices suited a pre-industrial era of small-scale, face-to-face politics conducted amongst a relatively homogenous people, and where power primarily resided at a local level. The twentieth century, in contrast, would require a new democratic system and a new set of democratic habits. The United States needed a democracy suited to an industrial and urbanized age: a society where citizens debated with others they had never met in national newspapers and across telegraph lines, and attempted to tackle problems of poverty, inequality, and concentrated economic power that would have been entirely beyond their predecessors' ability to grasp. Indeed, for many the crises of the industrial order had shown that the United States did not possess a truly democratic political order at all. "For years I accepted the theory as most of the rest of us accepted it, that we already had popular government, that this was government by the people," the Progressive Party's presidential candidate Theodore Roosevelt declared. But "[g]radually it came over me" that this was at best "half the truth." What the United States needed most of all was new "machinery for getting adequate and genuine popular rule."[1]

Now more than a century on, no one disputes that the first decade and a half of the twentieth century saw the radical reconstruction of American democratic politics, and that the loose coalition of political forces known

---

[1] Theodore Roosevelt, "How I Became a Progressive," reprinted in Carl Resek, ed., *The Progressives* (Indianapolis and New York: Bobbs-Merrill, 1967), 333. For the institutional transformations of the Progressive Era, see Stephen Skowronek, *The Making of the American State: The Expansion of National Administrative Capacities, 1877–1920* (Cambridge: Cambridge University Press, 1992), and Martin Sklar, *The Corporate Reconstruction of American Capitalism, 1880–1916* (Cambridge: Cambridge University Press 1988).

as "Progressivism" were largely responsible for that reconstruction.[2] The list of formal democratic transformations in the period was astonishing. At the level of the states, Progressives successfully lobbied for the widespread introduction of referenda, mandates, and initiatives to allow citizens to have a direct influence in the legislative process. They also oversaw the expansion of recall elections, the regulation of political parties, and direct primaries, all aimed at allowing party supporters to exercise control over their candidates. At the federal level, the era witnessed amendments to the Constitution to allow for the direct election of senators, the enfranchisement of women, and the radical empowerment of the federal executive, all also brought about with Progressive support.[3] The roll call of less formal efforts at democratic renewal was just as far-reaching. Across the United States, a whole host of interest groups and lobbying organizations sprang up to represent those previously excluded from mainstream politics.[4] The passion for democracy also moved far beyond the normal sphere of political life. These were the years when trade unions and Progressively inclined employers announced their intention to expand democracy into the workplace, when housing, parks, and playgrounds were rebuilt with the intention of engendering a deeper spirit of solidarity and understanding between urban citizens, and when some Progressive educationalists even tried to bring popular rule into the classroom.[5]

Yet despite the explosion of formal and informal democratic reforms, the democratic ideals that were shaped and articulated by intellectually engaged Progressives are deeply controversial amongst political theorists and political scientists today. A few commentators still see the Progressive

---

[2] For seminal introductions to Progressive politics, see James Kloppenberg, *Uncertain Victory: Social Democracy and Progressivism in European and American Thought, 1870–1920* (New York: Oxford University Press, 1986); Michael McGerr, *A Fierce Discontent: The Rise and Fall of the Progressive Movement in America, 1870–1920* (Oxford: Oxford University Press, 2003); Daniel Rodgers, *Atlantic Crossings: Social Politics in a Progressive Age* (Cambridge, Mass.: Belknap, 1998); David Thelen, "Social Tensions and the Origins of Progressivism," *Journal of American History* 56 (1969): 323–41; and Robert H. Wiebe, *The Search for Order, 1877–1920* (New York: Hill and Wang, 1967). For refreshing skepticism about the usefulness of the overarching term "Progressive," see Daniel T. Rodgers, "In Search of Progressivism," *Reviews in American History* 10 (1982): 112–32.

[3] See the discussions in Michael McGerr, *The Decline of Popular Politics: The American North, 1865–1928* (New York: Oxford University Press, 1986).

[4] For the crucial role of such organizations, see Adam Sheingate, "Political Entrepreneurship, Institutional Change, and American Political Development," *Studies in American Political Development* 17 (2003): 185–203.

[5] For examples, see Frederic Howe, *The City: Hope of Democracy* (New York: Charles Scribners and Sons, 1905), and Richard Jones, "Social Centers and Hymns for Democracy," *Common Good*, December 1913, 44–45. For excellent commentary, see Kevin Mattson, *Creating a Democratic Public: The Struggle for Urban Participatory Democracy during the Progressive Era* (University Park: University of Pennsylvania Press, 1998).

era as an age of heroic democratic reform—a time when activists aimed to free the United States from plutocracy and enable its citizens collectively to pursue a common good through revitalized civic participation—but most early twenty-first-century scholars view it with a far more jaundiced eye.[6] The criticism leveled against the Progressives is far from uniform, though. Some commentators disparage Progressive reformers for an excessive sentimentalism: suggesting that Progressives offered a utopian view of American politics often grounded in mythical and misleading appeals to "national unity" and "national destiny."[7] Others dismiss Progressives for prioritizing the politics of factional interest groups over national consensus and for investing too much power in elected and unelected elites at the expense of broader public participation in decision making.[8] Still others condemn Progressives for not knowing where they stood on the vital issues of the day, for introducing programs of reform that were internally inconsistent, and writing political theory that was all but incoherent.[9]

Paradoxical as it may seem, there is much of value in all of these critiques. That is partly because the Progressive movement itself was extremely diverse. As such, it is true that some Progressive reformers were overly optimistic in their expectation that American citizens could come together and agree upon a shared set of political values, whilst many others also acted disingenuously in the interests of a relatively small section of the whole society. Yet for all of their important insights these critiques also fail to capture the whole picture. They fail, in particular, to disentangle two crucial elements of the Progressives' democratic arguments: their ideal democratic theory and their short-term political strategy. This distinction was crucial to Progressive reformers, though, because they constantly sought to combine both a bold and optimistic vision of a more equal and inclusive democratic future and a ruthlessly realistic assessment of the shortcomings of the American democratic present. Failing to recognize that the Progressives

---

[6] For positive interpretations of much Progressive democratic theory, see Michael Sandel, *Democracy's Discontent: America in Search of a Public Philosophy* (Cambridge, Mass.: Belknap,1996), and Richard Rorty, *Achieving Our Country: Leftist Thought in Twentieth Century America* (Cambridge, Mass.: Harvard University Press 1998).

[7] See James Morone, *The Democratic Wish: Popular Participation and the Limits of American Government* (New Haven: Yale University Press, 1998), 97–124. For a more subtle critique, see Sheldon Wolin, *Democracy Inc.: Managed Democracy and the Specter of Inverted Totalitarianism* (Princeton: Princeton University Press, 2008), esp. 220.

[8] See Catherine Holland, "Democracy Beside Itself," *Political Theory* 34 (2006): 488–98; John Jordan, *Machine-Age Ideology: Social Engineering and American Liberalism, 1911–1939* (Chapel Hill: University of North Carolina Press, 1994); and R. Jeffrey Lustig, *Corporate Liberalism: The Origins of Modern American Political Theory* (Berkeley: University of California Press, 1982).

[9] See James Mileur, "The Legacy of Reform," in Sidney Milkis and James Mileur, eds., *Progressivism and the New Democracy* (Amherst: University of Massachusetts Press, 1999), 271.

were working at both of these levels mistakenly leads critics to describe Progressive positions as inconsistent, insincere, or wrongheaded simply by virtue of misidentifying short-term political strategies as long-term democratic ideals or assessing present-oriented policies as if they were principles of political aspiration.

Teasing apart the Progressives' democratic ideal theory from their political strategy of transformation is, then, fundamental to understanding Progressive democratic thought. When seen this way, positions some critics have dismissed as sentimental turn out to have been aspirational and policies that others have castigated as narrow-minded turn out to have been determinedly realistic. Analysis that disentangles these two aspects of the Progressive democratic theory also offers more than a new evaluation of the Progressives' own work, though. For the distinction that Progressives introduced between their long-term democratic theory and their immediate-term political strategy was not only important to them: it crucially shaped the American radical tradition of democratic political thought that followed them. The generations that followed the Progressives continued a conversation with them about both the ideal vision of democracy and the practical political means by which Americans might hope to realize that ideal. Any study of the possibilities inherent in that tradition must return to the democratic theory of the Progressive Era because it set the agenda for democratic reform for the remainder of the twentieth century.

Progressive Democracy

The political commitments of those labelled "Progressives" in the first decade and a half of the twentieth century were exceptionally diverse, often even conflicting. There were Progressives who championed the cause of the small businessman and those who welcomed the emergence of nationwide corporations; there were Progressives who hoped reform would emanate from the federal government and those who placed their faith in state administrations; there were Progressives who mobilized behind the newly emerging trade unions and those who dismissed the organized working class as the agents of economic faction.[10] But despite all of these differences, two essential and interconnected claims united all of those who campaigned under the Progressive banner. The first was that the United States was undergoing a radical social transformation at the beginning of the twentieth century as a result of rapid industrialization and urbanization. The second

---

[10] See Rodgers, "In Search of Progressivism."

was that the nation's cultural understandings, social values, and political systems would need to be dramatically reformed if the United States was to flourish in this new industrial age.

Amongst the multiplicity of Progressive voices, it was the social psychologist Charles Cooley who most ably articulated these two interrelated arguments in his 1902 masterpiece *Social Organization*. "[T]he present regime of railroads, telegraphs, daily papers, telephones and the rest has involved a revolution in every phase of life," Cooley contended. At the heart of that revolution was a paradox. On the one hand, industrialization had brought American citizens into ever closer contact with one another, had squeezed them into new urban streets, where they lived cheek-by-jowl in the way so poignantly portrayed by the painters of the Ashcan school.[11] Such citizens not only lived in closer proximity than they ever had before but they were also dependent on goods and services created by multiple others through an intricate and complex division of labor. There could be none of the rural "self-reliance" of American folklore in the industrial city.[12] On the other hand, these self-same industrializing forces also divided Americans from one another. Urbanization removed citizens from their traditional social settings, ripping families and communities apart and undermining the cultural expectations that had provided the social glue of the past. Meanwhile, the division of labor placed citizens in ever more specialized vocations. Few, therefore, could appreciate the work conducted by others within the same factory, let alone in the distant parts of the vast industrial complex that now stretched out across the United States. Citizens in the industrial age, Cooley thus complained, were more interdependent than ever before but also more detached. The crowds that jostled each other in the streets of the big cities were indisputably reliant on each other in crucial ways but they lacked the social bonds necessary to turn this mutual reliance into mutual acceptance, let alone mutual esteem.

This was a potentially explosive situation. Cooley contended that social discontent in the urban environment, while expected, could easily give way to serious social disorder that in turn could bring the peace and the prosperity of the entire nation tumbling down. It was a problem that demanded an immediate response. For Cooley, moreover, this response was to be cultural in character. American citizens in this interdependent industrial age, he explained, must somehow develop new norms and values consonant with the situation in which they found themselves. An interconnected, industrial

---

[11] See Robert Snyder, Rebecca Zurier, and Virgina Mecklenburg, *Metropolitan Lives: The Ashcan Artists and Their New York* (Washington, D.C.: National Museum of American Art, 1996).

[12] See Ralph Waldo Emerson, *Essays: Second Series* (London: Geoffrey Chapman, 1849).

society required, in particular, "common principles of kindness and justice," principles that could be shared between all members of the new order, enabling them to understand and empathize with each other, and even eventually feel bonds of attachment. As Cooley saw it, therefore, the task of the Progressive movement was to help all of the multiple, contrasting groups in urban society to identify these new common principles and shape these shared norms. Only then could Progressives hope to reassure urban citizens that a stable social order could return to the United States.[13]

This was a view that was all but universal amongst self-described Progressives. It shaped the stories of journalists such as Upton Sinclair, who revealed the worst excesses of capitalist production in *The Jungle* and *The Industrial Republic* and called for a new age of mutual concern to put them right.[14] It also lay behind the initiatives of social workers such as Jane Addams, Florence Kelley, and Paul Kellogg.[15] The "industrial city" must learn to "think in terms of the whole community," Kellogg insisted, if it is not to witness social unrest on an unprecedented and dangerous scale.[16] The same idea inspired Oswald Villard and W. E. B. DuBois as they founded the National Association for the Advancement of Colored People (NAACP). Citizens of the many races of the industrial United States would need to learn how to avoid "rancor of all sorts" if they were to live successfully together side by side in the new urban centers, DuBois reflected. It was only by identifying a new "common good for all Americans," black and white, that the nation could hope to avoid disaster and begin to dream of a better future.[17]

One group of Progressives sought to transform these cultural aspirations for a new spirit of communality into a more formal political vision. This was the so-called New Nationalist movement, led by the Progressive publicists Herbert Croly, Walter Lippmann, and Walter Weyl.[18] These three

[13] Charles Cooley, *Social Organization* (New York: C. Scribner's Sons, 1902), 83, 89.

[14] Upton Sinclair, *The Jungle* (New York: Doubleday, Page, and Co., 1906) and Upton Sinclar, *The Industrial Republic: A Study of the America of Ten Years Hence* (New York: Doubleday, Page, and Co., 1907).

[15] See Jane Addams et al., *Woman and the Larger Citizenship* (Chicago: Chicago Civics Society, 1914). For commentary, see Kathryn Kish Sklar, *Florence Kelley and the Nation's Work: The Rise of Women's Political Culture, 1830–1900* (New Haven: Yale University Press, 1995).

[16] Paul Kellogg, untitled MS in The Paul Kellogg Papers 3/28/12, Social Welfare History Archive, University of Minnesota.

[17] Editorial, "Introduction," *Crisis* 1 (1910): 11, and W. E. B. DuBois, *The Philadelphia Negro: A Social Study* (Philadelphia: Published for the University, 1899). See, too, Axel R. Schafer, "W. E. B. DuBois, German Social Thought, and the Racial Divide in American Progressivism, 1892–1909," *Journal of American History* 88 (2001): 925–49.

[18] On New Nationalism, see Maurice DiNunzio, ed., *Theodore Roosevelt: An American Mind* (New York: Penguin, 1995), esp. 16–18; Charles Forcey, *The Crossroads of Liberalism: Croly, Weyl, Lippmann, and the Progressive Era, 1900–1925* (New York: Oxford University Press, 1967); David Levy, *Herbert Croly of the New Republic: The Life and Thought of an American Progressive* (Princeton:

combined insights from across the broader Progressive movement into a new political program, advanced most frequently in the weekly periodical they established for the purpose, *The New Republic*.[19] As the label New Nationalist implied, the distinctive element of this political vision was its focus on the nation. Drawing attention to the vast scale of modern industrialization, the New Nationalists argued that it would only be possible to respond to the new social and economic challenges through concerted action on a national scale. In particular, they insisted that the difficulties thrown up by the complex pattern of economic interdependence in an industrial society required far more than piecemeal action from local authorities or voluntary groups. Nor could those problems be resolved by aspirations to cultural change alone. Rather, they required the oversight of a national political administration.

The core New Nationalist conviction, therefore, was that social distress, discontent, and disorder could only be avoided if the United States developed new "efficient governmental instruments," especially at the federal level. The instruments would allow a new generation of political leaders and bureaucratic experts to initiate intense, far-reaching, and concrete social and economic reforms in order to reduce the friction of the new social order.[20] The two major tasks of Progressives, then, was, first, to reform the structure of the federal government and then, second, to introduce a new era of national policymaking. Only this could ensure that "all is ordered" in industrial society and "not jumbled, nor left to the clash of egoistic individuals."[21] A newly reconstructed government could bring "plan where there has been clash, and purpose into the jungles of disordered growth."[22]

If government was going to be radically reshaped in this way, then so, too, was the process of electing and overseeing it. Croly, Lippmann, and

---

Princeton University Press, 1985); Marc Stears, *Progressives, Pluralists, and the Problems of the State* (Oxford: Oxford University Press, 2002); Ronald Steel, *Walter Lippmann and the American Century* (London: Bodley Head, 1980); and Edward Stettner, *Shaping Modern Liberalism: Herbert Croly and Progressive Thought* (Lawrence: Kansas University Press, 1994).

[19] For introductions, see Simon Nelson Patten, *The New Basis of Civilization* (New York: Mac-Millan, 1907); John R Commons, *Myself* (Madison: University of Wisconsin Press, 1964 [1934]); Josiah Royce, *The Philosophy of Loyalty* (New York: MacMillan, 1908); William James, *Some Problems in Philosophy* (London: Logmans, 1911); and John Dewey and John H. Tufts, *Ethics* (New York: MacMillan, 1908). For more on the intellectual sources of New Nationalist Progressivism, see Stears, *Progressives, Pluralists, and the Problems of the State*, 23–51.

[20] See Richard F. Bensel, *The Political Economy of American Industrialization, 1877–1920* (Cambridge: Cambridge University Press, 2000).

[21] Walter Weyl, "From Chaos to City," MS in The Walter Weyl Papers 2/7, Rutgers University Library.

[22] Walter Lippmann, *Drift and Mastery: An Attempt to Diagnose the Current Unrest* (New York: Michael Kennerley, 1914), 76.

Weyl demanded a "new democracy" for the United States: one "suited to the steam engine, the big factory, the great city, and the social relations corresponding to a complex, closely knit industrial system."[23] Such a democracy would, of course, be national in scope and primarily focused on federal government and federal elections. It would also, though, need to go beyond the petty party politics of old. What was required was a new and vibrant exchange of views across the entire citizen body, an exchange that would help the reconstructed federal government know whom precisely to focus upon when it engaged in social and economic reform and giving it a clear sense of what long-term goals to pursue.[24]

This was not an empty pipe-dream. The development of new technologies and the emergence of new media, the New Nationalists explained, made this kind of democratic exchange possible for the first time. Citizens could now directly communicate with one another across the vast expanse of the nation, discussing seriously the social and economic problems facing the country as a whole. No longer would citizens have to depend on the legislators to engage in discussion for them. The United States now had "at its disposal mechanisms for developing and exchanging opinions, and of reaching decisions, which are independent of representative assemblies," Herbert Croly contended. The railroad, the telegraph, and the newspapers had, as a popular refrain of the time had it, rendered "the nation a neighbourhood."[25] "Pure democracy," Herbert Croly concluded, "has again become not merely possible, but natural and appropriate."[26]

The initial advantage of this thoroughgoing democratic exchange was said to lie in its vital contribution to the technical and practical efficiency of a reformed national government. As Walter Lippmann explained, nationwide democratic debate could "furnish wisdom about multitudes" in a way that no other system could equal.[27] A vibrant national discussion would thus give those responsible for shaping a newly national policy the information they needed, helping them to identify the bases of the very "common good" that they should be pursuing in social and economic policy. But this was not the full extent of the New Nationalists' democratic vision. They also argued that this democratic process might initiate the very cultural changes

[23] Walter Weyl, *The New Democracy: An Essay on Certain Political and Economic Tendencies in the United States* (New York: MacMillan, 1912), 20–21.

[24] On anti-partyism, see Nancy Rosenblum, *On the Side of the Angels: An Appreication of Parties and Partisanship* (Princeton: Princeton University Press, 2008), 165–209.

[25] Willard A. White, *The Old Order Changeth: A View of American Democracy* (New York: MacMillan, 1910), 250.

[26] Herbert Croly, *Progressive Democracy* (New York: MacMillan, 1914), 265.

[27] See Walter Lippmann, *Preface to Politics*, (New York: Michael Kennerley, 1913), 116.

to which other Progressives had long aspired. By deliberating about the issues of the day, then, citizens across the nation might learn how to listen to and understand each other, helping them to develop empathetic and, eventually, solidaristic relationships. If they did that, they might also begin to pull together, to put aside their factional loyalties, and to think and act as a single national unit. Democratic discussion would thus encourage the "indispensable and increasingly powerful bond among the members of a modern industrial community" for which all Progressives longed.[28]

Here, then, was "a really educational theory of democracy." Democratic politics, in the form of ongoing, nationwide deliberation about the crucial challenges facing industrial society, would contribute in two crucial ways to national renewal. First, it would enable a newly empowered federal government to set the right objectives and pursue a common good suitable for an increasingly interdependent people. Second, it could also foster a spirit of togetherness, enabling Americans to overcome their divisions and develop increasingly strong ties with one another. Although the precise mechanisms remained vague, and fundamentally the detailed connection between citizenry and government was underspecified, the essential New Nationalist message was clear enough. Democratic deliberation focused on identifying shared goals and common values was fundamental if the United States is to "advance toward a better and deeper social and political union."[29] "The dynamics for a splendid civilization are all about us," Walter Lippmann argued, as nationwide democratic debate helped citizens "to co-operate on a large scale."[30]

Obstacles to the New Democracy

The New Nationalist Progressives were convinced that their democratic vision was necessitated by the times in which they lived. It was industrialization and urbanization that created nationwide interdependence and demanded that politics be redirected toward the common good. They did not, however, believe that the required democratic transformation would come about easily. In fact, Progressives of all sorts ceaselessly contrasted their democratic ideals with the realities of American political life in the early twentieth century.

---

[28] Herbert Croly, "The Obligation of the Vote," *New Republic*, October 9, 1915, 5.

[29] Herbert Croly, *The Promise of American Life*, (New York: MacMillan, 1909), 406, and idem, *Progressive Democracy*, 266.

[30] Lippmann, *Preface*, 317, and idem, *Drift and Mastery*, 145.

Part of their concern, of course, emanated from the increasing role that money appeared to play in electoral politics. Progressives were frequently to be found bemoaning the corruption of American political parties and worrying about the emergence of a new corporate plutocracy. Democratic mechanisms could not identify a truly common good if elections and the deliberations that preceded them were shaped by unjust economic circumstances.[31] Surprisingly, though, it was not financial inequality and its consequences that Progressives thought posed the most significant obstacle to the attainment of their desired new democracy. Their greatest fury was reserved for the capacity of the prevailing political, and especially the institutional, order of the United States to block progress. The political order was said to be unable to respond quickly and effectively to the changing needs and demands of the American people; it was also considered to be incapable of securing the necessary democratic engagement of citizens.[32] As the Progressive fellow-traveler Randolph Bourne put it, the new social and democratic spirit was effectively "barred from politics" in the United States by the prevailing institutions.[33] America was stuck with "a political system" designed for a "totally different civilization"; a system that "keeps our politics in bondage."[34]

To Progressives' eyes, the primary obstacle facing democratic renewal was the constitutional settlement itself. The United States Constitution, almost all Progressives continually complained, had been drawn up to govern a rural society by framers who were skeptical about direct democratic input into political decision making and who were more concerned with preventing the abuse of power than with creating a national government capable of intervening in every aspect of social and economic life.[35] Such a constitution was, therefore, entirely unsuited to the possibilities of politics in an industrial age. This unsuitability pervaded almost every aspect of the Constitution. It was especially troublesome in the form of the federal system, which excessively limited the authority of the national government; the separation of powers between legislature and the executive branch, which made coordination between the branches cumbersome at best, impossible at worst; and the doctrine of judicial review, which allowed just nine conservative Supreme Court justices to strike down Progressive legislation even if it made it through the legislature in the first place. This was a constitutional settlement, Herbert Croly complained, within which

---

[31] See Richard L. McCormick, *The Party Period and Public Policy: American Politics from the Age of Jackson to the Progressive Era* (New York: Oxford University Press, 1986).

[32] Lippmann, *Preface to Politics*, 255.

[33] Randolph Bourne, "American Uses for German Ideals," *New Republic*, July 1, 1916, 118.

[34] Lippmann, *Preface to Politics*, 286, and idem, *Progressive Democracy*, 314.

[35] See Croly, *Progressive Democracy*, 43, and Weyl, *New Democracy*, 15–16.

"[e]xecutives, legislatures, and courts were all granted abundant power to prevent others from doing things, and very little to do anything themselves."[36] It was a "rigid and authoritative traditional creed" that served only to "subordinate the collective will to rules."[37]

The political order that followed from such a constitution was thus decidedly not a system designed to encourage citizens to reflect on a changing common good, to provide them with opportunities to decide upon new courses of political action, or to empower a central administration to respond to their needs and aspirations. As Walter Weyl so evocatively put it, although "no King was set to rule over America" in 1781, the Constitution that replaced the monarchy "was more subtly subversive of the popular interest than might have been a dozen Georges."[38]

The Constitution's apparent ability to withstand efforts at change further exacerbated these concerns; it was still held in too high a regard by a large section of the citizenry to make any sort of direct attempt at wide-ranging reforms likely to succeed. As Walter Lippmann insisted, the founding fathers had "put their faith" in a distinctive institutional structure and "it has been part of our national piety to pretend that they succeeded."[39] Progressives also worried that even if the Constitution were to become vulnerable to challenge, the more superficially democratic elements of the existing American political order, especially the federal and state legislatures and the existing political parties, were probably incapable of rising to the task. Legislatures and parties were, after all, blighted by corruption. As Walter Weyl argued, legislatures across the United States tended to be controlled by one of the two main parties and the parties themselves were often "controlled by the ring; the ring, by the boss; the boss, by the trust."[40] Even when parties were not tainted in this way, though, Progressive critics worried they still failed to give voters a meaningful choice at election times. The real cleavage in American politics in the early twentieth century, Progressives argued, was that "between Progressives and non-Progressives," but this cleavage was not reflected in the division between the Democratic and Republican parties, both of which contained members of both Progressive and non-Progressive allegiance.[41] Somehow established party loyalties had become fixed in the United States on other cleavages, including race, locality, and social class, all of which the Progressives saw

---

[36] Herbert Croly "State Political Reorganization," *Proceedings of the American Political Science Association* 8 (1911): 128.

[37] Lippmann, *Preface to Politics*, 286, and Croly, *Progressive Democracy*, 314.

[38] Weyl, *New Democracy*, 317.

[39] Lippmann, *Preface to Politics*, 14.

[40] Weyl, *New Democracy*, 63.

[41] Croly, *Progressive Democracy*, 2.

as far less important. The party system failed to offer real opportunities to those seeking radical change. It was a "strange and monstrous thing," the *New Republic* reported, that even the putatively democratic parts of the American political order seemed impregnable "to the experience of a changing time."[42]

Progressives thus joined forces to condemn what they saw as the deeply undesirable *fixity* of the American political order. What was needed, they argued, was a democratic revolution that could "burst the frame apart."[43] The American people would have "to move in a body" to challenge the prevailing order, in the hope that one day it might "crumble to the ground" under concerted pressure, Herbert Croly explained.[44] What this meant was that the existing political institutions would have to be bypassed and a new order created from elsewhere.

It was for this reason that some Progressives began to demand mechanisms of "direct democracy." Citizens should be empowered to bring their own issues to the legislative agenda by means of "initiatives"; they should be allowed to veto other pieces of legislation by means of referenda; they should be able to control electoral candidates by means of direct primaries, "mandates," and recall elections for those who failed to follow their promises; they should also be able to overturn judicial review in cases where conservative judges stood out against popular opinion. Such mechanisms would bypass the courts, the legislatures, and the parties and allow the people to speak directly themselves. "[T]he establishment of equal suffrage, direct primaries, the initiative and referendum," Jane Addams argued, entailed that "the political organization of the nation can never again get so far from the life and the needs of the people."[45]

This appeal to direct democracy is the single project most associated with Progressive democratic thought in more recent scholarship.[46] Its record of actual achievement was far-reaching. Experiments in direct democracy took place across the United States throughout the Progressive

---

[42] Editorial, "The State's Right to Experiment," *New Republic*, February 3, 1917, 8. See, too, Sidney Milkis, "Progressivism, Then and Now" in Milkis and Mileur, eds., *Progressivism and the New Democracy*, 12–14.

[43] Lippmann, *Preface to Politics*, 13.

[44] Croly, "State Political Reorganization," 216.

[45] Jane Addams, "The Progressive's Dilemma," in Kellogg Papers 35/331.

[46] See, amongst an enormous literature, Arthur Ekrich, *Progressivism in America: A Study from Theodore Roosevelt to Woodrow Wilson* (New York: New Viewpoints, 1974); Thomas Goebel, "A Case of Democratic Contagion: Direct Democracy in the American West, 1890–1920," *Pacific Historical Review* 66 (1997): 213–30; and Austin Ranney, *Curing the Mischiefs of Faction: Party Reform in America* (Berkeley: Unviersity of California Press 1975). For an alternative view of the origins of party reform, see Alan Ware, *The American Direct Primary: Party Instutionalization and Transformation in the North* (Cambridge: Cambridge University Press, 2002).

Era, transforming politics at both the state and federal level. In 1913 the Seventeenth Amendment passed, ensuring the direct election of United States senators; women were enfranchised by the Nineteenth Amendment seven years later. At the state level, the Progressive Era saw twenty states introduce some form of initiative or referendum allowing citizens a direct say in the legislative process, and an incredible forty-seven states introduce some form of regulation of political parties, including direct primaries aiming to ensure that citizens themselves could play a role in the selection of candidates.

For some in the Progressive movement, these measures satisfied the very essence of the Progressive demand for democratic renewal. Not only may direct democracy of this kind "check much of our residual corruption, not only may it directly give the people a larger measure of political control than they now possess," one Progressive outlined, "but it may have even greater merit of being a vast school of democratic education."[47] Both democratic transformation and the politics of the common good were, it seemed, to be secured through mechanisms of direct democracy.

But not all Progressives welcomed the reforms so warmly. Many New Nationalists dismissed such methods as ill-suited to their essential purpose. The initiative and referendum seemed to Herbert Croly, for instance, as nothing but a "barren and mischievous addition to the stock of democratic institutions." Direct democracy of this sort displayed a worrying tendency to empower local and minority interests rather than to redirect democratic attention toward the identification and pursuit of a nationwide common good. "A democracy should not be organized so that the alert and vigorous minority can easily make its will prevail," Herbert Croly argued. "It should be organized so as to stimulate the liveliest possible political interest over the widest practicable political area. Such agencies of minority rule as the initiative and referendum in their ordinary form fail absolutely to contribute to the accomplishment of this necessary democratic purpose."[48] By encouraging citizens to mobilize support for particular ends in initiatives or to veto them in referenda, Croly continued, political power was handed over to "groups of individuals who occupy no intimate or responsible relation to the state administration or to the whole body of state public opinion." Such people would not be interested in seeking the common good; they would "merely want to push their own ideas or advance their own interests."[49]

[47] Weyl, *New Democracy*, 310.
[48] Croly, *Progressive Democracy*, 270, 308.
[49] Croly, "State Political Reorganization," 129–30. See, too, the more extended discussion in Stears, *Progressives, Pluralists, and the Problems of the State*, 78–83.

These concerns were not only the result of worries about particular instances of institutional design. They reflected a far more profound Progressive anxiety: doubts about the capabilities of the existing citizen body itself. All democratic institutions were to be judged on their contribution to a more coordinated response to the problems of industrialization and to the development of a greater spirit of national unity, but American citizens were not ready and able to employ the power provided to them by direct democracy in that way.[50] Croly, Lippmann, and Weyl all argued that Americans were individualists by inclination, with a tendency to focus on themselves and only to extend real loyalty to their families and perhaps to their local neighborhoods and voluntary societies. Such individualism had grown up steadily over the generations: originating from the religious convictions of the first settlers, reinforced by the experience of entrepreneurial expansion to the west and the open frontier, and entrenched still further by the rights-obsessed negativity of the American political order, with its emphasis on individual protections rather than on collective duties.[51] The result was that American citizens shared little sense of the larger social unit to which they belonged; they had, in the British commentator H. G. Wells's term, "no sense of state."[52]

Although democratic engagement was intended in the ideal to engender a deeper national spirit, then, Progressives worried that mechanisms of direct democracy would be more likely to spark greater argument and disunity than to set America on course for a politics of national unity. This disquiet had a profound impact on the New Nationalists' assessment of political possibility in early-twentieth-century America. All of their work was predicated on the need to craft a national politics of the common good, yet the prevailing attitudes of American citizens—not just their individualism, but their localism and their loyalties to ethnicity too—seemed to render a democratic path to such a good all but impossible. Can the "potentially democratic masses unite?," Walter Weyl asked in 1912. "Can the Maine lumberjack, the Negro lawyer, the German saloon keeper, the Montana farmer—men of different race, religion, and language; of different political traditions, of different economic status, of different social outlook . . . so compromise [their] conflicting claims . . . and thus compel a permanent victory?" It seemed unlikely. "The creation of democratic solidarity is halted by this multiplicity of cleavages," he concluded, and there appeared little that mechanisms of direct democracy could do about it. Such worries

---

[50] See Croly, *Promise of American Life*, 207.
[51] See Weyl, *New Democracy*, 36.
[52] H. G. Wells, *The Future in America: A Search After Realities* (New York: Harpers, 1906), 153.

were further exacerbated by widespread debates concerning mass immigration from Southern Europe and by the increased racial injustices faced by African Americans—especially, but not only, in the Southern states—further exacerbated these concerns. Far from exhibiting the virtues of a unified nationhood, the United States on this account seemed a "babel of traditions," where each and every group cleavage seemed as if it would "hamper and delay the formation of a national consciousness."[53]

This Progressive fear was exacerbated still further by a dangerously low evaluation of the cognitive capacities of citizens. Citizens in the early-twentieth-century United States were not only blighted by narrow loyalties but also by a more generic set of democratic inadequacies. "The one thing that no democrat must assume is that people are dear good souls, fully competent for their task," Walter Lippmann argued. Only "mystical democrats," he concluded, believe that American democratic practice "expresses the will of the people and that that will is wise."[54] Such skepticism was partly the result of a generalized disdain for the culture and practice of less well-off Americans, and especially Americans who were members of minority racial and ethnic groups, of the sort that had long characterized elite political theory.[55] It was, however, also widely held in more genuinely Progressive circles. Even the radical African American activist W.E.B. DuBois expressed concern that many poorer and minority American citizens were "not fit for the responsibility of republican government," going as far as to suggest that the absence of "the right sort of black voters" was just as much of an obstacle for those campaigning for racial harmony as "oppressive legal barriers."[56]

This conviction was further reinforced by the work of a new generation of political psychologists, especially that of Gabriel Tarde and Graham Wallasm, which carefully and persuasively elucidated the role of irrationality, short-sightedness, hatred, and bigotry in the political processes of all

---

[53] Weyl, *New Democracy*, 239, 347. For extensive discussion of these debates, see Gary Gerstle, "Liberty, Coercion, and the Making of Americans," *Journal of American History* 84 (1997): 524–58, and Desmond King, *Making Americans: Immigration, Race, and the Origins of the Diverse Democracy* (Cambridge, Mass., and London: Harvard University Press, 2000).

[54] Lippmann, *Preface to Politics*, 115.

[55] For detailed examinations of the use of such ideas in American history, see Desmond King, *In the Name of Liberalism: Illiberal Social Policy in the USA and Britain* (Oxford: Oxford University Press, 1998), and Rogers M. Smith, *Civic Ideals: Conflicting Visions of Citizenship in U.S. History* (New Haven: Yale University Press, 1998).

[56] See W. E. B. DuBois, "The Evolution of Negro Leadership," in Louis R. Harlam and Raymond W. Smock, *The Booker T. Washington Papers* (Chicago: University of Chicago Press, 1979), 9:175–78. For discussion, see William Jordan, "'The Damnable Dilemma': African-American Accommodation and Protest during World War I," *Journal of American History* 81 (1995): 1566.

actually existing democracies.[57] Democratic politics as it currently existed was, Tarde and Wallas explained, blighted both by the prevailing psychological characteristics of citizens—including individualism, factionalism, narrow-mindedness, and laziness—and by the tactics employed by professional politicians, which tended to exacerbate the worst of those tendencies. Democratic politics was a mess of conflicting interests whereby individuals and groups pursued their own goods at the expense of the goods of their fellow citizens through mechanisms of mobilization, campaign, and argument that drew on the worst aspects of human character.[58]

This argument took firm hold in New Nationalist circles, where a great distaste at the campaigning strategies employed by the political parties, especially in urban areas, was combined with a sense that the majority of citizens appeared to deserve little better. "[M]any of our political evils," Walter Weyl insisted in the *New Republic*, are due "to defective political machinery," but many others are caused by the "crowd-like action of ignorant and irresponsible constituencies."[59] Electoral appeals in such a democracy were based on patronage and emotion, short-term sectional interest and bigotry, rather than on attempts to identify a shared common good, and they were so at least partially because those were the kinds of appeals to which citizens appeared to respond. All of this meant that whilst the constitutional settlement might indeed keep American politics "in bondage," a shift to direct democracy might simply worsen the problems the industrializing United States faced by further releasing the spirit of social conflict. If citizens could not be trusted, then they should not be empowered.

Progressive reformers were thus caught in their own version of the paradox of politics. Their vision of a future ideal society was clear enough: theirs would be an America where citizens debated the common good together, took collective responsibility for identifying responses to the challenges their nation faced, and were able to pass those responses on to an easily permeable governing machine that would be capable of pursuing a coordinated policy on the basis of those publicly decided responses. Theirs would be a fully democratic America, one that possessed a spirit of national solidarity and was assisted by a government of real purpose and capacity. Yet the realities of even the most democratic elements of American politics as currently constituted made anything approaching that ideal vision extraordinarily difficult to realize. Demands for more direct democracy appeared a potential solution to some Progressives, but not to all. The more skeptical

[57] See Gabriel Tarde, *The Laws of Imitation* (New York: Henry Holt and Co., 1903), and Graham Wallas, *Human Nature and Politics* (London: Constable and Co., 1910).

[58] Lippmann, *Preface to Politics*, 302.

[59] Walter Weyl, "The Sovereign Crowd," *New Republic*, October 9, 1915, 266.

needed to be sure that citizens empowered with new democratic powers would make the right use of them; they needed to know that such a democracy would really enable the United States to transcend the individualism, factionalism, and irrationality of the present and move toward the deliberative politics of the common good that the future apparently demanded. But such reassurances would not be forthcoming. These Progressives possessed a blueprint of an ideal democracy but they only had non-ideal citizens with which to build it. It was a paradox that left Walter Lippmann "fearfully puzzled."[60]

Political Strategies for the New Democracy

Daunting as the challenge of this paradox was, the Progressives did not shirk it. Unlike many of their twenty-first-century counterparts, they neither abandoned the tasks of real-life politics altogether nor shelved their long-term ideals, turning to short-term political strategizing instead. Rather, these Progressives believed that whilst it was vital not to overlook the limitations of existing democratic practices and citizen habits, it was also crucial not to be overawed by them. It was true, Herbert Croly said, that the limitations of actually existing citizens meant that "the success of a thoroughgoing democracy" could not simply be "prophesized," as some of his more utopian colleagues had perhaps assumed, but such a democracy might still nonetheless be "consciously created." That creation would, of course, be exceptionally difficult. It would require both "an uncompromising faith" in the underlying "moral value of democracy" and a clear-sighted understanding of the political limitations of the present.[61] What Progressives needed, Croly concluded, was an approach to politics that was sincerely committed to the realization of a long-term ideal but that also built up from an unsentimental understanding of the politics of the early-twentieth-century United States. As Walter Weyl so eloquently put it, the move toward democracy would require Progressives to be "compromising in action" even as they were "uncompromising in principle."[62]

The approach to politics that followed from this dual commitment itself had two initial dimensions. The first emphasized the importance of

---

[60] Walter Lippmann, Letter to Learned Hand, September 4, 1916, in The Learned Hand Papers 106/15, Law School Library, Harvard University.

[61] Croly, *Progressive Democracy*, 173.

[62] Weyl, *New Democracy*, 269. For commentary on this general trend, see Leon Fink, *Progressive Intellectuals and the Dilemmas of Democratic Commitment* (Cambridge, Mass.: Harvard University Press, 1997), esp. 13–51.

developing plans for far-reaching institutional reforms that would be capable of transforming the habits and practices of the citizenry itself. It was no good recommending institutions that were dependent on such a transformation already having occurred, as much of the direct democracy agenda had appeared to presume. Instead ideas for new political institutions would have to explain how those innovations themselves could elicit the citizen habits necessary for democratic renewal. Institutional design, Herbert Croly thus argued, should be founded on the idea that good citizenship does not just emerge naturally but always needs "to be aroused, elicited, informed, [and] developed."[63] The underlying belief was clear: if citizens were situated in the right kind of democratic, political institutions they might be able to overcome their own limitations and rise to the challenge of creating a politics of the common good. As Walter Lippmann contended, a new institutional order was the best way to ensure that American citizens "think of the whole nation."[64]

Progressives of this kind thus spent an enormous amount of time and intellectual energy in identifying the kinds of institutional changes that might encourage citizens to develop the habits that they believed were necessary to their idealized democracy. This had both a critical and a constructive aspect. Critically, existing institutional arrangements were blamed for perpetuating "do-nothingness" on the part of government and factionalism and individualism on the part of citizens. The judicial-review powers of the Supreme Court, the limitation of executive authority through the doctrine of separation of powers, and aspects of federalism were all therefore to be dismantled. Constructively, they were to be replaced by institutions that created incentives for citizens to pursue common values and to develop a spirit of national solidarity. An extraordinarily diverse set of precise plans was proposed, ranging from new electoral systems for gubernatorial elections through a radical extension of the powers of the executive branch to the extension of democratic mechanisms to organizations outside the usual scope of politics.[65]

Such institutional reforms, however, would themselves have to be enacted politically, and that meant that citizens (or at least some of them) would have to be made to want them. As Lippmann had it, no "amount of architect's plans" alone "will build a house. Someone must have the *will* to build it." The second dimension of the Progressive approach to politics thus concerned the ways in which citizens could be aligned behind the necessary

---

[63] Croly, *Progressive Democracy*, 304.

[64] Lippmann, *Preface to Politics*, 104.

[65] For a summary, see "Conclusion," in Mileur and Milkis, *Progressivism and the New Democracy*, esp. 259–88.

task of institutional reconstruction. That in turn would demand serious strategic thought. It would not be enough simply to propagate the message and to hope that people would flock behind it. As Lippmann vigorously argued, "[o]nly the pathetic amateur deludes himself into thinking that, if he presents the major and minor premise the voter will automatically draw the conclusion." Rather, "the successful politician—good or bad—deals with the dynamics—with the will, the hopes, the needs, and visions of men. . . . So long as you rely on the efficacy of 'scientific' demonstration and logical proof you can hold your conventions in anybody's back parlor and have room to spare."[66]

That meant, of course, that Progressives might sometimes have to engage in the very kind of politics that they wished in the long run to transcend: the politics of manipulation, of coalition building, and even of factional mobilization. The worst characteristics of the citizen body would have to be enlisted in the task of their own abolition. But Progressives would have to be careful as they played with these forces, for they must not employ political strategies that would actually worsen the very tendencies that their reforms were meant to undermine. "We can't beat the Hearsts by using their methods," Walter Lippmann once said of the politics of the media mogul and his kind, because "we'd nearly be Hearsts in the end."[67]

The task these Progressives set themselves was, therefore, fiendishly difficult. They took some heart, though, from the direction that reform was already taking. Herbert Croly thus argued that even though most of the plans for "direct democracy" were misguided, that was not a reason to turn against democratizing trends in general. There was some hope that key elements of good citizenship might emerge as a result of the experience of slowly improving democratic engagement. He thus insisted, for example, that the expansion of democratic opportunities offered by the Constitutional amendments providing for the direct election for United States senators and the enfranchisement of women were to be welcomed, even in the prevailing non-ideal circumstances of the present. "The one sufficient justification for granting the vote to both men and women prior to the more general distribution of . . . mental alertness and social sympathy and aspiration," Croly outlined, "is the expectation that the vote itself will help educate the voter in the essentials of democratic citizenship." Citizens, he explained, "will never rise to the level of their necessary political obligations unless their sense of

---

[66] Lippmann, *Preface to Politics*, 220, 217–18.

[67] Walter Lippmann, Letter to Learned Hand, September 4, 1916, in The Learned Hand Papers 106/15.

responsibility is stimulated by a generous opportunity to act upon it. They cannot be prepared for the vote except by practice in voting."[68]

This argument was also extended to the politics of pressure groups that these Progressives hoped would be drawn into standard channels of democratic policymaking rather than kept on the outside. "Instead of proposing as did certain reformers a few years ago to drive special interests out of politics," Croly continued, "the object of a really educational political organization should be to drive them out from being behind the law or away from illegal or antisocial conspiracy into politics." Just in so far as those special interests "are made to argue their case in public and to prove their social value by reasons which appeal to other special groups of interest and opinion," he concluded, "they may tend to become a useful part of social organization."[69] Democratic participation by such groups, the editors of the *New Republic* explained, would "promote a sense of public responsibility and a disposition to make personal sacrifices" and even help foster "livelier human sympathies, intellectual alertness, adaptability and tenacity," enabling even those who disagreed to come together and share "an imperturbable faith in the great democratic enterprise of indefinite and social improvement."[70]

These arguments often offered little more than a classically Tocquevillian hope that individualistic, self-interested citizens would become more open-minded and kind-spirited when exposed to the experiences of democratic policymaking. They were deeply unsatisfactory as responses to the Progressive version of the paradox of politics, though, because they presumed that relatively small-scale changes in the institutional order could bring about a sweeping change in the attributes and attitudes of American citizens. Even most Progressives found the suggestion that a nationwide spirit of solidarity could be constructed simply from an exchange of views between special interest groups thoroughly unconvincing. There was, however, one other political development that appeared to offer a more compelling cause for optimism, one institutional change that seemed to the Progressives to offer a rather more concrete means of reconciling the pursuit of the long-term goal with the short-term means; it involved the politics of executive leadership.

The emergence of powerful, more-or-less directly elected single-person executives in place of the plural executives that had long characterized most state constitutions and of the gradual enhancement of the power of the

---

[68] Croly, "Obligation of the Vote," 8, 5.
[69] Croly, *Progressive Democracy*, 320–21.
[70] Editorial, "The Newer Nationalism," *New Republic*, January 29, 1916, 321.

federal executive were amongst the primary characteristics of Progressive-Era politics. This focus on the executive was an approach to politics embodied especially in the presidency of Theodore Roosevelt and by his later campaign as the candidate of the Progressive Party in the election of 1912. But it was also seen in the widespread enhancement of gubernatorial power and in the increasing focus on gubernatorial candidates in progressively inclined states, especially in the Midwest and parts of the South. New Nationalist Progressives believed that this development more than any other in contemporary politics enabled crucial aspects of their short-term ambitions and their long-term goals to be combined. Indeed, it often seemed that the extension of executive leadership was "the distinctive fact" about Progressive politics.[71]

The short-term advantages of focusing on single candidates for executive office were obvious to radical reformers: popular individuals like Theodore Roosevelt, Robert La Follette of Wisconsin, and Charles Aycock of North Carolina had proven ability to mobilize a broad range of support behind them, giving Progressives the chance they needed to burst through the old frame imposed by the constitutional settlement, by established citizen prejudices, and by the entrenched party system, and set about a dynamic process of reform.[72] This individual advantage was rapidly turned into political theory. A successful candidate might be elected largely on account of charisma, Herbert Croly argued, but when the candidate also offered a reform platform he could also justifiably claim to have "obtained office by a definite program of legislation." In such circumstances, "this body of public opinion would constitute him as the political leader of the state with full power to carry out its will," and a new political dawn might be expected to follow.[73]

Crucial as these opportunities might be, the longer-term advantages of concentrating on executive politics were often considered to be more important still. Croly, Lippmann, and Weyl believed that a focus on executive leadership enabled individual political issues to be brought together into a coherent whole for the first time in American history. If politics was rendered through the single person of a president or a governor rather than through legislatures in which each member was responsible to some determinate factional interest, then a form of political unity could be forged out of the disunity of prevailing democratic politics. Effective executive leadership, Jane Addams suggested, could "focus the scattered oral energy of our vast nation" and "direct it into practical reforms."[74] Walter Lippmann's

---

[71] Lippmann, *Preface to Politics*, 302.

[72] See Croly, *Progressive Democracy*, 297, and Lippmann, *Preface to Politics*, 24.

[73] Croly, *Progressive Democracy*, 303.

[74] Addams, "Progressives Dilemma."

description was grander still. Such a leader, he argued, "makes social movements conscious of themselves, expresses their needs, gathers their power and then thrusts them behind the inventor and the technician in the task of actual achievement."[75] And in so doing he moves forward the project of a coordinated response to the newly industrialized nation's problems.

This unity was partly a practical matter. A single-person executive was simply better able to trace the relationships between diverse elements of polity and tie them together and he would be better placed also to represent a broad constituency of interests rather than one section of the community. But for many Progressives the importance of executive leadership transcended even these advantages. Indeed, it often appeared that the singularity of the president as an individual would come to represent the unity of the nation itself; there was something almost Hobbesian about the Progressive vision of the offices of governor and president. Moreover, if Americans could be directed to think about the political issues of the day through the eyes of one man and one office, then they could be drawn into democratic engagement with him. By encouraging people to engage in debates focused on the program offered by a single leader, the interest of the people would be awakened and the citizen body organized and vitalized. But more importantly still, the focus on a single person would eventually lead citizens to think about politics from the perspective of a single, united, people. Croly thus argued that "the value of executive leadership" consists in its "peculiar serviceability not merely as the agent of prevailing public opinion" but also as the "*concentrator* of such opinion."[76]

This was a view that was not restricted to the New Nationalists. It spread right across the broader Progressive movement. Faith in the transformative role of executive politics became a hallmark of Progressive agitation. In Cleveland, Ohio, the Progressive mayor Tom Johnson, who died in office, was memorialized in the public square with this inscription:

> Beyond his party and beyond his class
> The man forsook the few to serve the mass
> He found us groping leaderless and blind
> He found us striving each his selfish part
> He left a civilization with a civic heart.[77]

---

[75] Lippmann, *Preface to Politics*, 302.

[76] Croly, *Progressive Democracy*, 304.

[77] See Edward Bemis, "Tom L. Johnson's Achievements as Mayor of Cleveland," *Review of Reviews*, May 1911: 558–60, and David J. Goldberg, *Discontented America: The United States in the 1920s* (Baltimore: The Johns Hopkins University Press, 1999), 3.

Nothing that the more academically oriented theorists of Progressivism could have written would have stated the argument more clearly.

It is for these reasons that the presidential election of 1912 mattered so much to Progressives of almost all stripes. They were confident that the newly formed Progressive Party had in Theodore Roosevelt a candidate who could meet all of those demands, a man indeed who had already demonstrated these talents whilst in office as president as a Republican from 1901 to 1909. Roosevelt, Walter Lippmann opined, "is a man of will in whom millions of people have felt the embodiment of their own will." Whilst he was president, he "wanted what the nation wanted; his own power radiated power; he embodied a vision; Tom, Dick and Harry moved with his movement."[78] Here was a man with unparalleled rhetorical skills, with broad popular appeal, who was able to engage in the skulduggery necessary for electoral success but was also committed to most of the Progressives' fundamental aspirations. With Roosevelt as candidate of the Progressive Party, he could draw the cause forward, educating and inspiring the citizenry as he did so. As president he could transform America.

These hopes came, of course, to nothing, wrecked by Woodrow Wilson's ability to capture key Progressive votes as the Democratic Party candidate in 1912, and then by Roosevelt's abandonment of the Progressive Party after the election and the party's subsequent collapse.[79] This failure caused intense soul-searching within the Progressive movement and was followed by deep division. Some Progressives followed Wilson after 1912, others switched allegiance to the Socialist Party, and still others abandoned mainstream politics altogether and headed off for a life of quiet, academic contemplation.[80] Even without that failure, though, many critics would still have dismissed the Progressive concentration on executive leadership as naive, elitist, or both. The Progressives' leadership-centered political theory was, of course, written before the rise of Fascism, at a time when very few American political commentators were as conscious of the dangers of demagoguery and overly powerful individual leaders as they would be a decade or two later. Nonetheless, it should have been clear at the time that Progressives were overly willing to place both political faith and practical responsibility in the hands of one man and one branch of government. Indeed, they often appeared almost wilfully blind in this regard, and seemed to think that if they

---

[78] Lippmann, *Preface to Politics*, 220, 221.

[79] See Amos Pinchot, *History of the Progressive Party, 1912–1916* (New York: New York University Press, 1958).

[80] See Eugene Tobin, *Organize or Perish: America's Independent Progressives, 1913–1933* (New York: Greenwood, 1986).

could find just one effective leader, then the limitations of the citizen body would simply disappear.

It is wrong, however, to dismiss the Progressive approach to democratic transformation in its entirety because of this one error, as many deliberatively minded critics have been wont to do.[81] At least in the years after 1912 and the failure of Roosevelt's presidential bid, senior Progressive thinkers and activists began to doubt that first-class leaders were the solution to the perceived democratic deficit in American politics. Some, indeed, began to concede that there was little more reason to believe that decent leadership was going to emerge in American democracy than there was to think that the broader citizenry of its own accord was going to become capable of exercising democratic power with responsibility and in the spirit of national solidarity. After 1912, then, the Progressives were in effect back where they started. If executive leadership was not going to be the mechanism by which the non-ideal democracy of the present was transformed into the ideal democracy of the future, they would have to look elsewhere.

Political Strategy Beyond the State

In the search for a more stable resolution of the paradox of politics after 1912, the Progressives began to look beyond the orthodox political process itself, turning instead to broader questions of the distribution and exercise of power in society at large. This was not an entirely new direction. Some in the Progressive movement had long considered issues in what would now be called "civil society" to be essential components of the process of democratic renewal and had castigated their colleagues for overlooking the less formal parts of the political process. Walter Lippmann argued in 1912 that American reformers were wrong to overestimate "the importance of nominations, campaigns, and office-holding." "If we are discouraged" by failings on the larger political scene, he observed, "it is because we tend to identify statecraft with the official government which is merely one of its instruments. . . . [W]e have mistaken an inflated fragment for the real political life of the country."[82]

In moving out beyond formal politics, Progressives were drawn to the one realm that had sparked their initial interest in democratic renewal: modern industry. It was reform of the governance of industrial life, they

---

[81] See James Nuechterlein, "The Dream of Scientific Liberalism: The New Republic and American Progressive Thought, 1914–1920," *Review of Politics* 42 (1980): 167–90.

[82] Lippmann, *Preface to Politics*, 56.

argued, that might provide the means for democratic reconstruction. This began with a worry. Progressives were deeply concerned with the tensions of the industrial workplace in the early twentieth century. They were partly worried, of course, about the economic and social inequalities that attended industrial labor and about the social division and unrest that might attend those inequalities. But their primary emphasis was on the dramatic mismatch between their democratic ideals and the experience of everyday life in the workplace. American industry, these Progressives argued, was a form of "autocracy." It was a world in which workers had to do exactly as they were told by their employers or risk destitution. Such autocracy, the *New Republic* outlined, was "an outrage upon the very principle of democracy." It was an outrage, moreover, with profound effects for the traditional politics, as the experience of working day to day under the arbitrary powers of an employer was said to "destroy the self-respect and moral integrity which is essential to good citizenship."[83]

The experience of absolutism in the industrial realm was thus said to lead ineluctably to its acceptance in the political. As the Progressive jurist, and later Supreme Court justice, Louis Brandeis put it, the governance structure of the industrial workplace was breeding a "nation of slaves."[84] It was no surprise that the emergent working classes were unable to exercise their duties as political citizens with any degree of skill and responsibility when their everyday lives were shaped by the experience of "servitude." "The greatest problem which is before the American people in this generation," Brandeis continued, "is the problem of reconciling our industrial system with the political democracy in which we live."[85]

The creation of some form of democracy in industry, therefore, came to be seen as a vital prerequisite for the creation of a better democracy in American politics. As such, it was given far more importance than any other potential reform in the writings of post-1912 Progressives.[86] But unlike other potential social changes, democracy in industry could not be created from above. The federal government simply did not have the power—or, with Wilson at the helm, the will—to involve itself in the reorganization of industrial governance. State-led initiatives might have more chance of

---

[83] Editorial, "Autocracy in America," *New Republic*, April 28, 1917, 366.

[84] Louis Brandeis, "On Industrial Relations," reprinted in Louis Brandeis, *The Curse of Bigness* (New York: Kennikat, 1962 [1914]), 81.

[85] Louis Brandeis, "Industrial Co-operation," reprinted in Brandeis, *Curse of Bigness*, 35.

[86] For contemporary commentary, see William R. Bassett, *When the Workmen Help You Manage* (New York: Century, 1919), and Charles W. Eliot, *The Future of Trade-Unionism and Capitalism in a Democracy* (New York: Putnam, 1910). See, too, Howell J. Harris, "Industrial Democracy and Liberal Capitalism, 1890–1925," in Nelson Lichtenstein and Howell Harris, eds., *Industrial Democracy in America: The Ambiguous Promise* (Cambridge: Cambridge University Press, 1996), 43–66.

making it past the legislature, but they were likely to run afoul of judicial review.[87] "[I]n industry as in politics," the *New Republic* similarly insisted, "there must come such devolution of authority. Welfare work and all reform from above are valuable only in so far as they aid and do not obstruct the uneven progress of the wage-earner toward industrial democracy."[88] The primary agent for any process of industrial democratization had, therefore, to be located within industry itself.

It was as such that Progressives turned with great expectation to the expanding American trade union movement. It "is labor organized that alone can stand between America and the creation of a permanent, servile, class," Walter Lippmann contended. It was an argument that Lippmann made with incredible force and unexpected radicalism. "Unless labor is powerful enough to be respected it is doomed to a degrading servitude," he asserted. "Without unions no such power is possible. Without unions industrial democracy is unthinkable" and "without democracy in industry . . . there is no such thing as democracy in America." "Only through the union can the wage-earner participate in the control of industry," Lippmann concluded, "and only through the union can he obtain the discipline needed for self-government."[89]

This call for the empowerment of trade unions and for a rapid increase in their input into industrial decision making was not restricted to Lippmann. In the five years between the collapse of the Progressive Party and the United States' entry into the First World War, it became the single most important theme in Progressive writing in general, and in *New Republic* editorializing in particular. "When employers refuse to negotiate with the unions," the *New Republic* continually argued, "they are denying to their employees the very substance of citizenship."[90]

Yet the advocacy of increased power for trade unions was not without its difficulties. Most importantly, it was unclear to many Progressives, even to those closest to the union movement, that trade union activity was always conducive to the construction of a nationally minded, empathetic, and broadly solidaristic spirit of citizenship. There were, after all, aspects of trade unionism that appeared to display the same limitations, especially the same factionalism, as the Progressives had identified in the political realm.

---

[87] See Julie Greene, *Pure and Simple Politics: The American Federation of Labor and Political Mobilization* (New York: Cambridge University Press, 1998).

[88] Editorial, "The Tolerated Unions," *New Republic*, November 7, 1914, 12.

[89] Lippmann, *Drift and Mastery*, 81.

[90] Editorial, "Unionism vs. Anti-Unionism," *New Republic*, September 23, 1916, 178.

If it was important to place faith in unions, it was also crucial to recognize that trade unions are not "always right still less always wise."[91]

These concerns had two dimensions. The first concerned the actual policies of the unions, and especially their perceived tendency to promote the economic interests of their members at the expense of the general industrial interest of the broader society. For Brandeis and others, it appeared that "the trade unions were too hasty in making up their minds to oppose" efforts at industrial improvement. This opposition was especially pronounced in response to the frequent recommendations of Taylorite efficiency engineers, whose "time and motion studies" suggested numerous improved techniques of production in the first two decades of the twentieth century. Brandeis and colleagues rather naively regarded these self-described "industrial experts" as impartial technicians with only the good of the nation at heart, but they were widely discredited within trade union circles.[92] The second dimension revolved around the tactics that unions often employed in pursuit of their goals, especially strike actions, industrial sabotage, and even, on occasion, violence. In Brandeis's mind, these disruptive tactics were associated with the apparent rise of "syndicalism" and with the radical industrial unionism of "Big" Bill Heywood's Industrial Workers of the World (IWW), and there was real fear in Progressive circles that other unions might follow the IWW in the direction of profound and dangerous forms of social conflict.[93] "We do not believe that the labor movement will gain by a syndicalist philosophy, based on contempt for public opinion," the *New Republic* insisted. The trade union movement's best hope "still lies, we believe, in the ideals and methods of democracy."[94]

Progressives thus found themselves faced with essentially the same dilemma with regard to the limitations of industrial citizenship as they had faced with regard to political citizenship. All of their fundamental principles led them to demand a rapid and radical democratization of industry, but they also feared that the chosen agents of such democratization would be tempted to pursue their own interests at the expense of others', displaying exactly the kind of narrow-mindedness that they thought blighted citizens in the polity at large. If trade unions did this they did not offer hope.

[91] Editorial, "Tolerated Unions," 12. See, too, the discussion in Melvyn Dubofsky, *When Workers Organize: New York City in the Progressive Era* (Amherst: University of Massachusetts Press, 1968).

[92] Louis Brandeis, "How Far Have We Come on the Road to Industrial Democracy?" reprinted in Brandeis, *Curse of Bigness*, 43.

[93] See Joyce L. Kornbluh, *Rebel Voices: An IWW Anthology* (Ann Arbor: University of Michigan Press, 1968).

[94] Editorial, "The Public and Trade Union Policy," *New Republic*, October 7, 1917, 237.

Rather, they threatened to unleash the drastic social disorder Progressives had always feared rather than bringing the United States closer to the civically focused, nationally spirited democracy that they craved.

Here, though, the issue could not be ducked. Conflict in industry was coming anyway, Progressives believed. It was an unavoidable consequence of the move toward an industrial economy, especially in the American context. Trade unionism would thus continue to rise, whether Progressives and their allies and enemies desired it or not. Workers were not going to be satisfied with what employers offered them forever and there was nothing even well-placed Progressives could do to avoid that. Progressives had, therefore, to develop a response to its demands and its tactics. As Lippmann explained, "the demonstration of King Canute settled once and for all the stupid attempt to ignore a moving force."[95] In the battle of the industrial workplace, Progressives would have to take a side, and ensure, too, that they made a difference. "The task of shaping [trade union] policy so that it may not flare out in futile insurrection, but shall become a powerful, continuous pressure upon society for its own reform, is absolutely fundamental to human progress," the *New Republic*'s editors charged.[96]

Once they had reached the realization that industrial conflict was unavoidable in itself, the decision that the New Nationalist Progressives came to was surprising, especially for a movement that had dedicated itself to governmental efficiency and national unity.[97] For despite all of their concerns, New Nationalist Progressives nailed their colors firmly to the mast of the trade union movement. "The trade union is a crude young democracy," the *New Republic* conceded, but "there is both unity and a principle" to it. "[W]age-earners stand united for common purposes, for common defence," and deserve Progressive loyalty out of respect for those commitments. And that loyalty was not grudging. Progressives rallied to the cause of unions' right to organize collectively. They offered staunch defenses of individual actions and they provided vigorous support for the right to strike itself, which they described as a right that "labor cannot *on any terms* surrender."[98] Most remarkably of all, though, they justified occasional acts of industrial coercion and even violence by those trade unions involved in the harshest of conflicts. Trade union politics in the early twentieth century was not the politics of reasonable persuasion, of deliberation across groups about the common good. It was, rather, the vigorous pursuit of economic

---

[95] Lippmann, *Preface to Politics*, 221.

[96] Editorial, "Toward Labor's Power," *New Republic*, August 5, 1916, 8.

[97] For the traditional view, see Jordan, *Machine-Age Ideology*; Nuechterlien. "Dream of Scientific Liberalism"; and Wiebe, *Search for Order*.

[98] Editorial, "Tolerated Unions," 12; emphasis in original.

interest, often conducted in the most conflictual of circumstances. But Croly, Lippmann, Weyl, and colleagues did not shy from that.

The Progressives' defense of this kind of disruptive, disorderly, and potentially factional politics was not simply a response to individual crises. Rather, Progressives began to argue that this kind of struggle was essential to democratic progress, even if it initially seemed to be a nondemocratic form of politics itself. Its advantages were thus general and not particular. "Those who deplore the use of force in the labor struggle," Walter Lippmann outlined, "should ask themselves whether the ruling class of a country could be depended upon to inaugurate a program of reconstruction which would abolish the barbarism that prevails in industry."[99] The question was, of course, rhetorical. "We are not civilized enough to meet an issue before it becomes acute," Lippmann continued. "We were not intelligent enough to free the slaves peacefully—we are not intelligent enough to-day to meet the industrial problem before it develops [into] a crisis. That is the hard truth of the matter. And that is why no honest student of politics can plead that social movements should confine themselves to argument and debate, abandoning the militancy of the strike, the insurrection, the strategy of social conflict."[100]

Although such arguments were redolent of those defending revolution, this was not intended to be an open-ended call to workers to take up arms. Indeed, most mainstream Progressives urged unions to avoid violence as often as they could and were sharply critical of the insurrectionary language of Heywood and the IWW. Strikingly, however, their reasoning was grounded more in practical considerations than in ethical ones. In contrast to the revolutionary ages of the eighteenth and nineteenth centuries, violent methods were unlikely to work in the modern industrial state, and that is why they were to be discarded. Walter Weyl explained this in detail in his most extensive treatment of the subject in *The New Democracy*. "Effective arms have become too costly and too difficult of concealment," he suggested. Whilst the "barricades" of the nineteenth-century Paris Commune were "built of cobbles," "modern streets are built of asphalt." And in any regard, the state and the employers could mobilize their agents of repression in "the briefest time" and with extensive and often conclusive force.[101] If trade unions were to employ coercive measures of their own, they would be better advised to conduct themselves stealthily, always staying as close

[99] Lippmann, *Preface to Politics*, 279.
[100] Ibid., 277–78.
[101] Weyl, *New Democracy*, 256–57.

to public opinion as their radical demands would allow, and selecting their particular political strategies with skill and judgment.

Even if they did not tend to advocate violence, though, the Progressives still had to explain why it was legitimate for a section of society like industrial labor to employ any sort of political coercion in order to get its way. The essence of their democratic theory, after all, resided in a nationwide discussion about the common good, not in the bargaining and strategizing of sectional interests associated now with democratic realism. Yet here they were defending the right of one increasingly strong movement to impose its will not through deliberation, discourse, and reason but by withdrawing their labor or by taking to the streets. In responding to that challenge, Progressives offered four distinctive and crucially important arguments.

The first insisted that as governing authorities and employers frequently made use of coercive tactics against the trade unions, it might occasionally be acceptable for unions to respond in kind. The United States was not, after all, a fully fledged democracy yet, and thus the kinds of obligations that would legitimately fall upon citizens of such a democracy did not always apply in the present. In an ideal democracy citizens would behave deliberatively toward each other, putting aside their personal ambitions for the sake of the common good, but early-twentieth-century America was not an ideal democracy and in this light it was at least fair that clashing sectional interests should be allowed to use similar methods in their competition with one another.

The difficulty with this first argument, of course, was that it said little about how this clash of factional interests could be transcended. Progressive political recommendations were meant to be transformative—to concentrate on the possibility of *improving* American democratic practice rather than solely on conducting it as was. The second Progressive defense of trade unionism thus suggested that the tendency toward sectionalism and coercive politics was a temporary one in the union movement and would ebb away as the movement became stronger and more confident. "It is the weak unions, the unorganized and shifting workers, who talk sabotage and flare up into a hundred little popgun rebellions," Walter Lippmann suggested. "But where unions can meet the employers on a real equality, as railroad workers can, there you will find very little insurrectionary talk."[102] As unions won battles against their employers, or against the state, therefore, they would tend to cease to be confrontational. Indeed, in this regard the Progressives often argued that it was in the very nature of trade unionism to work solidaristically and with civic spirit and that that nature would flourish with the

---

[102] Lippmann, *Drift and Mastery*, 87.

passage of time and as unions became more fully recognized as an unavoidable element of the industrial order. The "discipline and concert" required by trade union activity would be a precursor to the broader discipline and concert that would be required in a truly communal America.[103]

This perspective sometimes took a bolder form in the third Progressive argument for trade union politics, which suggested that the experience of trade union struggle itself—especially struggle in the noble cause of industrial democratization—could provide profound educational opportunities. Such struggle, Progressives explained, required union members to build solidarity with comrades, to think strategically, and to learn to take effective action, whilst all the while pitting themselves against injustice and democratic exclusion. All of these, of course, were skills and attributes that would be in great demand in an improved democracy, which would help union members to overcome the individualism, laziness, and irresponsibility that Progressives believed blighted modern citizenry in America at large. Trade union struggle might not quite be fully democratic citizenship—it was too disruptive and factional for that—but it was better than individualism, alienation, and disengagement.

Once again it was Walter Lippmann who provided the clearest exposition of this view. As he saw it, trade union activity provided an experience of a vigorous form of fraternity that many American citizens had not enjoyed since childhood. If union members cast their minds back to their younger days, Lippmann colorfully explained, they would recall their memberships in gangs of street kids. Within such gangs there had been a great sense of solidarity, of shared purpose, as well as fine displays of courage and action against adversity. Adults should remember that these gangs offer "a fine experience even though a few windows get smashed," Lippmann concluded. For "all their faults and misdirected energy," both unions and gangs provided "loyalty to something larger than the petty details of the moment" and as such they could both contribute to the democratic transformation of America.[104] Unity would come through struggle.

The fourth argument in defense of this kind of coercive politics built on this endorsement of the experience of struggle but raised it to another level. It celebrated the opportunities that radical trade union action provided for the broader reconstruction of American society, its economy, and its politics. As we have seen, political experimentation was of crucial importance to these Progressives. Locked in an outmoded political system that prevented fast and effective response to the changing needs of its people, the United

---

[103] See editorial, "Tolerated Unions," 12.
[104] Lippmann, *Drift and Mastery*, 231.

States had to become willing to try new things. In the long term, it had to move to a nationally rather than locally or individually focused politics, to expand democratic opportunities at work and in politics, and to listen and learn from new leaders; in the short term, almost any dramatic change was considered to be better than the uniformity and inertia of the prevailing political order. An occasional outburst from the trade union movement could, therefore, magnify the opportunities for experiment. It would reshape the incentives that applied to ordinary citizens, shocking them out of their complacency and urging them to think anew about the direction of the nation. It would also provoke a reaction from the more entrenched political powers, making them realize that they could not continue to ignore the industrial transformation forever.

"Whoever is working to express special energies is part of a constructive revolution," Progressives thus urged.[105] In a world of vigorous industrial conflict, where workers occasionally took to the streets or stopped producing the goods upon which large sections of the public had come to depend, the citizenry at large could be thus shown that politics really *matters*. In such a situation, new political opportunities would constantly present themselves. Politics thus "ceases to be a game and becomes identified with the realities of life."[106] It would be better, of course, if democratic renewal could come about through the reasoned conversation amongst citizens or at the behest of some great and benign leader, but after the collapse of the Progressive Party in 1912 neither of those seemed likely to occur; other routes would have to be pursued. If a better democracy had to be shocked into existence, then so be it.

Here, then, was the Progressives' final paradoxical resolution of a paradoxical situation. As the radical historian Charles Beard summarized, the prewar Progressives always contended that the United States required a new democracy, one that would celebrate the "larger unity" of the American people. After the failure of their other political efforts, however, they also came to believe that such a democracy might only be brought about through a "stormy unfolding of ideas and interests, in conflict and tension, in thought and experience."[107] American citizens of the early twentieth century, these Progressives held, were not yet capable of focusing on the nation at large. They might occasionally be guided to do so, especially if they had great leaders to inspire them or new institutions to re-educate them, but those strategies by themselves were unlikely to have the dramatic effect required.

[105] Lippmann, *Preface to Politics*, 66.
[106] Croly, *Progressive Democracy*, 315.
[107] Charles Beard, "The Promise of American Life," *New Republic*, February 6, 1935, 351.

The Progressives set out, therefore, to enable the complete transformation of the political understandings of the American citizenry through a process of social unrest. That was, no doubt, a risky and an unsettling business. It required that an increase in actual social conflict might have to precede the emergence of a new democratic order. Some would caution against that risk, but most Progressives themselves were certain that there was no alternative. The solidity and fixity of the prevailing political order had prevented other more peaceable efforts at Progressive reform. It could only be undone through a vigorous and disruptive series of actions.

To some, this route to democratic change appeared not only dangerous but distinctly undemocratic. Others, though, saw it as placing the onus back on the citizenry as a whole, and though potentially chaotic, it at least was in keeping with the core aspects of the democratic ideal itself. "A free man can always commit suicide," Herbert Croly reminded his readership in 1915, but that is not reason enough to enslave him. "It remains to be seen what kind of democratic community the American people will choose to be," but they should have the chance to try.[108]

The Progressive Legacy

Progressive democratic thought often appears to have been riddled with inconsistencies. This was a movement that desired a stable, communal, democratic order: one where the citizenry would discuss issues of shared concern in a spirit of national solidarity and expect an expert and empowered national government to act upon citizens' common desires and aspirations. It was also, however, a movement that sometimes placed extensive faith in individual leaders, despite worries of elitism and demagoguery. At other times the movement embraced the politics of trade union conflict and interest group coercion, despite the undemocratic and factional implications of such action.

These inconsistencies are, however, more apparent than real. They can largely be explained by reference to the crucial distinction between ideal theory, on the one hand, and transformative political strategy, on the other. Seen in this way, the Progressives were sincere in their desire to build the sort of democracy of which a modern-day deliberative democrat might have been proud. They were, however, also constantly aware of the obstacles that stood in their way and they sought relentlessly to find ways of overcoming those obstacles. Their eventual advocacy of the politics of trade union

---

[108] Croly, *Progressive Democracy*, 244.

conflict might be more redolent, therefore, of a particularly strident form of "realism" than of "deliberation," but it was intended to be the immediate means of achieving a political transformation, rather than to be reflective of the ultimate ideals of democratic politics. Disruption was the mechanism by which a national politics conducted in the interests of the common good could be constructed. It was not to be the end state.

In thinking about the need to separate the two forms of democratic theorizing—the ideal from the strategic, the principled from the practical—the thinkers and activists of the Progressive Era began a trend in radical democratic theory that would be felt throughout the twentieth century. This is not to say that the Progressives were right, either at the level of ideals or strategy. Their aspirations for a politics of the common good might well have been naive and sentimental, blind to the fact that the factional interests of which they so often despaired were essential elements of a modern industrial society, rather than just passing characteristics. Similarly, there were clearly good reasons to doubt whether allowing excessive powers to accrue to executive leadership or endorsing coercive and factional conflict within the trade union movement could in fact transform American democracy in the ways that the Progressives hoped.

It is also important to note that the commitment to the efficacy of disruptive action was only very selectively applied. Although most New Nationalists were eventually enthusiastic about trade union unrest, they remained much less willing to support other forms of radical action. Most importantly, they were almost entirely blind to efforts to rectify racial injustice. As Walter Weyl summarized, most of his fellow Progressives were convinced that "the present democratic movement" should "move forward, leaving the problem of Negro suffrage to one side."[109] It was a shocking omission and one that would haunt both radical democrats and the United States for years to come.[110]

All of this implies that the Progressives needed to say much more than they did about why they believed the limited form of radical direct action they endorsed would be capable of bringing about a new democratic

---

[109] Weyl, New Democracy, 343.

[110] See the discussion in Cornel West, Democracy Matters: Winning the Fight Against Imperialism (New York: Penguin, 2005), esp. 52–53. There were a few exceptions to this general trend. For a first-hand example, see Ray Stannard Baker, Following the Color Line (New York: MacMillan, 1908), and for excellent commentary, Elizabeth Lasch-Quinn, Black Neighbors: Race and the Limits of Reform in the American Settlement House Movement, 1890–1945 (Chapel Hill: University of North Carolina Press, 1993), and Eileen L. McDonagh, "The 'Welfare Rights State' and the 'Civil Rights State': Policy Paradox and State Building in the Progressive Era," Studies in American Political Development 7 (1993): 225–74.

order characterized by the pursuit of a genuinely common good for all Americans. That said, their successors did not spend their energies discussing apparent inconsistencies in Progressive thought. This was partly due to the Progressives' considerable political success, but it was also due to the intrinsic interest of the Progressive account of political change. These successors did not accept it all at face value. Certainly they wondered whether the early-twentieth-century Progressives had set the right course and whether their political recommendations would indeed help to realize their democratic ideals in the very non-ideal circumstances of the American political present. They accepted, however, their predecessors' key distinction between the task of outlining a democratic ideal that was not yet embodied in the politics of the United States and prescribing a set of citizen behaviors that might help that democratic ideal to be realized in a future political order. This was the debate that would shape the American radical democratic tradition throughout the twentieth century. The Progressives initiated it and they are crucial to the story for that reason.

CHAPTER TWO

After the Breach

Radical democratic theory in the Progressive Era offered an idiosyncratic combination of deliberative ideals and distinctly nondeliberative methods. Progressives longed for the day when the United States could conduct its politics in accordance with a spirit of nationwide solidarity: a time when a public-spirited citizenry would be actively engaged in ensuring that a powerful government machine effectively served the common good. They also believed, however, that the existing American political order posed a mighty obstacle to that goal, an obstacle that could only be removed through the exercise of exceptional leadership or through the power of radical social disruption. Put simply, the new democracy could only be built if there were far-reaching change to the American political order, and such change demanded dramatic rather than deliberative politics.

It was for this reason that almost all the leading Progressives welcomed the United States' entrance into the First World War in 1917, despite the untold suffering and loss of life that would ensue. Nothing, after all, would disrupt the prevailing political equilibrium like a conflict of this scale. It would be impossible to fight the war abroad without root-and-branch reform at home. Progressives thus saw the outbreak of hostilities as the opportunity that they had hoped presidential politics and social protest offered in the decade before. In order to respond to the military, economic, and political demands of the conflict, the nation would have to open itself to radical social and political experimentation, they argued. The political machinery of the United States would be reconstructed—with power taken away from the states and invested in a newly invigorated federal executive—and, just as importantly, the social attitudes of the nation would be radically harmonized and collectivized. Here was the chance, Progressives contended, to construct the "intellectually serious . . . centralized democratic state" for which they had long called.[1] Here, too, was the moment when the American people might finally put their characteristic individualism and factionalism

[1] Graham Wallas, Letter to Learned Hand, September 2, 1916, in The Learned Hand Papers 44/16, Law School Library, Harvard University.

to one side and turn to a more patriotic cause. Progressives and their allies insisted that even the injustices and divisions of race might be overcome, with W. E. B. DuBois famously reporting that war might enable black and white Americans to "close ranks shoulder to shoulder," with each putting aside their "special grievances" in a collective struggle to save democracy for the world.[2]

The conflict in its initial stages appeared to confirm at least some of these hopes. Despite being elected on a decentralizing platform, Woodrow Wilson's wartime administration embraced the New Nationalists' suggestions for institutional reform of the federal government almost in their entirety. The executive bureaucracy was vastly expanded and staffed with technocratic experts sympathetic to Progressivism. Wilson also established a Committee for Public Information with the specific aim of rendering "a single person of the great body of those who call themselves Americans."[3]

But the optimism did not last long. It soon became evident that although the wartime reconstruction of American politics and society was far-reaching, it was neither going to bring their democratic ideals any closer to realization or even serve the Progressives' own short-term political goals. If anything, it appeared to make their goals more distant than ever at both a social and an institutional level.

The first anxiety concerned particular citizen attitudes that the war was encouraging. While the war undeniably made large sections of the public more patriotic—more decidedly "American" in their allegiance—it did not seem to render them any more willing to deliberate about a shared common good. Indeed, quite to the contrary, wartime citizens flocked behind exclusionary rather than inclusionary causes. Organized groups going by such names as the Better American Federation, the National Association for Constitutional Government, and the National Security League rejected leftists, immigrants, African Americans, drinkers, and gamblers as "un-American," classifying them as unworthy of membership in the new patriotic republic.[4] The second anxiety concerned the structure of government

---

[2] W. E. B. DuBois, "Close Ranks," *Crisis* 8 (1918): 111. For insightful commentary, see Mark Ellis, "'Closing Ranks' and 'Seeking Honors': W. E. B. DuBois in World War I," *Journal of American History* 79 (1992): 96–124.

[3] Woodrow Wilson, cited in Robert Schaeffer, *America in the Great War: The Rise of the War Welfare State* (New York: Oxford University Press 1991), 6–7.

[4] See the files in The League for Industrial Democracy Records 49/3/1, The Tamiment Institute, New York University. See, too, Gary Gerstle, *American Crucible: Race and Nation in the Twentieth Century* (Princeton: Princeton University Press, 2002), 81–127; Oscar A. Hilton, "Public Opinion and Civil Liberties in Wartime, 1917–1919," *Southwestern Social Science Quarterly* 28 (1947): 201–24; William Jordan, "'The Damnable Dilemma': African-American Accommodation and Protest during World War I," *Journal of American History* 81 (1995): 1562–83.

itself. The federal executive had been rendered technically more effective by Wilson—of that there was no doubt—but, despite expectations, it appeared no better attuned to serving the Progressives' idea of the common good. Indeed, by the end of the war, the new powers of the federal government were far more often turned against Progressive allies—trade unionists, educators, social reformers, and radicals—than they were employed in their cause.[5] As a transatlantic war gave way to an uneasy peace at home in 1918, Progressives were left deflated once again, their hopes and expectations "shocked into disintegration."[6] The first attempt to transform democratic politics in the twentieth-century United States had failed.

The years that followed the war thus witnessed a thoroughgoing re-examination of Progressive democratic ideals and Progressive political strategies. That re-examination was led by three giants of American political thought—Walter Lippmann, Reinhold Niebuhr, and John Dewey—and the argument between them is now the stuff of academic legend. Throughout the 1920s and 1930s, Lippmann, Niebuhr, and Dewey vigorously disputed key aspects of Progressive democratic theory. They argued about whether it was right to strive for a democratic politics focused on the common good, about whether a modern citizenry could ever be brought into meaningful deliberation about such a good, and about the methods of transforming the current political order into a better one for the future.

Unlike Progressive thinkers, who are generally criticized today, these interwar disputants are frequently championed by latter-day democratic theorists. Deliberative democrats most often eulogize Dewey, seeing him as a philosophically sophisticated and politically sincere advocate of a communicative politics of the common good. Indeed, he is often cast as the intellectual father of deliberative democracy in America.[7] Realists, on the

---

[5] See David Kennedy, *Over Here: The First World War and American Society* (New York: Oxford University Press, 1980); Stuart Rochester, *American Liberal Disillusionment in the Wake of World War I* (University Park: Pennsylvania State University Press, 1977); Marc Stears, *Progressives, Pluralists, and the Problems of the State: Ideologies of Reform in the United States and Britain, 1909–1926* (Oxford: Oxford University Press, 2002), 127–41; James A. Thompson, *Reformers and War: Progressive Publicists and the First World War* (Cambridge: Cambridge,University Press, 1987).

[6] John Dewey, "A New Social Science," *New Republic*, April 6, 1918, 292.

[7] See, especially, James T. Kloppenberg, "Deliberative Democracy and Judicial Supremacy," *Law and History Review* 13 (1995): 393–411; Cass R. Sunstein, *The Partial Constitution* (Cambridge, Mass.: Harvard University Press, 1993); Robert Westbrook, "Pragmatism and Democracy: Restoring Dewey's Faith," in Morris Dickstein, ed., *The Revival of Pragmatism: New Essays on Social, Thought, Law, and Culture* (Durham: University of North Carolina Press, 1997). For a more critical take, see John Patrick Diggins, "Philosophy Without Foundations, Politics With Illusions," *Reviews in American History* 12 (1993): 116–20, and James Hoopes, *Community Denied: The Wrong Turn of Pragmatic Liberalism* (Ithaca: Cornell University Press, 1998).

other hand, just as often turn to Lippmann and Niebuhr, contending that they provided the first American democratic theory that dispensed with the myth of the common good whilst still maintaining a vision of democratic politics suitable for those with a radical agenda.[8] Either way, both camps of early-twenty-first-century democratic theorists agree on two things: they contend that the interwar writings of Lippmann, Niebuhr, and Dewey offered future generations insights of far greater power than those of their Progressive predecessors, and that those insights can be meaningfully categorized as either deliberative or realist in essence.

These interpretations do not, however, do full justice to the contributions of any of the participants—the Progressives, Lippmann, Niebuhr, Dewey, their many contemporaries—nor do they help us understand the evolution of the American radical democratic tradition. As with the Progressives, in order more fully to appreciate those contributions we need to pay far closer attention to the distinction between ideal theory and non-ideal theory—or, to put that another way, between long-term democratic goals and short-term political strategies—than have the deliberative democrats and realists. As before, such an analysis reveals crucial dimensions of these theorists' democratic thought that have otherwise gone unnoticed. This is not to say that there was no dispute between Lippmann, Niebuhr, and Dewey, nor to suggest that aspects of their democratic theory were not significant improvements on what had gone before. It is, instead, to contend that their arguments both perpetuated and augmented an American radical democratic tradition that had begun with the Progressives and that would continue after the Second World War. The arguments between these three theorists, as well as those between a legion of less well-remembered contemporaries, thus played a vital role in reshaping that American radical democratic tradition. They engendered change in both its ideal aspirations and non-ideal strategies and bequeathed future generations a revised democratic theory that continues to offer a inspiring glimpse of the democratic future despite being grounded in the almost unbearable constraints of the interwar years.

[8] See Casey Blake, "Public Intellectuals Without a Public," *American Quarterly* 41 (1989): 577–82; John Patrick Diggins, "Power and Suspicion: The Perspectives of Reinhold Niebuhr," *Ethics and International Affairs* 6 (1992): 141–61; Wilson Carey McWilliams, "Reinhold Niebuhr: New Orthodoxy for Old Liberalism," *American Political Science Review* 56 (1962): 874–85; and Eyal J. Naveh, *Reinhold Niebuhr and Non-Utopian Liberalism: Beyond Illusion and Despair* (Brighton: Sussex Academic Press, 2002).

An Age of Reaction

The war wreaked havoc on Progressive democratic thought. Almost all of the Progressives' key strategies and many aspects of their democratic ideals were tested and found thoroughly wanting. Most importantly, Progressives emerged from the war desperately disappointed at the way in which a radically empowered federal executive had chosen to employ its new authority. They were particularly concerned at the Wilson administration's perceived hostility to trade unionism, its repression of political opposition, and its censorship of the radical press. The war and immediate postwar years witnessed the United States' first real "red scare," and for all its protestations to impartiality, the Wilson administration lent its full support to the panic. In 1917 it pressed Congress to pass a restrictive Espionage Act, following it a year later with an even more restrictive Sedition Act. By the end of the war both acts, and other supporting measures, had been employed to the full. The Socialist presidential candidate Eugene Debs had been tried and imprisoned for allegedly inciting resistance to the war-recruitment effort. The leader of the IWW, "Big" Bill Heywood, had been forced into exile in the Soviet Union. Many trade unions loyal to the American Federation of Labor had been bullied into a series of disadvantageous "no-strike" deals. And, most worryingly of all for Progressive publicists, the Postmaster General Albert Burleson had removed the Communist *Masses* and the moderate *Intercollegiate Socialist* from the U.S. mail, censored the African American *Chicago Defender*, and even threatened the liberal *Nation* and the *New Republic* itself with the same fate if they refused to toe the administration's line.[9]

Given such a climate, the war and immediate postwar years were deeply uncomfortable for any American who dreamt of building a more equitable, let alone deliberative, democratic order. It seemed to most Progressives that the administration had been captured by a single sectional interest: "the business men of this country," the *New Republic* complained, have become "for the period of the war the licensed agents of the government" and they had done little but abuse their position.[10] Although some Progressives acquiesced in the face of the challenge—with Walter Lippmann even accepting a post in the administration itself—most responded by distancing themselves from the government. Lippmann aside, the leading New Nationalists once again became Wilson's foremost critics. More fundamentally, they abandoned their previous support for an empowered federal executive

[9] See note 5, above.
[10] Editorial, "The Passing of Sectionalism," *New Republic*, June 15, 1921, 61.

entirely. What they had intended as a process of "nationalization," these Progressives complained, "has degenerated into centralization." The federal executive had ceased "to provide an improved machinery for carrying out the collective purposes of the American people" and had begun instead to serve only sectional ends. Their conclusion was more startling still. Within three years of the end of the war, the New Nationalist theorists were demanding that the American people need to "be aroused, not as formerly for the purpose of accelerating the work of nationalization, but for the purpose of checking it."[11]

Unfortunately for Progressives, there was little sign that American citizens were ready to come to their aid. Although some groups like the newly founded American Civil Liberties Union (ACLU) and the decade-old National Association for the Advancement of Colored People (NAACP) did mobilize to try to support the repressed, many more organizations emerged to encourage the repression still further. The list of such enterprises appeared almost endless. The Anti-Saloon League and broader prohibition movement secured the ratification of their amendment; the campaign against East European and East Asian immigration emerged victorious with the restrictive Johnson-Reed Act of 1924; white vigilantes killed twenty-three African Americans in Chicago in 1919; and supporters of big business ensured the widespread eradication of collective bargaining, and often of trade union representation altogether, in a series of "open shop" drives in the early 1920s.[12]

The spirit of this age was astutely captured by F. Scott Fitzgerald's depiction of Tom Buchanan in *The Great Gatsby* in 1925. Gatsby's nemesis, Buchanan is an intolerant brute, deeply fearful of the changes that had swept across an industrializing America in the previous decades, unintelligent yet happy to argue that "science" has proved the necessity of protecting the advantages that have historically accrued to the "Nordic race" in America.[13] In combining this reactionary social outlook with bullish self-confidence, Fitzgerald's Buchanan perfectly symbolized the newly strengthened sense of the power of political reaction in the early 1920s, the power that so terrified the Progressives.

[11] Ibid., 61.

[12] See Alan Dawley, *Struggles for Justice: Social Responsibility and the Liberal State* (Cambridge, Mass.: Belknap, 1991), 172–217, and Desmond King, *Making Americans: Immigration, Race, and the Origins of the Diverse Democracy* (Cambridge, Mass.: Harvard University Press, 2000), esp. 85–126.

[13] See Ronald Berman, "America in Fitzgerald," *Journal of Aesthetic Education* 36 (2002): 38–51.

The Disappearing Nation

A new American nation had indeed been built in the war years, but it was not the nation that the Progressives had dreamt of. As the *New Republic* explained, it was one forged not "by candid and tolerant discussion" but "by waves of emotional compulsion which roll up huge and furtive majorities" of citizens, majorities which, moreover, were the creation "of fear, of downright coercion, or of unmanageable necessity."[14] There was little here to which increased democratization appeared to provide any kind of solution. Indeed, most Progressives had a strong sense that the democratizing reforms they had witnessed over the last decade or so—including women's suffrage, the direct election of senators, and the introduction of initiatives, referenda, and mandates—had each served to exacerbate the problem at least as much as they had resolved it.

In the prewar years Walter Lippmann had argued that Progressives could afford to place some faith in democracy even in the non-ideal present, in so far as "the age is rich with varied and generous passions."[15] By the early 1920s, though, it appeared to Lippmann and his colleagues that American passions were distinctly less various than they thought and certainly far from as generous. Where Progressives had once feared that the American citizenry was excessively individualistic, they now worried that the United States was rather an excessively homogenizing nation, critical of difference, skeptical of change, and willing to employ the full force of a newly empowered government machine to assert their will.

What all of this meant was that it was clear to Progressives by the early 1920s that it was not only the executive branch that was at fault. Indeed, it might not just be the strategic transformation that was misguided. The whole basis of the Progressives' idea of democratic renewal increasingly appeared to have been misconceived.[16] The war had precipitated a dramatic break with the political order of the past, it had encouraged many Americans to think of themselves as members of a single nation, and it had provoked a substantial increase in manifold forms of political mobilization, but it had not moved the United States closer to the democratic ideal for which Progressives of all stripes had hoped.

It was in this light that key Progressive theorists began to question that ideal itself, and especially to cast doubt on the notion that an industrialized

---

[14] Editorial, "The Making of an American Nation," *New Republic*, October 31, 1923, 242.

[15] Walter Lippmann, *Preface to Politics* (New York: Michael Kennerley, 1913), 318.

[16] See Malcolm Wiley, "Review: The Phantom Public and Others," *Social Forces* 4 (1926): 854–58, and Sidney Kaplan, 'Social Engineers as Saviors: Effects of World War I on Some American Liberals,' *Journal of the History of Ideas* 17 (1956): 347–69.

society should possess a democratic politics focused on the identification and pursuit of a single "common good." Reflecting on their own disillusion in 1921, the remaining New Nationalists noted that the instinctive resistance to the homogenizing trends of the war years had jolted them into accepting a new social theory. They now recognized that although the industrialized United States was composed of interdependent groups, just as they had always claimed, it was nonetheless still far from "an economically homogenous society of similarly occupied and like-minded people." Rather, American society, like all large societies, "is a community of diverse classes, occupations, races, as well as discordant sections and of insubordinate individuals."[17] It quickly became commonplace amongst Progressives to emphasize the essential incompatibility of the groups and individuals who made up the modern United States. The prewar idea that a nationwide common good provided the bedrock conceptual commitment of Progressive democratic theory was dead.

The early postwar Progressives thus openly embraced a form of pluralism. It was a position that enjoyed considerable vogue in the first few years of the 1920s. Almost all of the Progressives who had survived the war argued that it was crucial for any future renewed democracy to attend to the fundamental distinctions between different groups in society, rather than try to supersede or transcend them.[18]

The implications of the idea were profound, both in terms of the long-term ideal and in terms of the immediate political strategy. Seeing through newly pluralist eyes, Hebert Croly insisted in the early 1920s that American citizens should "become increasingly attached to centers of allegiance and social activity other than the state." There should be "built up" within the nation, "class, trade, and professional associations which will compete with the state" for their loyalty.[19] Such claims were a dramatic shock to the Progressive conceptual order even in their mildest form, but at times the argument went to remarkable extremes. This was the age in which many previously moderate trade unionists seriously considered the advantages of syndicalism, and many campaigners for racial justice replaced allegiance to the accommodationist, integrationist NAACP with a commitment to

[17] Editorial, "Making of an American Nation," 242.

[18] See Walter Lippmann, "A Clue," *New Republic*, April 14, 1917, 316; Norman Wilde, "Plural Sovereignty," *Journal of Philosophy* 16 (1919): 658–65; Norman Wilde, *The Ethical Basis of the State* (Princeton: Princeton University Press, 1924). For commentary, see William Y. Elliott, *The Pragmatic Revolt in Politics: Syndicalism, Fascism and the Constitutional State* (New York: MacMillan, 1928); Hoopes, *Community Denied*; and Ronald Steel, *Walter Lippmann and the American Century* (London: Bodley Head, 1980), esp. 162–68.

[19] Herbert Croly, "The Future of the State," *New Republic*, September 15, 1917, 181.

Marcus Garvey's back-to-Africa movement.[20] In his final, unpublished book, *The Breach of Civilization*, even Herbert Croly concluded that the wartime experience had instructed all democratic reformers that they must remember that in complex societies "the law of irrepressible conflict is much nearer the truth than the law of fulfillment and progress."[21]

In developing this case, American Progressives began to look for inspiration overseas, and they found it, especially in the work of the British Socialist Harold J. Laski and, to a slightly lesser degree, that of his close colleagues, G.D.H. Cole and R. H. Tawney. Laski, Cole, and Tawney had made a significant name for themselves in the United States during the war by using newspaper and journal columns to argue vociferously against the repressive wartime powers of the state. Emphasizing the state's in-built tendency to be captured by a small, usually privileged section of society instead of its capacity to represent the common good, these three insisted that the best hopes for reformers lay in resistance to central government and in the protection and eventual empowerment of other diverse groups in society, including most notably the trade union movement.[22]

Despite its origins in Britain, it was an argument that was quickly taken up in America, especially on the left of the Progressive movement and by younger scholars and activists who had not been so closely associated with the nationalism of the prewar days. Prominent postwar Progressive commentators, including Arthur Gleason, Jessie Hughan, Alvin Johnson, and Ordway Tead thus self-consciously sought to construct an American equivalent of this British "Socialist Pluralism."[23] There was a bookstore, The Sunwise Turn, in New York City that specialized in British pluralist literature, and some enthusiasts even founded a journal, the *Freeman*, in order to propagate the message. The purpose of the *Freeman*, its editors reported, was to be "cynical about political governments in general, and still more cynical about government in Washington," and thus to encourage radical activists and thinkers to look for alternatives to government as the loci of

---

[20] See John Murphy, "The IWW: An American Export," *Socialist Review* 11 (1920): 196–200, and Theodore Kornweibel, "Apathy and Dissent: Black America's Negative Responses to World War I," *South Atlantic Quarterly* 80 (1981): 322–38.

[21] Herbert Croly, *The Breach of Civilization*, Microfilm in The Felix Frankfurter Papers, Law School Library, Harvard University, 16.

[22] See Stears, *Progressives, Pluralists, and the Problems of the State*, 141–45.

[23] See Arthur Gleason, *Inside the British Isles* (New York: Century, 1917); Arthur Gleason, *What the Workers Want* (London: George Allen and Unwin, 1920); Jessie Hughan, "Guildsmen and American Socialism," *Intercollegiate Socialist* 7 (1920): 165–68; Alvin Johnson, "Revolutionary Reconstruction," *New Republic*, December 15, 1920, 80; and Ordway Tead, "Guilds for America," *Intercollegiate Socialist* 7 (1919): 31–33.

reform.[24] "It is time," Arthur Gleason argued, "that our statesmen, our social experts, our writers, and our industrial leaders begin to study" pluralism, for even if they do not, soon "they will be forced to accept it."[25]

Of the more established figures in the Progressive movement, it was Walter Lippmann, a personal friend of Harold Laski's from the latter's days at Yale and Harvard, who was most heavily influenced by the British variant of pluralism. Initially, Lippmann had been skeptical of Laski, seeking to hold on longer to the old Progressive notion of a democratic politics focused on the discovery of a nationwide, American common good. "[M]y own hopes," he told the *New Republic* in 1919, "are in what might be called the latent public." Such a "public," he contended, must at some point "arise and assert the supremacy of confidence over fear, of reason and charity over suspicion and hysteria," and when it so prevails, it will "restore the good humour of America."[26] But Lippmann abandoned this aspiration in the early 1920s, driven both by the intellectual power of Laski's pluralist critique and by his deepening concerns with the intellectual and moral capacities of American citizens. Indeed, he soon began instead to shape a pluralist social theory that was in some ways more thoroughgoing than Laski's, even though its political ramifications would be far less radical than the British pluralist had imagined.

Lippmann's pluralism emerged in two books that established his academic reputation as a social and political theorist of the very first rank: *Public Opinion*, published in 1920, and its even more startling sequel, *The Phantom Public*, which appeared five years later. In both of these works, Lippmann returned to the psychological theories that had long undermined his faith in the cognitive capacities of the average citizen, but he now combined that concern with his newly found dedication to a pluralist social theory that emphasized the essential incompatibility of the interests, beliefs, and opinions of the various sectors that collectively made up American society. Bringing these two ideas together, Lippmann damned his previous Progressive theory almost in its entirety. Reformers should no longer hope that citizens will ever "find a unity which absorbs diversity," he argued, for such a hope was inevitably misguided.

Where Progressives had once called for nationwide democratic deliberation to identify a shared good, Lippmann now contended that such deliberation would throw little light on the core problems that faced the United States. The problems of the industrial age were just too complex to

---

[24] Editorial, *Freeman*, December 29, 1920, 362.

[25] Arthur Gleason, "The Discovery," *Survey*, May 19, 1917, 159.

[26] Walter Lippmann, "Unrest," *New Republic*, November 12, 1919, 322.

be tackled thoughtfully and intelligently in such discussions. "[M]odern society is not visible to anybody nor intelligible continuously and as a whole," he summarized. Given the extent of the differences between all of the various groups and associations in American society, and the intellectual limitations of their members, then, it was only possible to claim that "[o]ne section is visible to one section, another to another section, one series of acts is intelligible to this group and another to that."[27] Even if actual "common interests" do connect such groups at the level, say, of "scientific fact," they will be so deeply hidden that they will "elude public opinion entirely."[28]

Lippmann further insisted that such restricted vision on the part of citizens and their groups was not a passing stage, but rather was ingrained in the very nature of human beings. "Against this deep pluralism thinkers have argued in vain," he reported. "They have invented soul organisms and national souls, and oversouls and collective souls; they have gone for hopeful analogies to the beehive and the anthill, to the solar system, to the human body," but none captured the reality of social life better than pluralism.[29] Nor would any change in political machinery improve the situation; in fact, Lippmann dismissed that idea with even more vigor. "The democratic El Dorado has always been some perfect environment, and some perfect system of voting and representation, where the innate good will and instinctive statesmanship of every man could be translated into action. . . . But while the democratic theorist was busy at this, he was far from the actual interests of human nature." Progressives might have spent the prewar years fine-tuning institutional recommendations designed to elicit a deliberative focus on the common good, Lippmann concluded, but the average American citizen was never going to play his part. He "was interested in all kind[s] of other things."[30] It was an understandable judgment. This was, after all, the Jazz Age.[31]

Lippmann drew two practical lessons from these arguments. The first and most frequently remembered was a call for crucial political decisions to be taken out of the hands of the intellectually limited citizen body as a whole and vested instead in an informed, educated, and trusted elite. If the citizen

---

[27] Walter Lippmann, *The Phantom Public: A Sequel to* Public Opinion (New York: MacMillan, 1925), 167, 42.

[28] Walter Lippmann, *Public Opinion* (New York: MacMillan, 1922), 310.

[29] Ibid., 97. Lippmann did not cleave to this position for the remainder of his career, but neither did he return to his earlier Progressive vision. For later developments, see John Patrick Diggins, "From Pragmatism to Natural Law: Walter Lippmann's Quest for the Foundations of Legitimacy," *Political Theory* 19 (1991): 519–38.

[30] Lippmann, *Public Opinion*, 311.

[31] See F. Scott Fitzgerald, *Tales of the Jazz Age* (New York: Charles Scribners and Sons, 1923), and G.T.W. Patrick, "The Play of a Nation," *Scientific Monthly* (October 1921): 350–62.

body could not be expected to discover a common good, the argument outlined, the basic business of governing should be left to those who at least
had a chance of seeing some of the interconnections upon which all of these
diverse people were dependent nonetheless. The task of governing should
be ceded to a "specialized class whose personal interests reach beyond the
locality."[32] The second lesson is now more frequently overlooked but it was,
for Lippmann himself, more crucial still. For the purpose of *Public Opinion*
and *The Phantom Public* was essentially to demand that all democratic engagement was capable of ensuring was some kind of social peace between
different sectors of society, sectors that were always going to think of their
interests as incompatible at some level and between whom mutual understanding would always be limited. "When we speak" of a democratic solution to a problem, Lippmann thus insisted, we should mean no "more than
that two conflicting interests have found a *modus vivendi*."[33]

This recalibration was fundamental to the future of democracy, or so
Lippmann believed. The crucial difficulty with prewar Progressivism was
that it offered a false promise of nationwide community. This was an approach "where separateness of purpose is covered up and confused, where
false unities are worshipped, and each special interest is forever proclaim-
ing itself the voice of the people and attempting to impose its purpose upon
everybody as the purpose of all mankind." A new, pluralistically informed
democratic theory could right all these wrongs simply by ceasing to "look[]
for an identity of purpose" and instead "look simply for an accommodation
of purposes." Only if it did that—accepted that all the many sectors in a
complex modern society could never agree on more—would democracy be
able to survive in anything like a recognizable form. The alternative, the experience of the war years had shown, was that a "false ideal of democracy"
would "lead only to disillusionment and to meddlesome tyranny."[34]

Politics without the Nation

Lippmann's essentially pessimistic tone was perfectly suited to the spirit of the
times. Even those who cleaved to the older vision were struck by the power
of his argument and the clarity of his prose: "Mr Lippmann," John Dewey
wrote in a *New Republic* review of *Public Opinion*, "has thrown into clearer
relief than any other writer the fundamental difficulty of democracy."[35] But

[32] Lippmann, *Public Opinion*, 310.
[33] Lippmann, *Phantom Public*, 98.
[34] Ibid., 98, 255.
[35] John Dewey, "Public Opinion," *New Republic*, May 3, 1922, 288.

it nonetheless took a while for the full force of his theoretical message to be realized. Everyone understood, of course, that Lippmann had removed the faith in the common good and further reduced expectations about the American citizenry, but fewer people so quickly noticed that in so doing he had also reshaped understandings of the nature of political power itself.

Where the prewar Progressives had tended to see stability and order in political life emanating from the essential interconnectedness of a single national community, reinforced perhaps by a benign government that sought in general to serve the "common good," the pluralist Lippmann saw things very differently. In so far as social order was possible at all, he insisted, it would have to emanate from one of two sources. First, it could be derived from actual, concrete bargains struck by the potentially conflicting sectors in society as they pursued their self-interests and accepted the need for some form of modus vivendi. Or, second, and most likely, it could be enforced by the coercive power of the central state. The "present state," Lippmann argued, "is primarily an instrument of coercion" whose role was to ensure that the natural discontents of a plural society did not topple into dangerous disorder by the use or threat of physical force. The task of a democratic theorist, Lippmann thus insisted, was to deal with this fact of coercion: to develop a theory capable of responding to the essential role of state coercion in the political order rather than to hide from it or to wish it away.[36]

Although it took a few years, the importance of this message eventually resonated deeply with the broader community of theoretically engaged political commentators, and by the mid-1920s Lippmann had encouraged an obsession with coercion both as the fundamental characteristic of the modern state and as the central mechanism of coordination and control in any nation characterized by widespread social difference and disagreement. As the Columbia University political scientist Clarence Case noted, the prewar Progressive argument that national "unanimity" would somehow render coercion obsolete was now widely dismissed as a form of "insipid sentimentalism." Instead, the use of coercive force to secure order, either by the government or by some other agency, now appeared to be "a fact inseparable from life in society."[37] There could be no expectations of social stability, or of order, not even of governance itself, without it.

This claim dominated radical democratic theory in the mid-1920s. Some brave individuals did try to restore the old order. The respected novelist and

[36] Lippmann, *Public Opinion*, 295.
[37] Clarence Case, *Non-Violent Coercion: A Study in Methods of Social Pressure* (London: George Allen and Unwin, 1923), 413, 319.

public intellectual Waldo Frank, for example, produced *The Re-discovery of America* in a vain attempt to restore the vision of Herbert Croly, who, he argued, had "laid the foundation in modern, real terms, for the view of America as a democratic nation led by an aristocracy of spirit."[38] What was needed, Frank thus insisted, was a renewed effort to discover a shared American identity and to reject the dangerous and divisive coercive and pluralist spirit of the age. His argument was, however, roundly mocked by most left-leaning commentators. In rejecting "pluralism," one reviewer remarked, "Frank is driven . . . to accept the monistic logic of patriotic Americanism concealed in a different formula and definition of Americanism," but such a logic offered little to those disillusioned by their wartime experiences. By concentrating on a nationwide deliberative politics and "rejecting the necessity for political reorganization through all available means of *power—political, industrial ideological—*" this commentator continued, "Frank becomes a positive danger to those forces engaged in challenging the domination of Big Business." The time for such overoptimistic, "metaphysical mysticism" had passed. A new era of "realism" had begun.[39]

As this second argument implied, the intellectual trends away from Progressivism and toward coercive pluralism were dramatically reinforced by political developments in the 1920s. It was a decade that was particularly cruel to Progressive personnel and to Progressive political expectations. Walter Weyl and Herbert Croly died in the early part of the decade, as did Arthur Gleason and Randolph Bourne, young activists who had promised to replace the initial generation of New Nationalists.[40] Others, like Ordway Tead, withdrew from politics entirely, exhausted by the impact of the war and the apparent failure of the Progressive experiment.[41] The political process was also unrelentingly harsh on those who remained. Roosevelt's original Progressive Party was never successfully rebuilt after its failure in 1912 and efforts to create a Labor Party in its place similarly came to nothing late in the second decade of the twentieth century.[42] Later, the Farmer-Labor Party that originated in Wisconsin and Minnesota consistently failed to

---

[38] Waldo Frank, *The Re-discovery of America* (New York: Charles Scribners and Sons, 1929), dedication.

[39] Sidney Hook, "The Nonsense of the Whole," *Modern Quarterly* 5 (1930): 509, 506. See, too, Robert Morss Lovett, "Liberalism and the Class War," *Modern Quarterly* 4 (1928): 191–94.

[40] See collection of obituaries, The Paul Kellogg Papers 2/17, Social Welfare History Archive, University of Minnesota.

[41] See Ordway Tead, "Autobiography," in Leon Finkelstein, ed., *Thirteen Americans: Their Spiritual Biographies* (New York: Institute for Religious and Social Studies, 1950).

[42] See Robert Morss Lovett, "The Farmer-Labor Fiasco," *New Republic*, July 18, 1923, 198–200, and, for an overview, James Weinstein, *The Decline of Socialism in America, 1912–1925* (New Brunswick: Rutgers University Press, 1984), 272–74.

make any significant headway, and although Progressive forces rallied to run a spirited campaign for the presidency in 1924 under the candidacy of Robert La Follette, that effort also came to nothing and was followed by La Follette's own death a year later.[43] Although some historians have argued that there were some smaller-scale Progressive successes in the 1920s, especially as certain Progressive ideals were picked up once again by the Republican Party, it did not appear as such to Progressive activists and intellectuals themselves.[44] To those who had aimed so high in the prewar years, the failure of the La Follette bid "symbolized the burial of the Progressive movement as a political force."[45]

All of these anti-Progressive forces were exacerbated still further when the Depression hit in 1929, throwing millions into unemployment and poverty and intensifying the difficulties of social exclusion that the war years had first thrown up. The economic calamity engulfing the nation rendered the idea of an American national cause or spirit even more redundant than before, especially as the early efforts of Herbert Hoover's "do-nothing" Republicans and the struggling Democrats were largely met with disdain by left-leaning intellectuals. Even the rise of Franklin Delano Roosevelt, first to the Democratic nomination and then to the presidency, failed to reassure these critics that change could come to the United States through democratic politics of a Progressive kind. Despite the legislative excitement of Roosevelt's first hundred days, the opening months of the New Deal were roundly condemned by most radical commentators for selling-out Progressive aspirations to corporate interests and for failing fundamentally to reshape either the American economy or the American political order.[46] Whilst Roosevelt was prepared to battle "abstractions," such as

---

[43] See Nathan Fine, *Labor and Farmer Parties in the United States, 1828–1928* (New York: Russell and Russell, 1961).

[44] See Alan Brinkley, *Liberalism and its Discontents* (Cambridge, Mass.: Harvard University Press, 1998), 111–31; Otis Graham, *Encore for Reform: Old Progressives and the New Deal* (New York: Oxford University Press, 1967); and Ellis Hawley, *The Great War and the Search for a Modern Order* (New York: St. Martin's, 1979).

[45] For a contemporary perspective, see Abraham J. Muste, "Militant Progressivism?," *Modern Quarterly* 4 (1928): 332–41. For insightful commentary, see Ronald Feinman, *Twilight of Progressivism: The Western Republican Senators and the New Deal* (Baltimore: The Johns Hopkins University Press, 1981); Arthur S. Link, "What Happened to the Progressive Movement in the 1920s," *American Historical Review* 64 (1959): 833–51; and Richard Pells, *Radical Visions and American Dreams: Culture and Social Thought in the Depression Years* (Middletown, Conn.: Wesleyan University Press, 1973), 13.

[46] See John Dewey, "Prospects for a Third Party," *New Republic*, July 27, 1932, 278–79; editorial, "Twenty One Demands for President Roosevelt," *Common Sense* 1 (1933): 3–5; and George Soule, "Roosevelt Confronts Capitalism," *New Republic*, October 18, 1933, 269–70. For commentary, see Theda Skocpol and Kenneth Feingold, "State Capacity and Economic Intervention in the Early New Deal," *Political Science Quarterly* 97 (1982): 255–78.

"unemployment, Depression, and the like," the *New Republic* complained a year after the New Deal commenced, he was unwilling to recognize the concrete forces that were actually responsible for the evils facing the United States: "Henry Ford, the steel magnates, the packers."[47] What was required by the new crisis, voices across the Left insisted, were both economic experiments of a far more drastic scale than those proposed by Roosevelt's early New Deal and radical assaults on the antiquated political machinery of the United States that, just as before the war, was said to be the major obstacle to necessary reform.[48]

Realism, Coercion, and Power Politics

It was in this light that the few prewar Progressives who remained active in the Depression Era joined together with the next activist generation in a desperate search for a new vision and a new set of concrete political strategies that could initiate it. By the close of 1933, almost everyone on the American Left felt "the need for something really new."[49] The answer to that call came from a most unlikely source: a professor of Practical Theology at the Union Theological Seminary in New York, Reinhold Niebuhr.[50]

Niebuhr was well-steeped in the Progressive political tradition, having served as pastor to the German evangelical mission in industrial Detroit, and having campaigned against the worst excesses of Henry Ford's brand of capitalism in the automobile industry. His deeply profound influence on the American radical democratic tradition in the Depression Era, though, was dependent on one book: *Moral Man and Immoral Society*, published in 1932. There, Niebuhr employed the pluralism of the previous decade to explode any remaining Progressive attachment to a deliberative politics of the common good. At the heart of his alternative democratic theory was an acceptance of the inevitability of coercion in social and political life. "All social co-operation in a larger scale than the most intimate social group," Niebuhr outlined at the start of *Moral Man*, "requires a measure of coercion. While no state can maintain its unity purely by coercion neither can

---

[47] Soule, "Roosevelt Confronts Capitalism," 271.

[48] See Bruce Bliven, "Franklin D. Roosevelt: Patron of Politics," *New Republic*, June 1 1932, 62–64; John Dewey, "Prospects for a Third Party," *New Republic*, July 27, 1932, 278–79; Waldo Frank, "Will Fascism Come?," *Modern Monthly* 8 (1934): 464–66.

[49] George Soule, *A Planned Society* (New York: MacMillan, 1932), 27

[50] See Arthur M. Schlesinger Jr., "Reinhold Niebuhr's Role in American Political Thought and Life," in Charles Kefley and Robert W. Bertall, eds., *Reinhold Niebuhr: His Religious, Social, and Political Thought* (New York: MacMillan, 1956).

it preserve itself without coercion. . . . [I]t is never absent." "Ultimately," he continued, "unity within an organized social group, or within a federation of such groups, is created by the ability of a dominant group to impose its will." Clearly there was no room here for even a vestige of prewar Progressive ideals. In fact, Niebuhr took direct aim at the deliberative nationalism of previous decades: "only a romanticist of the purest water could maintain that a national group ever arrives at 'common mind' or becomes conscious of a 'general will' without the use of either force or the threat of force."[51]

Niebuhr was far more deeply concerned by the practical implications of this observation, though, than Lippmann or his colleagues had been. For whilst the pluralists of the 1920s had generally been content to notice the role that coercion played in politics and to hope that the necessary coercive power could both be effectively constrained and vested in a responsible and well-educated political elite, Niebuhr did not take such a benign view. He was too heavily influenced by arguments concerning the essential selfishness of human beings, derived from a combination of European Socialism and the theology of "the Fall," to believe that any individual group could be trusted to run the state fairly or impartially. To him, any group in possession of the ultimate coercive force embodied by the state machine would be tempted to pursue their own interests at the expense of the interests of others. "In every human group," he argued, "there is less reason to guide and check impulse, less capacity for self-transcendence, less ability to comprehend the needs of others, and therefore more unrestrained egoism than the individuals who compose the group [might] reveal in their personal relationships." Any group that was given the task of organizing society, or operating its political machinery, would inevitably thus go awry. "[H]owever social its intentions or pretensions," such a group would "always arrogate an inordinate portion of social privilege to itself."[52]

Niebuhr did not take this to mean that the pursuit of a better society was an entirely unworthy project. Instead, he suggested that it was necessary to seek a society characterized by "social justice," even amongst the corruptible and corrupted characters of contemporary politics. For Niebuhr, however, the content and meaning of this idea of "social justice" was not provided by the views of individuals or by the limited capacities of sectors of society and as such it could never be expected to emerge in deliberative politics. Rather, he offered a transcendent view of such justice. It inhered in objective states of affairs and not in people's views about those affairs. The idea was thus not subject to the same doubts as the idea of the "common good" might be as

---

[51] Reinhold Niebuhr, *Moral Man and Immoral Society* (New York: Continuum, 2005 [1932]), 5, 6.
[52] Niebuhr, *Moral Man*, xi, 6.

it was not dependent on any assessment of citizens' capacities to overcome their own limitations.

This is not to say that Niebuhr offered a particularly thoroughgoing account of what he thought justice actually entailed. He did not. Nor did he explain how human beings with their limited capacities would ever be capable of recognizing it or pursuing it. In *Moral Man*, he simply hinted that justice demands some form of equality, especially equality in access to power, resources, and opportunities. Any social or political effort that "aims at greater equality," Niebuhr argued, "has a moral justification which must be denied to efforts which aim at the perpetuation of privilege."[53]

The lack of clear conceptual detail was not considered a difficulty by Niebuhr, though, for he was certain that all that was needed was a general sense of purpose for politics. Indeed, the pursuit of a more philosophically pure account was a distraction from the question that really mattered: how could egalitarian ideals of justice be realized in the imperfect conditions of the human world? The crucial task for reformers was, therefore, not to develop a subtle and nuanced account of some putative ideal society but to work out how a generally more equal society could be brought about in the face of the inevitable limitations on human capacities.

For Niebuhr, the basic outline of an answer to that question was also wholly clear. Reformers must abandon any residual faith in the benefits of a democratically engendered social harmony, recognize the necessity of coercion in politics, and think hard about how coercion could be channeled to the cause of greater equality rather than greater privilege. Niebuhr's stated mission was to persuade aspirant reformers that they would have to think about political power anew. They would have to realize that some citizens got their way in politics not by persuading their fellows but by dominating them, not by fostering a spirit of consensus but by throwing themselves wholeheartedly into competition with their rivals, not by reaching out across factional boundaries but by better identifying potential friends and inevitable enemies.

Niebuhr was deeply worried, however, that such a mission sat ill with American reformers. Such reformers had, after all, been brought up with Progressive sentimentalism, a program that had been committed to achieving a democracy of national unity wherein different sectors of society provided each other with reasons and pursued an idealized common good. That kind of politics, Niebuhr contended, "completely disregards the political necessities in the struggle for justice in human society by failing to recognize those elements in man's collective behavior which . . . can never

[53] Ibid., 154.

be brought completely under the dominion of reason or conscience." Progressives thus need instead to accept that "collective power" like that exercised by the prevailing state and the privileged classes "can never be dislodged unless power is raised against it." Since reason is always, at least to some degree, the servant of interest in a social situation, social injustice cannot be attained by "moral and rational suasion alone," he concluded. "It must be taken for granted therefore that the injustices in society . . . will not be abolished purely by moral suasion." "Conflict is inevitable," the argument ended, "and in this conflict power must be challenged by power."[54]

All of this was, of course, intended to open the door to a whole host of political strategies aimed at securing greater equality in the long run whilst not being dependent on the creation of a more deliberative politics. Essentially, the pursuit of justice required that the disadvantaged organize politically in fierce defense of their own interests. For Niebuhr, that meant that even violent revolution should be placed back into consideration. American democratic reformers, Niebuhr insisted, "are wrong in their assumption that violence is intrinsically immoral." Violence can be the product of ill will or good will and can serve either the cause of justice or that of injustice. Moreover, given that all change in the social order was likely to come about through coercion, it would be merely squeamish to distinguish between coercing violently and nonviolently. The distinction was at best a tendentious one. "If a season of violence can establish a just social system and can create the possibilities of its preservation there is no purely ethical ground upon which violence and revolution can be ruled out," Niebhur argued, which meant that "the real question" facing reformers in the United States was, "What are the political possibilities of establishing justice through violence?"[55]

Niebuhr's own answer to that question was ambiguous. While he believed that there were clearly circumstances in which those at the bottom of the social order might usefully take up arms, they were relatively few and far between, and extraordinarily rare in modern America. Within the context of the United States, he worried, neither the organized working class nor tyrannized African Americans were likely to succeed in their objectives if they simply took up arms against their oppressors, however morally justified such an approach might be.[56]

In outlining such a response he was, of course, actually far closer than he realized to the position that Walter Weyl and other Progressive colleagues

[54] Ibid., xii, xiii, 93.
[55] Ibid., 113, 118, 119.
[56] Ibid., 136–41.

had outlined prior to the war. They, too, had insisted that strategies other than those of persuasion were required for drastic political change. They had also suggested that violence might be considered a morally acceptable form of transforming the political landscape, but that it was unlikely to be successful in the context of the modern American state.[57] Even if, however, there were far more similarities between Niebuhr's account and that of the Progressives than he allowed for, there was still no doubt that the tenor and structure of the argument was essentially different. Most importantly, although he did look forward to a better, more just order to come, Niebuhr did not conceive of coercive politics as a passing stage, a necessary strategic move in the transition from a non-ideal to an ideal democratic order. Rather, he believed that coercion of some sort, be it violent or nonviolent, was always going to be a part of the political process. He also believed that it would be necessary to maintain a constant struggle to ensure that such coercion was put to use serving the needs of the dispossessed at least as well as it served the needs of the privileged. His future was not a future of the deliberative pursuit of a nationwide common good and it was in this regard that his break from prewar Progressivism was absolute.

Progressive Renewal

By the beginning of the 1930s, the Progressive democratic theory that had held such sway in the early years of the century was in ruins. It had been pummeled, first, by the experience of the First World War, and then, second, by the intellectual response to that experience, especially in the form of pluralism and the attack on the idea of the common good as well as the new emphasis on the essential role of coercion in maintaining social and political order in a diverse society.

In this context, Niebuhr's vision of a coercive politics of social justice seemed attractive in many ways. As Niebuhr himself would later suggest, the brutal economic conflicts that the Depression released implied that "everyone but the ascetic is a participant in the brutalities of the social struggle now." [58] It also appeared increasingly unlikely that these conflicts could be transcended in the short term. The only question Niebuhr believed that it was worth asking of any social group is "on what side of the struggle they are," and it was a position that was widely endorsed.[59]

---

[57] See the discussion in the previous chapter.
[58] Reinhold Niebuhr, "After Capitalism—What?," *World Tomorrow* 16 (1933): 203.
[59] Ibid., 203.

Yet, whilst some did begin to adopt a revolutionary perspective compatible with Niebuhr's, something held mainstream Progressives back from a full-scale conversion to the coercive pluralism that characterized Niebuhr's thought in the early 1930s. The reluctance was, in part, the product of understandable anxiety about the openly adversarial nature of the Niebuhrite vision and what seemed to some to be unhelpfully "superficial thinking in regard to the necessity of violence." But more worrying for most was Niebuhr's failure to offer much in the way of concrete guidance. It was all very well to assert that it was important for everyone to take a side in the necessary struggle, Niebuhr's Progressive critics insisted, but one needed also to say something about how justice was actually—practically and concretely—going to be obtained. There was very little in the theologian's work, that is, on the key questions of *who* was going to provide the crucial agency of change—which social forces were actually going to be mobilized—and *what* they were going to do when they managed to capture the power that was now denied them. There was, in other words, much lacking from what Jerome Davis called the "presentation of his positive technique for achieving social and economic justice."[60] And the Depression needed a response, not just a rhetoric.

It was for this reason that many on the Progressive Left began to try to shape a new theory, one that combined elements both from the skeptical, pluralistic, and coercive work of Lippmann, Case, Niebuhr, and colleagues with key elements of the prewar Progressivism of Croly, Lippmann, and Weyl. This new combination was openly and widely discussed in Progressive weeklies and journals throughout the early 1930s and it was seen at its clearest in two books: George Soule's *A Planned Society*, and his friend Stuart Chase's *A New Deal*.

The crucial shift in Soule and Chase's work concerned the rehabilitation of at least some idea of a common interest. For these thinkers, although the postwar pluralists had been right to dismiss the average American citizen's ability to transcend his own world and grasp the common good of the whole nation, they had been wrong in further claiming that it followed that no such common good existed at all in the United States.[61] Just as Niebuhr believed that the fundamental meaning and value of justice transcended what actually existing individuals and groups actually thought about justice, Soule, Chase, and their colleagues argued that a substantial common good might in fact connect the interests of American citizens, independent of

[60] Jerome Davis, "Moral Man and Immoral Society," *Annals of the American Academy of Political and Social Science* 166 (1933): 231. See, too, L. M. Pape, "Moral Man and Immoral Society," *American Political Science Review* 27 (1933): 296–97.

[61] See Soule, *Planned Society*, 44.

whatever those citizens themselves thought divided them. This was particularly true, they argued, in the realm of economics, where every American could reasonably be said to share a common interest in the avoidance of misery and in the existence of some form of prosperity, even if they did not consciously understand their economic lives as interconnected or interdependent in any way. The pluralists were probably right that it was impossible to unite the American people in their "morals" or their "play" or their "love," Chase summarized, but they were wrong to think that they did not share a common interest in their "housekeeping."[62]

Soule and Chase thus resurrected an essential element of the prewar Progressive story—the possibility of directing politics toward service to the common good—even though they offered a radically hollowed out account of what such a good might contain.[63] As Robert MacIver celebrated, they believed in a common interest in the area of "economic control" at the same time as they accepted its irrelevance in the "domain of moralistic control."[64]

In addition to this renewed understanding of the place of the common good, Soule, Chase, and colleagues also returned to three further elements of the prewar Progressive vision. The first concerned the cause of economic distress. The Depression, they argued, was essentially due to the chaos of an unregulated and unstructured free market. It was the absence of effective planning and economic oversight that was to blame for the turmoil. The second involved the means by which the American machinery of government could relieve that distress. What was required was more effective coordination of the interdependent parts of a complex industrial society by a powerful, well-staffed, and purposeful federal government. "Of all idle Utopian dreams," Soule complained, "unlimited capitalistic competition is the most fanciful. We never really had it; we are getting farther from it every day. Why not frankly acknowledge that sensible management for collective purpose is the necessary goal, and see what we can do to achieve it? Why

[62] Stuart Chase, *A New Deal* (New York: MacMillan, 1932), 213. This argument again bore close affinities to the case made by the British socialist pluralists. See Stuart Chase, "On the Paradox of Plenty," *New Republic*, January 18, 1933, 258–60, and Stears, *Progressives, Pluralists, and the Problems of the State*, 168–98.

[63] It is worth noting, however, that Soule believed that the day for a more substantive common good might come. The "first objective naturally must be to raise the lowest standards of living, not to speak of providing everyone the assurance of enough to eat and wear. But, after such modest goals are achieved, it may appear that people really do not want to go much further in that particular direction. We may be more interested in the quality of our satisfactions than in that quantity" (*Planned Society*, 282).

[64] Robert MacIver, "The Ambiguity of the New Deal," reprinted in Howard Zinn, ed., *New Deal Thought* (New York: Bobbs-Merrill, 1969 [1933]), 57.

not devise our controls with that purpose in view, and mobilize around it?"[65] The third considered the obstacles to such action. Predictably, blame was laid in two directions: first, toward an outmoded constitutional settlement that prevented the government from taking quick and effective action; and, second, toward the continuing prevalence of a set of social norms and values amongst a large number of citizens that continued to laud laissez-faire capitalism even in times of economic distress and was seemingly hostile to collective action.

Taken together, these three elements left Soule and Chase with exactly the same kind of exasperation that had afflicted the prewar Progressives and with a similar sense of the place of the United States in a democratic temporal order. Unlike Niebuhr and Lippmann, then, who had drawn back from the idea that the non-ideal present in American government might give way to a more ideal future, Soule, Chase, and their colleagues restored the Progressive notion that the future could in all likelihood be made qualitatively and substantively better than the present.[66] If only the prevailing political structures could be reshaped in some way, and a new system of government constructed, then the United States would become a polity in which the common good, rather than the private interests of big business, could become the central purpose of its governing agencies, and within that sort of polity the economic system could be effectively organized for the benefit of all.

In many ways, this idea of cross-temporal transformation was even more important to the Depression-Era Progressives than it had been to their prewar predecessors. The battle to achieve it was certainly more dramatic. The United States, Stuart Chase insisted, needed a "cleansing, wholesome innovation. The shift of ambition and the goal of success toward public service, science, research, the arts, industrial management, statesmanship, and away from sheer accumulation, would be the happiest and most welcome change which could happen to contemporary civilization," he continued, and it was worth almost any risk in order to bring about the "revolutionary" change in political machinery and practice that was needed to bring it about.[67] "The bent toward fixity," Soule added, has to be "supplanted by the bent toward adventure." The United States must enter a "time of conscious history-making."[68] "Why," Stuart Chase asked with a distressingly revealing naivete, "should the Russians have all the fun of remaking the world?"[69]

[65] Soule, *Planned Society*, 183.

[66] On Niebuhr's rejection of this temporal perspective, see Pells, *Radical Visions*, 98.

[67] Stuart Chase, "A New Deal for America: The Road to Revolution," *New Republic*, July 6, 1932, 201.

[68] George Soule, *The Coming American Revolution* (London: George Routledge and Sons, 1934), 4.

[69] Chase, *New Deal*, 252.

Despite all these Progressive echoes, however, there was one fundamental difference between this vision and that of their prewar predecessors, and that concerned the place of citizen democracy. The prewar Progressives had held an unshakeable faith in democratic politics, both as a mechanism for change and as a crucial element of a more ideal future. Citizen engagement had, therefore, been crucial to prewar Progressivism. It simply did not feature in the Depression-Era variant. Instead, Soule, Chase, and their colleagues accepted almost without question Lippmann's postwar rejection of the efficacy and morality of participatory democratic politics in almost every form. If the necessary reforms were to occur, they argued, then Americans would have to strip away what they dismissively called the "democratic dogma."[70]

It was in this regard that the importance of Soule and Chase's rejection of the possibility of subjectively felt, mutually shared common good was most keenly felt. Postwar Pluralism, they argued, had demonstrated that American citizens could not *feel* a deep sense of national solidarity. Nor could they overcome their own private interests long enough actually to perceive the common interests that united them. Such citizens "cannot be amalgamated" into a single unit, Soule summarized in strikingly Pluralist language. Even though "the interest of the whole" exists in some objective sense, it can not be made democratically to "emerge from the jangle of the interest of the parts," as prewar democrats had supposed. Citizens would therefore have to "be led" toward an understanding of their commonality and, if necessary, forced to live their lives in ways that served the common good. In the absence of any spirit of solidarity or deep sense of collective engagement amongst the citizen body, the activities of diverse citizens must be effectively "coordinated" by the exercise of effectively wielded coercive power.[71]

This combination of Progressive collectivism and Pluralist democratic skepticism resulted in an elitist and hierarchical vision of social transformation and political power. There was, then, plenty of talk of the importance of executive leadership in Soule and Chase's work, just as there had been in the decades before. This time, though, it was the task of leaders actually to direct the behavior of economically active citizens according to their own vision of the economic good rather than to inspire those citizens to think and feel as a solidaristic unit or to involve them in any significant way in the major decisions of the day. "The drive toward collectivism leads toward control from the top," Chase insisted, and it was pointless and self-

[70] Ibid., 219.
[71] Soule, *Planned Society*, 37, 138.

defeating for any Progressively inclined politician to resist that conclusion. Only when the executive was empowered to direct and control the economic behavior of the nation, when it was freed from the hindrances of an outdated constitution, factional loyalties, individualistic norms, and from the interferences of an ill-informed and reactionary citizen body—only then could the United States government actually begin to serve the common good. It would take such an administration to enable real social and economic transformation, reshaping the social and economic order so that "instead of being individually at war with society, instead of being baffled and burdened by an irrelevant environment of social forces we shall be at work, through society, mastering our life and creating it as a whole."[72] It was here in postwar thought, not in prewar Progressivism, that the specter of an authoritarian politics of (pseudo-)scientific elitism really began to stalk the United States.[73]

Despite its horrific implications, Soule and Chase's vision found a great deal of support in the dark days of the Depression. Its influence was felt amongst many trade unionists, former Progressives, and even some of those connected with Franklin Roosevelt's new administration.[74] It also found some international admirers. Writing in a *New Republic* symposium on "the future of democracy," the British-based Irish Socialist George Bernard Shaw, for example, excitedly seized on the coercive undercurrent of such thought. "There is no antithesis between authoritarian government and democracy," he insisted. "All government is authoritarian; and the more democratic a government is the more authoritarian it is."[75]

Yet despite the enthusiasm for authoritarianism, there were two omissions from the theory as an account of how such change should occur. The first concerned the insight and trustworthiness of their putative executive elite. Soule and Chase's theory was entirely dependent upon the possibility that a cadre of expert planners, bureaucrats, technocrats, and political leaders were going to be able to understand the nature of a common good that most citizens were unaware of, come up with an effective plan to realize that good, and not be tempted to serve their private interests along the way. They did nothing, then, to answer Niebuhr's charge that such elites

---

[72] Ibid., 283.

[73] See John Jordan, *Machine-Age Ideology: Social Engineering and American Liberalism 1911–1939* (Durham: University of North Carolina Press, 1994).

[74] For contemporary overviews, see Paul Homan, "Economic Planning: The Proposals and the Literature," *Quarterly Review of Economics* 47 (1932): 102–22, and Rexford Tugwell, "The Design of Government," *Political Science Quarterly* 48 (1933): 321–32. For commentary, see Leon Fink, *Progressive Intellectuals and the Dilemmas of Democratic Commitment* (Cambridge, Mass.: Harvard University Press, 1997), 214–41.

[75] George Bernard Shaw, "The Future of Democracy," *New Republic*, April 14, 1937, 289.

were not to be trusted or to reassure the organized working class, African Americans, or other marginalized groups that their interests would not be overlooked by self-described experts drawn almost exclusively from the white middle class.

The second concerned the way in which such experts were meant to come to power in the first place. For having so roundly condemned the democratic method and having also dismissed the reformist (or revolutionary) potential of the American working class in the same way, Soule and Chase were in fact left without an account of how American politics was ever going to be transformed. As their most strident critic, John Chamberlain, had it, Soule and Chase's idea was "like a magnificent machine with no dynamo attached; there is nothing to start the conveyor belts moving."[76] Just as the actual agents of change had been absent from Niebuhr's vision, so they were from Soule and Chase's too.

In responding to this criticism, Soule, Chase, and their supporters offered three suggestions. The first two were desperately unconvincing. The first, unsurprisingly, turned to the potential of great leadership, especially executive leadership, with Soule suggesting, just as Croly once had, that exceptional individuals were capable of providing the "driving force" for large-scale change. The difficulty there, of course, was that Progressives could identify no such individual apart from Franklin Roosevelt, and attitudes toward Roosevelt and to the New Deal in general were far from wholly positive amongst self-described radicals in the 1930s. His first term was largely dismissed for its apparent timidity, and although there was more open appreciation in the second term as the president challenged the Supreme Court's constitutional objections to reform, very few radical commentators believed that reform lead by the president was likely to do all that was necessary to reconstruct the entire political order in the manner the Depression demanded.[77]

The second turned instead to the supposedly innate sense of the American people that "order" was better than "chaos." "We can count on the organizing disposition of mankind," Soule again insisted, eventually to lead the citizen body away from private interest and pluralist democracy and

---

[76] John Chamberlain, "A Planned Society," *Modern Quarterly* 6 (1932): 118. See, too, John Chamberlain, *Farewell to Reform: The Rise, Life, and Decay of the Progressive Mind in America* (New York: John Day and Co., 1933), 317–19, and Gerald Spenser, "A New Deal," *Modern Quarterly* 6 (1932): 102–3.

[77] See David Plotke, "The Wagner Act, Again: Politics and Labor, 1935–1937," *Studies in American Political Development* 4 (1989): 105–56, and Lizabeth Cohen, *Making a New Deal: Industrial Workers in Chicago, 1919–1939* (New York: Oxford University Press, 199).

toward the effectively administered regime of the future.[78] Such an argument, however, failed to convince not only because it depended on the very good sense of the citizen body that these thinkers had denied, but because even if it was true that citizens cleaved to order over chaos, that was a disposition that was unlikely to usher in an era of revolutionary turmoil of the sort the Depression-Era Progressives believed was required. A spirit of order was not going to engender a new political era in the United States.

The third response thus carried all the real burden of hope. It was borrowed from the earlier technocratic, utopian visions of Edward Bellamy and Thorstein Veblen and suggested that despite the general lack of interest in radical change amongst the American citizenry, there was, in fact, one small but influential section of the population capable of bringing about the necessary transformation.[79] That section was made up of the "intelligent minority" of engineers and scientists who were already at work in the economically advanced parts of American society. Within this group, the argument continued, there were individuals who saw themselves as members of a "new class" of political activists, capable of constituting "shock troop units in every community in the Republic," who could lead the way to a technocratic revolution, either violent or nonviolent.[80] These were the organizers and the technicians, people who understood the limitations of the prevailing economic anarchy and who could see past the anachronisms of the established political order into a more coordinated and a more just future. They were also equipped with the necessary intelligence for strategic action. They were therefore unlikely to be blinded by short-term sectional interests or dissuaded by the propaganda appeals of organized capital or conservative labor. This section of society, the argument concluded, was not subject to the limitations that afflicted other elements of the citizenry, and they could, therefore, be charged with ushering in the ideal future order even in the midst of a desperately non-ideal present.

Even on its own terms, however, this third argument also failed to satisfy. Paradoxically for those who prided themselves on their use of "science," it was a claim grounded far more in hope than evidence, for there was precious little to suggest that any significant number of "engineers and economic planners" were interested in mobilizing for political change in the 1930s. There were no noticeable organizations binding them together, no journals or newspapers of shared concern, and no effective voice in political debates. And even if such a group were to start to cohere socially

---

[78] Soule, *Planned Society*, 137, 153.

[79] See Edward Bellamy, *Looking Backward* (Toronto: G. N. Morang, 1897), and Thorstein Veblen, *The Engineers and the Price System* (New York: B. W. Hubesch, 1921).

[80] Chase, *New Deal*, 249.

and politically, it was also unlikely that they would possess the power to effect anything like the sort of far-reaching changes that Progressives of the Depression Era hoped for. "Watch them. They will bear watching," Stuart Chase insisted, but that was the best that he could offer.[81]

All expectations had thus been entrusted to a desperately weak challenger to the prevailing power of corporate capitalism. As John Chamberlain put it, it was an argument that was "simply not talking in terms of human material." Soule and Chase claimed not to be Utopians, Chamberlain continued, but their work most assuredly contained the very worst elements of Utopian theorizing, lacking as it did any account of the "human agency" that would have "the power to institute" their desired new regime.[82] There was, of course, a great irony here, for in decrying the possibilities of a citizen-led, democratic transformation, and embracing instead the reform potential of coercive power, this new generation of Progressives left themselves without an agent of change at all. On the account Chase, Soule, and their colleagues outlined, the inadequacies of the present could only be rectified by an agent that comprehended the problems of the economy, understood the nature of the common good, and possessed political power. But no such agent presented itself.

Indeed, it seemed almost impossible that one could. As Walter Lippmann himself so powerfully argued, this was the problem on which "the whole conception flounders." "Because a planned society must be one in which the people obey their rules, there can be no plan to find the planners: the selection of the despots who are to make society so rational and so secure has to be left to the insecurity of irrational chance."[83] It also, of course, had to be left to the insecurity of supposedly "irrational" citizens, for if the change that Soule and Chase desired was ever to be brought about, it would have to be initiated, to some extent at least, by the public itself. It was in this way that the paradox of politics—the difficulty of making an ideal society out of the non-ideal political material of the present—had struck again, right at the heart of the new Progressive vision.

The Crisis of Democracy

The problems of Depression-Era radical democratic thought were not all of Soule and Chase's own making. It was essentially the pluralist, coercive

---

[81] Ibid., 252.

[82] Chamberlain, "Planned Society," 118.

[83] Walter Lippmann, "Planning in an Economy of Abundance," *Atlantic Monthly* 159 (1937): 46.

critique of prewar Progressivism mobilized by Lippmann and Niebuhr that left much American political thought at a dead end. Initially, that critique had deprived Progressives of three faiths: in the potential of the citizen body itself, in the existence of a common good that could bind Americans together, and in the possibilities of a profoundly better political future. When the Depression hit and it became clear that Niebuhr's vision offered little by way of a practical solution, Soule and Chase attempted to resuscitate aspects of the Progressive vision. Responding both to the intellectual emphases of their time and to the depth of the crisis of the Depression, they chose to propound a slimmed-down conception of the common good and an expanded sense of the possibilities of a future order. But they did not to try to resurrect faith in the citizen body itself. They offered an almost millennial vision of the future, but one that said little to nothing about the role of the average citizen in decision making or about the processes of political transformation.

On this view, the ideal of democracy offered almost nothing to American citizens at all; what was required instead was obedience, order, and, hopefully, prosperity. The 1920s and early 1930s represented, therefore, the nadir of radical democratic thought in the United States of the twentieth century. It was a time in which hope for the future was all but entirely displaced by worries about the here-and-now and in which it no longer seemed appropriate either to design ideal democracies for the future or to hope for much in the way of far-sighted political agency in the present.

Despite the prevailing pessimism, though, not all was lost in those years. For at the same time as Lippmann, Niebuhr, and their colleagues were crafting a pluralist, coercive critique of Progressive political ideas, a few others were attempting to keep the more communitarian, democratic, and even deliberative aspects of the prewar Progressive vision alive. They were led, of course, by a radical intellectual whose influence would be felt far beyond the interwar years. He was John Dewey, and it is to his democratic thought, and the practical democratic politics that such thought both inspired and defended, that this study now turns.

CHAPTER THREE

Radicalism Americanized

The intellectual impact of the assault on the Progressive vision of democratic reform in the interwar years was profound. The fact that it came at the very time when many European nations were turning their backs on democratic politics entirely made its impact greater still.[1] By the mid-1930s, many American radicals were to be found openly wondering whether democracy had a future in the United States or whether, instead, it would be replaced by a Fascist-inspired form of corporate capitalism or by a Bolshevik-inspired class revolution.[2] Barely a month went by from the stock market crash until the outbreak of the Second World War without one of the organs of radical political thought holding a symposium on the future of democracy. "The very evolution of democracy . . . in every modern state is in the direction of concealed dictatorship," the popular left periodical *Modern Quarterly* reported as early as May of 1930. "The contempt for democracy which has grown up amongst a number of liberal thinkers in the last generation is but part of the reflection of the underlying decay of democratic institutions."[3] Even those who resisted this trend and remained committed to the democratic ideal were nonetheless unsure of how much democratic politics had to offer in the near term, especially given the desperate state of American social and political life during the Depression. "Should undemocratic means be used in the struggle for political and economic democracy?" the League for Industrial Democracy rhetorically asked at their 1939 summer conference. "Can means be separated from ends?"[4]

In amongst all the doubters, however, at least one much-celebrated voice appeared to hold out against the trend: that of John Dewey. Already well regarded as a philosopher before the First World War, Dewey shot to prominence in radical political circles after the conflict, quickly developing a reputation as the most persuasive advocate of an identifiably Progressive

[1] See Waldo Frank, "Will Fascism Come to America?," *Modern Monthly* 8 (1934): 464–66.

[2] See Sidney Hook, "On Workers' Democracy," *Modern Monthly* 8 (1934): 529–44.

[3] Editorial, "Democracy versus Dictatorship," *Modern Quarterly* 5 (1930): 398, 400.

[4] "Summer Conference 1939," The League for Industrial Democracy Papers 49/9/1939, The Tamiment Institute, New York University.

theory of democratic reform.[5] Dewey garnered plaudits for both his finely nuanced account of the nature of an ideal democracy and for his concrete suggestions for democratic reform. In both of these regards, Dewey appeared to be the most optimistic advocate of a "new kind" of democratic politics, at least in the 1920s. His approach was experimentalist, Pragmatist, but also distinctively deliberative, with a strong focus on the advantages of national communication.[6] Democracy, for Dewey, required a widespread conversation between all citizens: a conversation that would encompass all of the issues and concerns that were close to their hearts. At the very moment that Lippmann and Niebuhr were dismissing the possibility of any cross-sectional discourse, Dewey was placing it as the core of his political philosophy. He was also, moreover, insisting that it was an ideal that could be realized in the modern United States. If citizens were provided with enhanced educational opportunities and offered a real chance to influence the political decisions that shaped their lives, then a new democratic order could be built and the nation's problems could begin to be remedied.

Dewey's renown in this regard has remained intact. Indeed, some more recent commentators have gone as far as to suggest that all "subsequent American leftists" have failed to make "any advance on Dewey's understanding" of the crucial questions in democratic politics.[7] There is, however, far more to the story of Dewey's democratic theorizing, and the politics that it inspired, than the orthodox story allows. For despite his unstinting conviction that a new kind of democratic politics could be realized in the United States, Dewey was chastened by the challenges that democracy faced, just as his colleagues were, in the Depression years. Most importantly, although Dewey's commitment to some form of identifiably deliberative democracy as a long-term ideal did remain constant, his views as to how such a democracy could be built, by whom, and when, all radically changed as the Depression years progressed. By the end of the 1930s, he was advancing political recommendations that he would previously have condemned: political recommendations that more closely resembled those of Niebuhr and colleagues than those that were demanded by the prewar Progressives, let alone those that would be called for by orthodox deliberative democrats in the years to come. He did, however, give those arguments a distinctive

---

[5] For excellent overviews, see Robert Westbrook, *John Dewey and American Democracy* (Ithaca: Cornell University Press, 1991), and Alan Ryan, *John Dewey and the High Tide of American Liberalism* (New York: W. W. Norton, 1995).

[6] For contemporary commentary, see William Y. Elliott, *The Pragmatic Revolt in Politics: Syndicalism, Fascism and the Constitutional State* (New York: MacMillan, 1928).

[7] Richard Rorty, *Achieving Our Country: Leftist Thought in Twentieth-Century America* (Cambridge, Mass.: Harvard University Press, 1998), 31.

twist by emphasizing what he claimed was a characteristically *American* approach to the process of democratic transformation. Reform, he insisted, has to be rooted in traditional and well-established American values rather than shaped anew. As Dewey became more "radical," then, he sought simultaneously to make radicalism more "American."

Dewey was far from alone in crafting this new democratic vision in the later interwar years, even if he was undeniably the leading light amongst the intellectuals who propounded it. Indeed the last few years of the 1930s witnessed the re-emergence of a powerful radical democratic movement in both political theory and practice in the United States. It was a movement that set out both to save existing American democratic practices from the combined threats of Fascism and Communism and that strove to improve these institutions and to enhance the capacities of the citizens who lived and worked within them. The task of such a movement was, of course, immense. It had to overcome both the deeply ingrained intellectual skepticism of the time and to propose a viable response to the political, social, and economic turmoil that had been unleashed by the Depression. It likewise sought to develop a new account of both the ideal democratic order and the means by which such an order could be reached, and would do so by combining the best elements of early Progressive democratic thought with the most fruitful parts of the challenge posed by pluralism and proponents of coercive force. It was an attempt that was not always entirely convincing, but one that came to have an enormous influence in the years to come.

Maintaining the Faith

Despite already enjoying a significant reputation as a pragmatist philosopher and as a student of education, John Dewey had been a peripheral figure in the prewar Progressive movement.[8] He generally adhered to the outlines of the New Nationalism as sketched by Herbert Croly, the young Walter Lippmann, and Walter Weyl, and occasionally seemed to emphasize the importance of national solidarity even more vociferously than his colleagues had.[9] In the immediate postwar years, he remained a champion of that perspective, even in the face of the collapse of the Progressive faith brought on by the experience of World War One. In the first few years after the war, he

---

[8] See John Dewey and J. H. Tufts, *Ethics* (New York: MacMillan, 1908), and the discussion in Marc Stears, *Progressives, Pluralists, and the Problems of the State: Ideologies of Reform in the United States and Britain* (Oxford: Oxford Univerrsity Press, 2002), 46–49.

[9] For excellent commentary, see Alan Cywar, "John Dewey in World War One," *American Quarterly* 21 (1969): 578–94, and Ryan, *John Dewey*, 154–99.

penned two well-received works of political philosophy: *Reconstruction in Philosophy* and *Human Nature and Conduct*. Both of these works argued that the core of the Progressive account of democratic values and democratic practices remained essentially valid.[10] Seven years later, he published an even more vibrant defense of the Progressive perspective, *The Public and its Problems*, a book that was intended as a direct response to the skeptical pluralism of Walter Lippmann, and that has remained in print ever since.[11]

For all of his commitment to the essentials of prewar Progressivism, though, Dewey was stung by pluralism, and especially by Lippmann's critique of the idea of the common good upon which so much of New Nationalist Progressivism had depended. His previous support for a straightforward sense of national solidarity was undermined by the new realization that a modern industrial society was primarily characterized by a "plurality of changing, moving, individualized goods and ends." The pluralists had convinced him that "variety is more than the spice of life; it is largely of its essence."[12] The pluralists also compelled him to accept that even if a common good could be identified, no single government was ever likely to pursue it in an entirely trustworthy fashion. When "the state is involved in making social arrangements like passing laws" he explained, it always "acts through concrete persons," and those persons are susceptible to the same temptations and limitations that afflict all other human beings.[13] It had been to prewar Progressivism's detriment, he implied, that it had failed to insist loudly enough on the limitations of the agents of the state.

Despite these pluralistic leanings, Dewey did not join Lippmann in abandoning the conviction that Americans in the industrial age shared deep and important connections. Instead, following the British psychologist Graham Wallas, Dewey argued that Americans now lived in what he called "the great society": an era of advanced technology and transportation that inevitably generated close relations of interest between otherwise diverse citizens. Whatever the differences of opinion and circumstance between the various social groups in the modern United States, Dewey insisted that on account of this industrial transformation, they were "so intimately interrelated that what happens to one of them ultimately affects the well-being of all of them."[14] He also believed that such common interests could never be well served by competition between the groups but required instead the

---

[10] See John Dewey, *Reconstruction in Philosophy* (London: University of London Press, 1921), and John Dewey, *Human Nature and Conduct* (New York: Modern Library, 1922).

[11] See John Dewey, *The Public and its Problems* (Chicago: Gateway, 1946 [1927]).

[12] Dewey, *Human Nature and Conduct*, 308.

[13] Dewey, *Public and its Problems*, 18.

[14] John Dewey, *Lectures in China* (Honolulu: University of Hawaii Press, 1973 [1920]), 71.

creation of a cooperative rather than a competitive social and political environment. Thus the central task facing all radicals remained just as it had been before the war. It was to "devise means for bringing the interests of all the groups of a society into adjustment, providing all of them with the opportunity to develop, so that each can help the others instead of being in conflict with them."[15]

The crucial difference for Dewey in the 1920s concerned the precise nature of that "means." Whereas before the war he had expected citizens and governing authorities quickly to join together in the task of national renewal, he now accepted that many citizens might be deeply hostile to such an adjustment and he also conceded that governing authorities could not be straightforwardly trusted to bring it about in an impartial way. Pluralism and the experience of war itself had demonstrated that the state "has no hands except those of individual human beings" and that those hands were always subject to temptation.

Unlike Lippmann, Niebuhr, Soule, or Chase, Dewey began the search for an answer to this problem with the citizenry itself. The excesses of the war years, Dewey believed, might have demonstrated both that the United States "has no political agencies worthy" of the task of national renewal and that the citizenry currently failed to identify with an inclusive vision of national solidarity. But it had also revealed that the second of those problems would be easier to overcome than the former.[16]

This conviction became the central tenet of the renowned theory of "the public" that Dewey developed in the later 1920s. "The democratic public is still largely inchoate and unorganized," he suggested, but nonetheless "an organized, articulate public," which might otherwise be known as a "great community," was still a possibility in the United States. At present, the United States had developed a "great society"—a pattern of actual interactions and shared interests—without concomitantly "generating a great community," a subjective sense of shared belonging and mutual loyalty. As such, Americans felt detached and distanced from each other, alienated from their nation, and caught up in a "sweep of forces too vast to understand or master." That, Dewey insisted, was something that must be put right. American reformers thus needed to concentrate on "discovering the means by which a scattered, mobile, and manifold public may so recognize itself as to define and express its interests" collectively. Moreover, this "discovery is necessarily precedent to any fundamental change in machinery":

---

[15] Ibid.
[16] Dewey, *Public and its Problems*, 82, 109.

attitudinal change would have to precede political change.[17] As Dewey's biographer Robert Westbrook describes it and as noted above, "the great society" already existed, crafted by the "extensive webs of interdependence" that were themselves the inevitable product of industrialization. The "great community" was now to be constructed, and would be "marked by a shared understanding of the consequences of this interdependence."[18]

It was here, as has so often been noted, that the idea that would later provide the foundations for deliberative democracy first emerged in American political thought: Dewey's contention that "communication can alone create a great community."[19] It was a bold prescription. The "great community" could come into being even in a society as diverse as the United States if citizens could be drawn into intense, informed, and articulate conversation with each other. If citizens could discuss the ways in which their lives progressed, then they could begin to realize how they were, in fact, dependent on the provision of the same sorts of services, how they profited from the same sorts of social stabilities, and how they could flourish and develop more profoundly if they began to act in concert rather than in competition with each other. The "give-and-take of communication," Dewey summarized, is the only way to give each individual an "effective sense" of being a "member of a community . . . who understands and appreciates its beliefs, desires, and methods, and who contributes to a further conversion of organic powers into human resources and values."[20]

For this to take place nothing short of a revolution was required. But it was a revolution in the mechanisms and content of social communication rather than in political power and political institutions. "The highest and most difficult kind of inquiry and a subtle, delicate, vivid and responsive art of communication," Dewey outlined, "must take possession of the physical machinery of transmission and circulation and breathe life into it." If the press could be reformed, education enhanced, and social scientists led to explain their ideas and propagate their research to as many citizens as possible, then a real opportunity would present itself. In such a society, individuals would be in conversation with one another to such an extent that "the ever-expanding and intricately ramifying consequences of associated activities shall be known" across the citizen body.[21] Effective and improved communication would thus realize the potential for the "great community," the alert and self-conscious "public," to emerge in the United States.

[17] Ibid., 126–27, 109, 135, 147.
[18] Westbrook, *John Dewey and American Democracy*, 309.
[19] Dewey, *Public and its Problems*, 142.
[20] Ibid., 154.
[21] Ibid., 184.

In the 1920s, therefore, Dewey rejected what he saw as the postwar pluralists' excessive focus on "politics" and the coercive mechanisms of the state and argued instead that reformers should turn to the world of communication, media, and education if they wished to reconstruct American democracy.[22] As his protégé, the Minnesota political scientist Norman Wilde, summarized, Dewey intended to demonstrate that that unless American citizens broadly shared an "active interest in the common life, no political machinery will work." [23] It was useless to try to remove temptations in the governing elite, to hope that the common good could be served from above, before a common good had actually been identified by the citizen body itself.

This was, of course, never considered to be an easy task in itself. The pluralists had demonstrated that American social life as it was currently constituted was characterized by private interest, faction, and exclusion. But to Dewey's mind they had not proven that it was impossible for such difficulties to be overcome. Even if the challenge was a difficult one, moreover, it would have to be faced. Dewey believed no other route to reform could provide a stable alternative. "Until we can knit together again these fragments of the common life by the development of a unifying interest, we cannot hope to make *any* system work," Norman Wilde again explained. "The practical problem, then, is not primarily that of devising new machinery for carrying out the social will . . . but rather for the creation of the social will itself."[24]

Dewey thus sharply rejected the central pluralist claim that American citizens would never be able to overcome the intense sectional loyalties, private interests, and short-sightedness that divided them. He also dismissed the essentially coercive view of politics to which such pluralism had given rise. For all of his commitment to collectivism and the development of a nationwide spirit of solidarity, Dewey then described his position as a definitively "liberal" one. It was more closely related to the Jeffersonian tradition that most of his colleagues roundly condemned than to its more recent Nieburhite alternative. As such, effective communication was vitally dependent on the possibility of open debate. Only when citizens were free from excessive control by the state or other agencies, and only when they felt themselves to be thus, would they be able to exchange views about the most important aspects of their lives. It was crucial, therefore, for reformers to keep the faith with liberal essentials, including freedom of speech,

---

[22] See John Dewey, "Public Opinion," *New Republic*, May 3, 1922, 288.
[23] Norman Wilde, *The Ethical Basis of the State* (Princeton: Princeton University Press, 1927), 183.
[24] Ibid.

of the press, of assembly, and the like.[25] "I don't like the phrase academic freedom," Dewey told a group of adult educators in 1928, "because there really is nothing academic about freedom. Freedom of mind, freedom of thought, freedom of inquiry, freedom of discussion, *is* education, and there is no education without these elements of freedom."[26]

Such arguments applied just as much to the behavior of citizens as they did to the behavior of states. At the same time as Niebuhr and colleagues were urging citizens to engage in an openly adversarial politics, a politics that placed its emphasis firmly on power rather than on persuasion, Dewey was instructing citizens to do just the opposite. Democratic communication could only generate new forms of social cohesion if it was based on a mutually empathetic, open-minded, and considerate exchange of views. It was reason and moral suasion that would build the "great community," not a friend/enemy distinction. The primary role of the reformer in Dewey's eyes was, therefore, neither to prevent injustice and abuse by the privileged elite through a constant struggle for control of political power—as it was for Niebuhr—nor to lead unwilling citizens toward a communal future through effective executive action, as it was for Soule and Chase. Rather, it was to use all the devices available in the "great society" to protect and enable widespread discussion and to inform its participants. It was only in this way that the "great community" could emerge and factionalism subside.

This was not a call for state inaction, of course. Dewey was acutely aware that for such a conversation to take place, government would have to offer more in the way of education, information, and social welfare than it did at present, and certainly to do more than the liberals of the nineteenth century had anticipated. Dewey did not anticipate that it would necessitate much in the way of coercive power—in the 1920s, at least. "The state remains highly important," Dewey explained, "but its importance consists more and more in its power to foster and coordinate the activities of voluntary groups."[27] Indeed, the use of coercion would be more likely to provide an obstacle to the emergence of social harmony than an incentive to it given that state restraint was likely to stir up resentment between different groups and increase the likelihood of undesirable exclusions. It was the expansion and

---

[25] David Rabban suggests that Dewey was the only major Progressive to keep this emphasis on free speech in postwar writing. See David M. Rabban, *Free Speech in its Forgotten Years* (Cambridge: Cambridge University Press, 1997), 335–41.

[26] John Dewey, "Address to American Federation of Teachers, Local 5," in the The Abraham J. Muste Papers, Labor-Management Document Center, Cornell University.

[27] Dewey, *Reconstruction in Philosophy*, 204.

exercise of "freed intelligence" rather than compulsion that would provide the primary "method of directing change."[28]

Democracy Radicalized

This liberal democratic restoration of Progressivism infuriated Dewey's critics. They found it wildly overoptimistic in its communalism and were even more irritated by its apparent unwillingness to take the challenge of the psychological limitations of citizens seriously. Niebuhr thought the whole program was little short of absurd. He opened *Moral Man and Immoral Society* with a ferocious broadside against Dewey. "It is rather discouraging to find such naive confidence in the moral capacities of collective man, among men who make it their business to study collective behaviour," he opined. "They do not see that the limitations of the human imagination, the easy subservience of reason to prejudice and passion, and the consequent persistence of irrational egoism particularly in group behavior, make social conflict an inevitability in human history, probably to its end." According to this argument, Dewey and his supporters failed to understand that coercion of some sort is essential both to the securing of social stability and to the achievement of any sort of social justice, especially in so far as the latter involved the stripping of privilege from those who currently enjoyed it. "A higher degree of intelligence and a more acute rational perception might conceivably destroy class bias to some degree," Niebuhr conceded, "[b]ut it cannot abolish the egoism of a class" in its entirety. "It must be taken for granted," he insisted, "that the injustices in society, which arise from class privileges, will not be abolished purely by moral suasion" or cross-class conversation.[29]

Dewey must have expected this response, but he was stung by it nonetheless, especially so given the Progressive political failures of the 1920s and early 1930s, which were exacerbated by the Depression. As the 1930s opened, he found it increasingly hard to argue that reformers should dedicate themselves to the slow, steady development of social understanding through improved communication. After all, almost all other self-identified radicals agreed that drastic political action was required, either to rearrange the distribution of economic resources to ameliorate the condition of the

---

[28] John Dewey, *Liberalism and Social Action* (Amherst, Mass.: Prometheus, 2000 [1935]), 61.

[29] Reinhold Niebuhr, *Moral Man and Immoral Society* (New York: Continuum, 2005 [1932]), xvi, xvii, 93.

least advantaged or to wrest political power from those who exercised it, or both.

As the Depression deepened in the early 1930s, putting Dewey under the twin pressures of criticism and circumstance, he eventually began to concede that his argument was no longer entirely appropriate to the demands of the time.[30] By 1933 he had begun to accept that it would be extremely difficult to initiate the kind of cross-national political conversation of which he dreamt whilst political, social, and economic power was distributed so dramatically unequally. Writing in the new radical periodical *Common Sense*, Dewey thus conceded that real "[p]ower today resides in control of the means of production, exchange, publicity, transportation and communication. Whoever owns them rules the life of the country, not necessarily by intention, not necessarily by deliberate corruption of nominal government, but by necessity."[31]

Having considered the issue, moreover, he reached a predictable conclusion. Such power was currently concentrated in the hands of a small plutocracy, an elite that was continuing to prosper whilst the remainder of the United States languished in the Depression. It was simply not possible under such circumstances to initiate the broad social discussion that he had previously considered the essential precursor to political transformation. It was thus vital for reformers to strive to enact an egalitarian corrective to these circumstances before they turned their minds to the construction of a truly deliberative democracy. "[T]he creation of an order in which industry and finance are socially directed in behalf of institutions that provide the material basis for cultural liberation and growth of individuals," Dewey concluded in typically convoluted fashion, "is now the sole method of social action by which liberalism can realize its professed aims."[32]

He also recognized, however, that few of these reforms had been forthcoming, even from Roosevelt's early New Deal. It was as if the political elite did not understand the true nature of the problem, he fretted. To Dewey, it was as if "the reactionaries" had somehow seized control of the "army and police, and the press and the schools."[33] More worryingly it also appeared that the mass of American citizens were doing little to insist on the need for rapid and far-reaching social and economic transformation. Perhaps this was an example of the very citizen ignorance that his critics had always

---

[30] See Edward J. Bordeau, "John Dewey's Ideas about the Great Depression," *Journal of the History of Ideas* 32 (1971): 67–84.

[31] John Dewey, "The Imperative Need for a New Radical Political Party," *Common Sense* 2 (1933): 6.

[32] Dewey, *Liberalism and Social Action*, 60.

[33] Dewey, "Future of Liberalism," 34.

warned him about. If citizens were truly engaged in democratic debate and truly concerned with the situation of those around them, would they not have risen up and demanded the reform that was so clearly required? Dewey's answer indicated the final turnaround for the one-time optimist. It was "only because the mass of the people refuse to look facts in the face and prefer to feed on illusions, produced and circulated by those in power" that they failed to throw themselves into the task of political reform in the "profusion" that the times demanded.[34]

These were arguments that could have been written by Niebuhr or any of his many followers, and they prefaced a phase in Dewey's career that is far too often overlooked by his deliberative champions today. During this phase, Dewey clearly separated the long-term goal of a communicative democracy—to which he remained resolutely committed—from a short-term political strategy suitable for Depression-Era America that emphasized a series of distinctly nondeliberative approaches to the ongoing struggle. The latter was crucially necessary, Dewey now contended, if reformers were to remove the inequalities of power that prevented the realization of anything approaching the communicative ideal. In the mid- to late 1930s, therefore, Dewey was no longer committed to a deliberative realization of his deliberative goal. Instead, he emphasized that control of the commanding heights of the political machine was an essential precursor to the reconstruction of the American democratic order.

This moment in Dewey's thought reached its apotheosis in 1935. In that year he published *Liberalism and Social Action* in order to explain this turnaround in full, and to answer his radical critics. The book was intended to explain how it was possible to remain dedicated to enhancing "the place and use of socially organized intelligence in the conduct of public affairs" whilst also suggesting that communicative politics was currently unsustainable in the United States. Dewey held that in the present crisis it was essential to compete in a politics run by "individuals and parties" whose primary concern lay not in provoking broad discussion amongst citizens but "in capturing and retaining office and power," and run by "organized pressure groups" who conducted themselves through the "propaganda of publicity agents," rather than through the processes of experimental education.[35] Disconcerting though it was, this sort of politics could not simply be bypassed because it stood in the way of "accomplishing the great transformations" that the Deweyan understanding of democracy demanded. Instead,

---

[34] Dewey, "Imperative Need," 6.
[35] Dewey, *Liberalism and Social Action*, 53.

it provided the preconditions for working toward such a democracy in the future.

Dewey thus insisted that what was required was "a concrete program of action" capable of ensuring that those committed to egalitarian and inclusive democratic renewal could take power from the established parties and redirect the path of American social reform. The business now, he outlined, "is to bend every energy and exhibit every courage" in the political battle ahead. "[D]iscussion and dialectic . . . are weak reeds to depend upon for systematic origination of comprehensive plans," he suggested. However important such deliberative strategies would be in the future ideal democracy, they were too easily crowded out now by other, far less desirable practices, or by sectional loyalties, or simply by poor judgment. In the present situation, democratic action must "become radical," Dewey explained.[36]

Summarizing the argument, the *New Republic* suggested that in the past Dewey had placed "too much reliance on discussion as a solvent of conflicts," emphasizing "things like reason, persuasion, objective search for truth, free speech, education" in a way that was "so innocent as to be naïve."[37] What was required was political action that recognized the limitations of the prevailing order rather than simply hoped for a better future. It was time for those citizens willing to campaign for change to employ actions that were "buoyant, crusading, and militant" rather than conciliatory, discursive, and open-minded.[38] They must not hesitate to employ new, more dramatic political means if they were to right the terrible wrongs that blighted a United States reeling from the Depression.

Radicalism Americanized

For all his change of heart, however, Dewey still remained resolutely within the bounds of liberal democratic political action—indeed, he continually evoked the term "liberalism" to describe his political position. There had, he argued, to be a distinctly free and democratic means of securing democratic goals even if what counted as properly free and democratic action in the present would not necessarily count as such in a more ideal future. "Here," he concluded, "is the place where the problem . . . centers today." He was particularly insistent that radicals should resist any talk of "violence as the main method of effecting drastic change."[39] Whilst some in the

---

[36] Ibid., 93, 66, 73.
[37] Editorial, "Liberalism Twenty Years After," *New Republic*, January 23, 1935, 290–92.
[38] John Dewey, "Democracy is Radical," *Common Sense* 6 (1937): 11.
[39] Dewey, *Liberalism and Social Action*, 78, 67.

Depression had turned to Communism for solutions, and were attracted by the idea of revolutionary action, Dewey was relentless in his rejection of all such proposals. No program of action grounded in the direct and forceful overthrow of the oppressive classes would be capable of founding a new democracy, he insisted.[40]

This argument irritated the growing band of Communist intellectuals, of course, many of whom had hoped to recruit Dewey to the cause of the class struggle.[41] But Dewey's rejection of violence was more subtle than some of his fellow-traveling critics suggested. He had been tempted to endorse violent methods, he suggested in an intentionally disarming rhetorical move, because he appreciated that the current, unjust, and undemocratic regime was frequently dependent on illegitimate violence itself. But he turned his back on violent methods because, even if they were successful in the short term, they would involve too great a degree of social disruption and engrain too deep a sense of social hostility to be an effective way of crafting a more deliberative and socially cohesive future. "Force breeds counterforce," he explained. If Americans had learnt anything from observing the revolutions that had beset Europe over the course of the previous two centuries, it should have been that violent transformations of political power are very rarely followed by social stability. Violent revolution was a poor way to build a political system capable of eliciting social harmony and easing communication across different sections of society. "A revolution effected solely or chiefly by violence can in a modernized society like our own result only in chaos."[42] That, after all, was a lesson that Alexis de Tocqueville had provided a century before.[43]

Dewey thus concluded that what was required were other forms of political action: those resting somewhere in the middle ground between violent insurrection and communicative rationality. The remaining questions, of course, were how these sorts of political action were to be identified and whether they could ever be successful in shaping a new democratic order. On both scores, Dewey was confident that answers could be forthcoming. His optimism was based on a conviction that the fundamental values that underpinned Progressive understandings of politics were somehow still immanent in American social and political life, even if radical forces were currently in abeyance.

---

[40] See John Dewey, "Why I am Not a Communist," *Modern Monthly* 8 (1934): 135–37.

[41] See Andrew Feffer, "The Presence of Democracy: Deweyan Exceptionalism and Communist Teachers in the 1930s," *Journal of the History of Ideas* (2005): 79–97.

[42] Dewey, "Why I am Not a Communist," 137.

[43] See Alexis de Tocqueville, *Democracy in America* (London: Everyman Library, 1994 [1840]), esp. 2:327–29. See, too, Bordeau, "Dewey's Ideas about the Great Depression," 67–84.

The United States, after all, was at least already a partial democracy, Dewey explained. It was, therefore, a nation where the basic ideals necessary for the proper functioning of a democracy were already implicit in elements of the constitutional order and in the cultural understandings of the people at large. Key values such as liberty, equality, and community were thus ingrained in at least some aspects of the prevailing order and in the value-sets of many, perhaps even most, American citizens. What radical reformers needed to do, Dewey implored, was to call upon the better instincts of the American people, dragging these hidden liberal democratic ideals to the foreground. Reformers had to alert their fellow citizens to the enormous gulf between these ideals and the existing realities of a United States hit hard by the Depression and encourage them to demand that gulf be closed.

Such an argument had both practical and philosophical implications. Practically, Dewey insisted that the fact that so many Americans shared fundamentally democratic impulses would inevitably help citizens to settle upon forms of political action that were both effective in the necessary struggle and generally democratic in nature. Whilst historically nondemocratic countries might have no choice but to pursue democratic renewal through violent insurrection, this was not the case in the United States, he explained. Instead, American citizens should be able to think of means of bringing about far-reaching change whilst still staying true to their underlying political values. They would not be tempted by the "doctrine of the dictatorship of the proletariat, with its threats to exclude all other classes from civil rights, to smash their political parties, and to deprive them of rights of freedom of speech, press and assembly."[44] Rather, they would eventually be able to formulate a "concrete program of action" that was "vital and courageous" but also "open and democratic."[45]

This approach would have the added advantage of wrapping the radical political cause in the flag, allowing radicals to portray themselves as the true patriots, and encouraging citizens to campaign politically with the same level of emotional intensity that they invested in other national purposes, including war. Because the values of liberal democracy were so deeply rooted in America's heritage and mythology—Americans lived in the "tradition of Jefferson and Lincoln," Dewey explained—American citizens would not "weaken and give up" in the face of the challenge to democratic governance

---

[44] Dewey, "Why I am Not a Communist," 136.
[45] Dewey, *Liberalism and Social Action*, 91–92.

that the Depression posed, but rather give a "whole-hearted effort to make democracy a living reality."[46]

Philosophically, this argument was intended as a riposte to two fundamental criticisms of pluralism. First, Dewey believed that the shared democratic heritage and experience of American citizens meant that it was still possible to talk of a common good in American political life, despite all of the crucial differences that divided the United States. Sectionalism was not inevitable in American politics, even in the depths of the Depression. The potential for a "great community," or a coherent "public," was rich in America, ready to be forged by American citizens on the basis of their shared adherence to core democratic politics.

Second, Dewey's insistence on drawing on an essentially "American" radicalism was also intended as a response to the so-called paradox of politics that had so blighted reformers since the beginning of the twentieth century. It provided, that is, the basis for a new answer to the question of how it was possible to construct a better democratic future out of the very non-ideal material of the present. Dewey had long recognized that "the passage or transition" from the present to the future had always to draw on "something" already there, lurking in the chaos of the prevailing order. The future could not, he insisted, be made out of new cloth. The task of even the most ambitious radical thus had to begin with "the process of viewing and examining the present to discover what possibilities are resident in it."[47] Dewey's emphasis on an immanent spirit of democracy in the United States explained how that could occur. On this account, all reformers had to do was to entice American citizens to reflect on values that they already at least partially shared and understand better how those values could be better and more fully realized in a future political order. The material for political transformation was already there, latent in the people of America, just waiting to be drawn out.

Building a Movement

This position found a ready audience amongst democratic reformers in the mid-1930s. Some hard-nosed, skeptical radicals still, of course, rejected the vision as naively patriotic. Stephen Schmalhausen thought that even if Dewey "feels at home 'in my own country,'" that was "too bad" because

---

[46] Ibid. For commentary on this kind of argument, see Rogers M. Smith, *Stories of Peoplehood: The Politics and Morals of Political Membership* (Cambridge: Cambridge University Press, 2003).

[47] John Dewey, "Social Change and its Human Direction," *Modern Quarterly* 5 (1930): 423.

"America is urgently in need of philosophers possessed not only of intellectual clarity but more particularly of spiritual courage."[48] But many commentators were much more excited and it was easy to see why such a position was so attractive, especially as it so explicitly related the ideals and the practices of democratic reform to some underlying sense of American national identity. In reviewing *Liberalism and Social Action*, the editor of *Common Sense* suggested that Dewey had offered "the synthesis between liberalism and radicalism which many, who are unwilling to swallow dogmative faith in violence, have been craving."[49]

In addition to all of its other advantages, such an account helped overcome the concern that radicalism was somehow ill suited to American national culture. Right-leaning critics had, of course, long argued that radicalism of all sorts was a foreign invention dragged into the United States by immigrants, especially those from Eastern and Southern Europe, and at odds with indigenous political ideals.[50] Although American radicals had always rejected such a characterization, there was no better way of doing so than by tying radical aspirations to widely held views of American identity. What that meant for democratic reform in the United States, *Common Sense*'s editor Arthur Bingham pointed out, was perfectly sketched by Dewey's argument: although radicals must be "prepared to struggle," they must also continually demonstrate that such a struggle could be conducted in the "American way," that strategies for change were "fitted to American traditions and American habits."[51] "Radicalism," Bingham concluded, must be "Americanized."[52]

A new generation of radical democrats in the late 1930s were therefore captivated by the idea that a more assertive form of political action somehow grounded in American values and in American political heritage offered a new way of countering the evils of the Depression and of beginning the job of building a new democracy in the United States. What they were not immediately certain about, however, was what that idea actually meant in practice. If this was to become anything more than a set of vague generalities, it had to be translated from principle to concrete politics.

---

[48] Samuel Schmalhausen, "The Logic of Leninism," *Modern Quarterly* 5 (1930): 460.

[49] Arthur Bingham, "Liberalism and Social Action," *Common Sense* 4 (1935): 28. The attractions of this argument were not reserved to Dewey and his followers. For broader appeal, see Michael Denning, *The Cultural Front* (London: Verso, 1997), and Gary Gerstle, *Working-Class Americanism: The Politics of Labor in a Textile City, 1914–1960* (New York: Cambridge University Press, 1989).

[50] See Gerstle, *Working-Class Americanism*, 166–73.

[51] Editorial, "Toward What Goal?," *Common Sense* 1 (1933): 3.

[52] Arthur Bingham, "What Does American Mean?," *Common Sense* 4 (1935): 24.

In one sense, that might have seemed straightforward. The basic notion of an "Americanized radicalism" could have helped reformers identify the paths *not* to travel, including that of violent revolution. Even that sort of argument provoked reflection, though, as some of the most radical commentators were keen to remind their readers that the republic of the United States itself had originally been forged out of revolution and civil war. George Soule thus argued that "true" Americans believe in liberalism and democracy, free speech and free assembly, as Dewey had always argued, but they also believe in the "legitimacy of revolution." Seen in this way, the American tradition was a revolutionary tradition and so an Americanized radicalism should also be at least partially revolutionary. The heroes of the past were not just the reason-givers of the founding convention, or the drafters of the Thirteenth and Fifteenth amendments to the Constitution, Soule continued, but the minutemen of the Revolutionary War, the soldiers who had fought in the Union army, and statesmen like Washington and Lincoln who had led them in those violent struggles. When American citizens dedicated themselves to the value of the Declaration of Independence, Soule concluded, they were committing themselves "not merely to the revolution that [their] forefathers helped to make" but also to "any new revolution that may be justified in the interest and reason of the common man."[53]

Whatever the bravado of the language, though, "revolution" for Soule and his colleagues did not actually mean violent overthrow or insurrection: that was both too dangerous and too unlikely to bring the results desired. So while some Communists, and especially those associated with the Popular Front in the late 1930s, tried directly to associate the American Revolution of the eighteenth century with the class revolution of the twentieth, that was not the road taken even by the most radical of non-Communists. Few were enthused by Marxist-inspired class-struggle or by Fascist attempts to forge a new nation of racial purity. They also turned their backs on mavericks like Huey Long and Father Coughlin, whose radical populism enjoyed a momentary vogue in some quarters in the mid-1930s.[54] It was impossible, the radical democrats of the *New Republic* and *Common Sense* argued, to reconcile the demagoguery, corruption, and willingness to employ force of Long and Coughlin with the American liberal and democratic ideals to which they largely continued to cleave.[55] Indeed, when Long was assassi-

[53] George Soule, *The Future of Liberty* (New York: MacMillan, 1936), 7. For further versions of this argument, see Denning, *Cultural Front*, 126–31.

[54] See Alan Brinkley, *Voices of Protest: Huey Long, Father Coughlin and the Great Depression* (New York: Vintage, 1983).

[55] Editorial, "Cutting and Leadership," *Common Sense* 4 (1935): 2–3. See, too, Selden Rodman, "After Roosevelt, the Kingfish?," *Common Sense* 2 (1933): 15–17.

nated, the news was reported deeply unsympathetically. It served simply as a reminder that "[f]orce begets force and those who rule by the sword shall perish by the sword."[56]

The new generation instead proposed what was to be a peculiarly democratic revolution. Even Soule conceded that the "only sensible preparation" for a new democratic order "is the fullest possible use of traditional American liberties—free speech, free association, the ballot-box, defense of democracy and equality."[57] It was vital to have the strength and the courage of previous generations, and to use stories of American revolutionary ideals and American revolutionary history in order to promote that courage, but it was neither necessary nor wise to mimic the past's insurrectionary actions precisely.[58]

It thus remained difficult to work out exactly what the new strategy was thought to entail in positive terms. As a *Common Sense* editorial on "obtaining power" admitted in 1935, although the basic idea of combining American ideals with a practical struggle for far-reaching change was a good one, "radicals have yet to find a formula that will provide a bridge to their well-thought-out goal."[59] All of this confusion was partly due to the fact that Dewey and his colleagues were self-confessed "amateurs in what is called practical politics."[60] Intellectual reformers in the Depression Era were simply not well versed in the means of political struggle, Dewey insisted, in part because the disappointments of the war had led many to abandon the political organizations with which they had previously been associated and in part because they often found it hard to stomach the need to put their long-term aspirations for a discursive, reasoned democratic order on hold. "It is in organization for action" that American reformers are "weak," he continued, because those committed to the sort of free exchange of opinion and belief tended to prize the more academic skills of reasoning and persuading rather than those of mobilizing, organizing, and strategizing. They had always balked in the past at the "discipline, ardor and organization" that was required for effective participation in the competitive political process.[61]

[56] Editorial, "News Behind the News: Huey Long's Death," *Common Sense* 4 (1935): 4.

[57] Soule, *Future of Liberty*, 181.

[58] For excellent discussions of rival Communist versions of this argument, see Denning, *Cultural Front*, 126–31; Gary Gerstle, *American Crucible: Race and Nation in the Twentieth Century* (Princeton: Princeton University Press, 2002), 128–86; and Julia Micklenberg, *Learning from the Left: Children's Literature, the Cold War, and Radical Politics in the United States* (New York: Oxford University Press, 2006), 85–124.

[59] Editorial, "On Obtaining Power," *Common Sense* 4 (1935): 3

[60] John Dewey, "Prospects for a Third Party," *New Republic*, July 27, 1932, 278.

[61] Dewey, *Liberalism and Social Action*, 91. See, too, John Dewey, "The Future of Liberalism," *Journal of Philosophy* 22 (1935): 225–30.

Throughout the late 1930s, therefore, Dewey and colleagues struggled to craft suggestions for political action that were both radical and in accord with identifiably American values. In doing so, they created a number of organizations, all of which focused on developing new political strategies to disrupt the prevailing order and initiate far-reaching change, but without the need for violent insurrection. The most important of these were the League for Independent Political Action (LIPA), of which Dewey was the chair, and the League for Industrial Democracy (LID), of which Dewey was president.[62]

LIPA's purpose was to create a new political party to rival the Democratic Party and to drive the program of reform on still further. It was a dream that owed much to the original plan for a Progressive Party under Theodore Roosevelt in the prewar years. LIPA aimed to construct a cross-class alliance, where party loyalty would be based not on material interest or sectional interest, but on an ideological commitment to the social and political transformation of the United States in accordance with the democratic ideals implicit in American political culture.[63] "The present struggle in this country is something more than a protest of a . . . class, whether called the proletariat or given another name," Dewey explained. "It is a manifestation of the native and enduring spirit against the destructive forces that are alien to democracy," and a new political party was required to bring that struggle directly into electoral competition.[64] Such a party would "unify the forces of social change" by emphasizing "the solidarity of the exploited *many* against the profit-making *few*," rather than by building loyalty from any one particular section of society.[65]

Within LIPA circles, the buildup to the presidential election of 1936 was accompanied by feverish speculation that a new cross-class party could effectively challenge the Democrats from the left. Such predictions were not intended to be "mere sentimental ardour": too much energy was put into the effort for that.[66] Yet it was clearly far from clear-sighted realism either. Indeed, looking back now, it seems that most of those involved with LIPA were subject to naive bursts of utopian optimism. "We predict," the move-

---

[62] See *Annual Reports* in The League for Industrial Democracy Records 49/9, The Tamiment Institute, New York University, and LIPA, "News Bulletin," 1.

[63] See Arthur Bingham, "The State in Theory and Practice," *Common Sense* 4 (1935): 28.

[64] John Dewey, "Democracy is Radical," *Common Sense* 6 (1937): 10. See, too, the editorial "Not a Labor Party," *Common Sense* 5 (1936): 3–4, and the editorial "New Deal or New Party?," *Common Sense* 6 (1937): 3–5.

[65] League for Independent Political Action, "News Bulletin: League Prepares for Action," *Common Sense* 1 (1933): 1 See, too, Robert Morss Lovett, "The Coming of a New Party," *New Republic*, August 31, 1932, 77–78, and the editorial "Toward a New Party," *New Republic*, May 22, 1935, 33–34.

[66] John Dewey, "Prospects for a Third Party," *New Republic*, July 27, 1932, 278.

ment reported in *Common Sense* in 1935, "that within six months" a new party "will have taken definite shape, and that its program will be under discussion in every city and hamlet in America."[67] In fact, of course, no such party emerged and Roosevelt's New Deal Democrats continued to dominate the politics of reform.

LIPA tried to make the best of this situation, of course. After Roosevelt's landslide victory in 1935, its leaders argued that many of his votes were, in fact, best understood as an endorsement neither of the president himself nor of the Democratic Party, but rather as an expression of support for the very notion of reform. "In the huge Roosevelt majority there are millions whose stand is to the left of the President," the *New Republic* reported, and those voters are "demonstrably capable of taking independent political action in 1940."[68] Even if no successful independent political force had emerged, the argument continued, vibrant discussion of the idea had provided a powerful incentive to New Deal Democrats not to ignore this boldly reforming constituency. The radicalism of the so-called second New Deal in the years immediately proceeding and following the 1936 election was explained by this pressure. LIPA advocates insisted that it was only because Roosevelt and his allies had been looking over their shoulders at gathering LIPA strength that "the New Deal has come to mean something very different" from the excessively mild reform program they associated with the early years of the first administration. Following Roosevelt's campaign against the Supreme Court, LIPA congratulated itself still further. The New Deal, they insisted, was "gradually becoming all that the third party forces . . . could hope for."[69]

Such an interpretation was undeniably self-serving. Although individuals in Roosevelt's administration were influenced by some of the arguments of Dewey and his colleagues, it is highly unlikely that they paid much attention to the LIPA threat. The movement for a third party never had any significant electoral muscle. But the failure of this project did not spell the end of efforts to transform the ongoing political struggle. For at the same time that LIPA was advancing the cause of partisan reform, the selfsame thinkers and activists were working within the LID to draw industrial action into the mix. If the radical democratic project could no longer be through a new political party, the best alternative lay with the radical trade union movement, and especially with the Congress of Industrial Organizations (CIO).

---

[67] Editorial, "For a Commonwealth Party," *Common Sense* 4 (1935): 2.

[68] Editorial, "Toward a Labor Party," 98.

[69] Editorial, "New Deal or New Party?," *Common Sense* 6 (1937): 5.

Assertive Americanism

The CIO began its life as a loose coalition of trade unions that broke away from the American Federation of Labor (AFL) in 1935 but rapidly became the most strident single agency for radical reform in the United States.[70] No single organization better captured the troubled relationship between short-term struggle and long-term idealism in the Depression Era than the CIO. Even its founding moment seemed the perfect symbol for the age. On October 19, 1935, at the AFL's annual convention in Atlantic City, the leader of the United Mine Workers (UMW), John L. Lewis, flattened the AFL's vice-president William Hutcheson with one blow from his fist after Hutcheson had tried to stop the expression of dissent from a radicalized group of rubber workers.[71] The next day, Lewis gathered forty colleagues for an emergency meeting and began the process of breaking away from the AFL and forming a new confederation of unions committed to a more radical, inclusive, and dramatic style of unionism. Within a year the CIO was as good as fully formed and was seeking to organize industries that had never known effective labor representation, taking the battle for collective bargaining directly to the employers all over the country, and continually challenging the Roosevelt administration to live up to the promises it had long made to working people.[72]

Crucial though it became to the radical imagination in the late 1930s, transforming the CIO into a liberal agent for radical transformation was no easy business. As the *New Republic* reported, after Lewis and the CIO appeared on the political scene the central question facing reform intellectuals was whether "a skilful left swing to the jaw" was mindless violence capable of engendering nothing but antisocial disruption or whether it was simply "good pragmatic science," action of the sort needed to initiate the socially desirable transformation for which Dewey and colleagues had longed.[73] The cause of the concern was straightforward: the CIO's tactics might not have been violent in themselves but they were undeniably coercive and they frequently provoked a violent response. The CIO thus sought to influence

---

[70] See Robert H. Zieger, *The CIO, 1935–1955* (Chapel Hill: University of North Carolina Press, 1995).

[71] See Edward Levinson as cited in Irving Bernstein, *Turbulent Years: A History of the American Worker, 1933–1941* (Boston: Houghton Mufflin, 1970), 397. See, too, the excellent description in the editorial "Five Rounds," *Time*, October 28, 1935, 3–4.

[72] On Roosevelt's early promise to labor, see the editorial "Collective Bargaining Again," *New Republic*, February 13, 1934, 6. For extensive and informative discussion, see Nelson Lichtenstein, *State of the Union: A Century of American Labor* (Princeton: Princeton University Press, 2002), 20–51.

[73] Kenneth Burke, "Liberalism's Family Tree," *New Republic*, March 4, 1936, 115.

the outcomes of American politics not through rational persuasion of the sort that Dewey had previously championed but through direct action, and it often conducted that action in ways that seemed to pay scant attention to the ideals to which liberals and Progressives had attached themselves. Radicals had, therefore, to ask themselves whether Lewis was simply another Coughlin or Long or whether he, and his movement, represented the new political beginning for which radicals had been desperately searching since the onset of the Depression.

From the moment that Lewis's fist knocked Hutcheson to the floor, then, the political methods of the CIO were mired in controversy. This was a movement that was not to be intimidated. Seeking desperately to overcome the shocking weaknesses of interwar trade unionism, the CIO leadership was dedicated to employing whatever tactics were necessary to revivify labor organization, even if that meant taking the struggle directly to the plant or to the streets or to Washington D.C. As the movement's most astute analyst has explained, in all of its efforts the CIO constantly sought to project an image of "manly strength," "[i]ts picket line confrontations, its military-like logistical innovations, its centralized organizing campaigns, and its enormous public demonstrations" making it often appear as an "irresistible juggernaut" that would overcome opposition by its sheer size and power and that would brook no opposition.[74]

Throughout the late 1930s, the CIO conducted itself in a way that terrified rivals, worried neutrals, and thrilled supporters, picking battles with employers and politicians who had never expected to face a challenge from organized labor, and winning many of the struggles that it initiated. It was unsurprising, therefore, when its actions were eventually met with repressive force from both employers and from the state. When efforts were made to organize steelworkers in the midwest in 1937, company-employed guards and police turned directly on striking workers. On Memorial Day dozens were killed or wounded in Chicago, and in the months that followed others were struck down in Cleveland, Youngstown, and Massillon, Ohio. By the end of the year, at least eighteen CIO activists were dead, and many more workers and bystanders left injured.[75]

Even before such dramatic developments, many radical commentators had rallied behind Lewis's CIO. Incredibly, some even linked the struggle to the nonviolent resistance movement for Indian independence then capturing the attention of the world, incredulously suggesting that Lewis

---

[74] Zieger, *CIO*, 2.
[75] Ibid., 62.

handled himself with the nobility and self-denial of a Gandhi.[76] Others, however, were more troubled. Despite the sense that economic and social justice demanded action by the organized working class, a *Common Sense* editorial thus pondered in 1937, "one cannot help wondering how far that democratic goal can be achieved through industrial warfare, and whether class struggle may not defeat its own ends." As the CIO unleashed a "new wave of great strikes over the country," they concluded, "it is well for those who believe in an ideal of society rising above internecine war to weigh the relation of those strikes to that ideal."[77] For some, this approach was wrong both in principle and in practice. It was wrong in principle because strike action constituted "a sort of blackmail by which a small minority of the employees of an industrial corporation seek to dictate both to management and to their fellow workers."[78] It was wrong in practice because it was likely to result in more rather than less social tension. It was natural that many employers, consumers, and sections of the public at large would feel deep "resentment" if the CIO should seek to forward its goals by attempting to "inconvenience," "threaten," or "dominate."[79] Democracy might demand economic justice, the criticism went, but this was not the way to achieve it.

The crucial test of the relationship between the CIO and radical democratic theorists came in late December 1936, when members of the United Automobile Workers (UAW) began a sit-down strike at the General Motors plant in Flint, Michigan, in support of their demand for union recognition from the company.[80] The sit-down was a dramatic innovation in the repertoire of American protest. The workers occupied the plant and organized a whole new structure of civic life inside it. In addition to making their own meals, they held meetings to discuss the politics of the day, put on plays lampooning the employers, and held classes in economics and labor history. They also successfully resisted legal efforts by General Motors to retake the plant, with Lewis masterminding negotiations and court challenges outside the plant and the workers themselves physically repelling forceful attempts by the company and the police to enter it, using water hoses, wrenches, and other forms of resistance available on the shop floor.

[76] See Martha Gruening, "Non-Violent Resistance," *New Republic*, May 22, 1935, 55, and Richard B. Gregg, *Non-Violent Resistance* (New York: MacMillan, 1935).

[77] Editorial, "Flint and a New Social Order," *Common Sense* 6 (1937): 3.

[78] Editorial, "Is the Sit-Down Unfair?," *New Republic*, February 17, 1937, 32.

[79] Editorial, "Flint and a New Social Order," 5.

[80] See Sidney Fine, *Sit-Down: The General Motors Strike of 1936–1937* (Ann Arbor: University of Michigan Press, 1969), and Jim Pope, "Worker Lawmaking, Sit-Down Strikes, and the Shaping of American Industrial Relations, 1935–1958," *Law and History Review* 24 (2006): 45–113.

This was not industrial anarchy, though. There was studied determination to resort neither to physical violence nor to damage of the machinery itself, and discipline amongst the workforce was exceptionally high. In fact, there was a clear militarism about the Flint operation. As one sit-downer himself put it, "it was like we were soldiers holding the fort. It was like war."[81] It was as if the Paris Commune had come to the twentieth-century Midwest.

The novelty of the sit-down strike alone was enough to capture attention, but the discussions that it provoked went to the heart of the problems of democratic theory. Most radical reformers were sympathetic to the cause of union recognition and collective bargaining for which the UAW was fighting, but they needed to ask themselves more seriously whether the forcible seizure of property and the establishment of an almost autonomous workers' society, even if only for a short period, was a legitimate form of action. Were the long-term ideals helped or hindered by such a move?

For some, the answer was clearly not. The long-time editor of the *Nation* and founder of the NAACP, Oswald Villard, thus wrote an open letter to Franklin Roosevelt condemning "lawlessness on either side in labor disputes" and arguing that "every time labor violates the law or seeks to take it into its own hands, it does itself tremendous harm. It alienates supporters, sloughs off friends, and strengthens those employers who resort to corruption and trickery, to brass knuckles, clubs, and tear gas."[82]

Contrary to almost all expectations, though, Villard was very much in the minority. The vast majority of radical democratic theorists and activists relentlessly backed the strikers. Indeed, for them, Flint was a landmark in the struggle for democratic transformation. It was even celebrated as the start of a "new social order."[83] A whole host of arguments were mustered in support of the sit-down, but two in particular resonated profoundly. The first suggested that the primary advantage of the sit-down strategy was that it revealed where violence really lay in the prevailing political order. "The sitdown is the most effective form of strike," Robert Morss Lovett explained, because "it eliminates violence" on the part of the workers themselves and "places responsibility for it squarely on the police." Most importantly, it demonstrated that the only way that the current distribution of resources could be maintained was if it was imposed upon a reluctant population by the use of violent coercive force. The sit-down was thus "a forcible reminder to workers, to management, to shareholders, and to the public that legal title is not the final answer to the question of possession." That final answer

---

[81] Zieger, *CIO*, 51.

[82] Oswald Villard, "A Letter FDR Ought to Write," *Nation*, June 6, 1937, 729.

[83] Editorial, "Flint and a New Social Order," 5.

actually lies in the willingness of the privileged to reinforce their claims by use of violent power.[84] If democratic theory was hostile to violence, therefore, it should not be hostile to the peaceful occupation of property by those who were the most vulnerable in society, but rather to the forceful recapture of that property by those who already owned much and who only used what they owned to perpetuate their own advantage. Seen this way, the Flint sit-down was not a case of "force repelling force," as Villard and critics had claimed, but a case of peaceful occupation being used to reveal that it was the privileged who really relied on force and would continue to do so unless the political order was radically reconstructed.[85]

The second argument began with a similar insistence on the *inequality* of the two parties involved: the workers and the employers. These were not two groups equally well-placed to negotiate their differences or to deliberate about their shared interests and potential common goods, nor were they located within a system of industrial decision making that was true to any sort of democratic ideal. Rather, General Motors conducted itself as a sort of industrial autocracy, insisting on dictating the terms and conditions of service without input from the workers themselves, and thus rendering their workers as good as "slaves of the Depression."[86] In such circumstances, the *New Republic*'s editors insisted, labor should be free to behave in almost any way that might contribute to the transformation of the industrial and broader political order. "No obligations can exist upon organized labor until its organized status is established and recognized," they bluntly argued. "The development of anything like industrial constitutionalism or democracy in industry requires at the very least that both parties meet on something approaching an equal footing," and if the sit-down led to such an improvement it was a desirable contribution to democratic politics.[87] The underlying claim here was straightforward: "the debate over legality seems to us entirely off the point," just as arguments about violence were. "In all this clod of words, it is as well to stick to first principles: the best status for industry is genuine collective bargaining."[88] And if the employers would not recognize that then they should be forced to accept it.

---

[84] Robert Morss Lovett, "A G.M. Stockholder Visits Flint," in Howard Zinn, ed., *New Deal Thought* (New York: Bobbs-Merrill, 1968 [1937]), 216.

[85] See Hartley Barclay, "We Sat Down with the Strikers and General Motors," *Mill and Factory* 2 (1937): 33–40.

[86] See Lichtenstein, *State of the Union*, 26.

[87] Editorial, "Labor Wins in Court," *New Republic*, April 21, 1937, 308.

[88] Editorial, "Mr. Lewis and the Auto Strike," *New Republic*, February 3, 1937, 399. See too, the editorials "The Sit-Down," *New Republic*, January 20, 1937, 342–43, and "The Sit-Down and Fascism," *New Republic*, March 31, 1937, 225.

All of this combined to leave radicals like George Soule insisting that the CIO was both shaping the future of American democracy and honoring the past of the American democratic tradition. When one reflects on the challenges CIO unions faced, he continued, "one is reminded of the tyrannies and abuses of power listed in the Declaration of Independence. Representative government in industry . . . is denied, and the denial enforced by every means of violence, intimidation, and corruption that the . . . employers can devise."[89] "Since the tradition of democracy runs deep in the United States," Soule concluded, it is the "opponents" of the CIO who always "stand at a disadvantage in debate." The CIO's struggle was a struggle for the future of the American democratic ideal.

This was an argument that the CIO's unions, and especially John Lewis himself, were always enthusiastic to make. Despite its use of direct action methods, the CIO was not antidemocratic, Lewis always insisted, and neither was it anti-American.[90] Rather, it was a crucial player in the struggle to fend off challenges to the actually existing democratic order during the Depression and was in the process of building a better democracy in the United States. The cultural symbolism of the CIO constantly reinforced these themes: the sit-down strikers emerged from their occupation in Flint waving American flags; the CIO's posters and pamphlets almost invariably carried cartoons of Washington and Lincoln; and the CIO's theme song, "Solidarity Forever," was sung to the tune of the "Battle Hymn of the Republic."[91]

The philosophical idea behind these symbols was also continually emphasized and often explained with great sophistication. Democracy, CIO supporters argued, depends on equality between parties and in the circumstances of the 1930s such equality could only be attained through the full assertion of labor's power. "I think that the workers in the automobile industry and the workers elsewhere who are trying to organize here in our country are entitled to the support of every thoughtful American," Lewis explained, because "the organization of the workers in the mass production industries, to a point where they may become articulate in voicing their grievances and stating their ideals and objectives, will be the greatest contribution toward the preservation of political democracy in America."[92]

[89] Soule, *Future of Liberty*, 96–97.

[90] See Gary Gerstle, "The Politics of Patriotism: Americanization and the Formation of the CIO," *Dissent* 33 (1986). See, too, the editorial "What is Americanism?," *Partisan Review* 3 (1936): 3–16.

[91] See Gerstle, *American Crucible*, 152–53.

[92] John L. Lewis, "The Struggle for Industrial Democracy," *Common Sense* 6 (1937): 8–11.

An Industrial Democracy Without Democracy

It sometimes appeared that the CIO would move beyond its short-term strategy of disruption to produce a full-throated call for a wholly new social and political order, an order based on the idea of democracy in industry. "If we are to have political democracy in this land of ours, we must also have industrial democracy, democracy in our industrial establishments which will recognize that the rights of those who work for a living are equal with the rights of those who merely profit from the labor of those who work for a living," Lewis frequently argued.[93] The Flint sit-down was thus justified by its role in ensuring "the coming of industrial democracy to the men in these great plants."[94]

This talk of "industrial democracy" and of the role of trade unions in promoting it was, of course, strikingly reminiscent of prewar Progressivism. Herbert Croly, the young Walter Lippmann, Walter Weyl, and colleagues had frequently placed emphasis on the need to involve workers in industrial decision making in the hope and expectation that this would create more open-minded, empathetic, and critically able citizens in society at large. In the late 1930s this argument made a dramatic comeback.[95] The CIO, Ordway Tead explained in 1939, "is a democratizing agency" because it relates "natural associations of kindred workers to their calling, to their employers, and to organized society in a way designed to assure a more equalized consideration" of the interests of all.[96]

The CIO's aspirations also occasionally seemed to go beyond the prewar Progressive ideals, especially by positing racial inclusion within the industrial-democratic equation. As Gary Gerstle has argued, the CIO's radically democratic interpretation of American ideals was sometimes employed to tie "the nation's civic tradition of equality and fairness" directly to fights against racial prejudice and discriminatory practices in the workplace.[97] Many in the lower levels of the CIO thus sought to organize African American and ethnic minority workers in multiracial unions for the first

[93] Lewis, "Struggle for Industrial Democracy," 11.

[94] John Brophy, senior advisor to Lewis, cited in Gerstle, *American Crucible*, 152. See, too, Victor Reuther, *The Brothers Reuther and the Story of the UAW: A Memoir* (Boston: Houghton Mifflin, 1976).

[95] For extensive discussions, see Milton Derber, *The American Idea of Industrial Democracy, 1865–1965* (Urbana: University of Illinois Press, 1970); Gerstle, *Working-Class Americanism*, 182–87; and Bernard Johnpoll and Mark Yenburgh, eds., *The League for Industrial Democracy: A Documentary History* (Westport, Conn.: Greenwood, 1980).

[96] Ordway Tead, *New Adventures in Democracy: Practical Applications of the Democratic Ideal* (New York: McGraw Hill, 1939), 92.

[97] Gerstle, *American Crucible*, 154.

time. The UAW's constitution called for all workers to "unite in one organization regardless of religion, race, creed, color, political affiliation or nationality."[98] In some places such efforts met with significant success. Over half a million previously un-unionized African American workers would eventually become members of CIO affiliates. CIO progaganda was even willing to recognize that African Americans possessed a "higher moral right to challenge their oppressors" than any other sector of American society.[99]

Despite such encouraging signs, though, the scope of the CIO's vision of a future industrial democracy was nowhere near as far-reaching as it initially appeared. Crucially, and as was not the case in the Progressive Era, the justification of radical trade unionism in the 1930s involved little or no discussion of the possibilities of active participation by workers in political or economic decision making either in the short term or the idealized long term. Rather, the CIO's vision of industrial democracy was strictly concerned with the rebalancing of industrial and political power. When Lewis and his supporters insisted they were building an industrial democracy, then, they were talking about the immediate preconditions for more equal bargaining and not about initiating their members in the ways of deliberation or the pursuit of social harmony. Those loftier ambitions associated with the Progressive Era and with Dewey's arguments in the 1920s were almost entirely forgotten. The industrial democracy the CIO was building was a democracy of equal partners in collective bargaining, not one of collective deliberation about the future of the nation.[100]

The argument in defense of this absence was clear. This was not the time, Lewis and his supporters believed, for idle speculation about what the ideal democracy in industry would look like. It was, instead, the moment when the basic preconditions of any sort of democracy would have to be laid. That in turn required engagement in a sometimes brutal conflict on terms that the unions had not chosen but from which they would not flinch, and such a conflict could not be won by training participants in the politics of deliberation or rational persuasion. For all of its clarity, though, the ramifications of this argument were profound. Most importantly, the primary virtues of CIO

---

[98] Article 2 of the constitution of the International Union of United Automobile Workers of America (1936).

[99] See Robert Korstad and Nelson Lichtenstein, "Opportunities Found and Lost: Labor, Radicals, and the Early Civil Rights Movement," *Journal of American History* 75 (1988): 786–811; Margaret Lamont, "The Negro Unionist," *Modern Quarterly* 10 (1937): 15; and Niebuhr, *Moral Man and Immoral Society*, 154. For broader commentary, see Thomas Gobel, "Becoming American: Ethnic Workers and the Rise of the CIO," *Labour History* 29 (1988): 173–98.

[100] See Nelson Lichtenstein, "Great Expectations: The Promise of Industrial Jurisprudence and its Demise, 1930–1960," in Nelson Lichtenstein and Howell Harris, eds., *Industrial Democracy in America: The Ambiguous Promise* (Cambridge: Cambridge University Press, 1996), 113–41.

activity lay in organization, discipline, and struggle. The CIO was, therefore, always a top-down organization where the emphasis was placed on taking effective action against recalcitrant employers. It was also an outcome-oriented organization, where the outcome involved an improved position for working American citizens though without those citizens necessarily being involved in the decision making processes. As the editors of the *Modern Monthly* noted, "the C.I.O. wants only those strikes which are run under its leadership; it wants the workers to stick to its line and not advance beyond it."[101]

John L. Lewis once argued that the only real objection to the sit-down strike that employers could muster was that "it is effective."[102] Insofar as the CIO and its admirers almost entirely bypassed the question of citizen education, virtue, and democratic improvement, they could almost have added that the organization's "effectiveness" was the only real argument in its favor. For all the talk of founding radical action on distinctly American values and in a distinctly American tradition, the defense of the Flint sit-down strike, and of the CIO generally, suggests that in many ways it was the more skeptically pluralist vision of Reinhold Niebuhr that emerged triumphant from the arguments in democratic theory during the Depression years. Five years before Flint, after all, Niebuhr had counseled strongly against the search for compromise or accommodation prior to the existence of equality between the negotiating parties, arguing that "an adjustment of a social conflict, caused by the disproportion of power in society, will hardly result in justice as long as the disproportion of power remains."[103] It was an argument that was strikingly close to those offered by a host of intellectuals and reformers in the late 1930s.

Despite the invocation of a liberal democratic Americanism, very few in the CIO talked of the long-term ideal comprising open dialogue, deliberation, and the pursuit of a new social harmony, fewer still of an inevitable cohesion in the American nation. Instead, almost everyone insisted on the importance of struggle, of the need to take forceful action to ensure the radical recalibration of political, economic, and industrial power in the United States. It was as if the combination of the pluralist and coercive political theory of the 1920s and early 1930s, the desperate economic circumstances of the Depression, and the dramatic emergence of the CIO as a powerful force of change were too much for the remnants of Progressive political thinking to bear. Even Dewey's faith in the efficacy of using "democratic

---

[101] Editorial, "Striking for a New America," *Modern Monthly* 10 (1937): 2. See, too, Staughton Lynd, *"We Are All Leaders": The Alternative Unionism of the Early 1930s* (Urbana and Chicago: University of Illinois Press, 1996), esp. 1–18, and Zieger, *CIO*, 67–71.

[102] Editorial, "Mr Lewis and the Auto Strike," 399.

[103] Niebuhr, *Moral Man and Immoral Society*, xv.

means" to realize "democratic ends" was undermined by the confluence of these factors, all but ceding the Progressive strategy to the discipline and order of the quasi-militarism of the CIO.

The Legacy of the Depression

Beyond the CIO itself, the precise conceptual story of Progressivism in the post-Depression period was more complicated. What had really broken out in the late 1930s was a temporary truce between those who believed in the inevitability of coercion in politics and those who hoped for a more deliberative future. Almost all Progressive and liberal democratic thinkers thus accepted that the circumstances of the time called for political action that was more radical, more dramatic, and even more coercive than that which would have been accepted by many of them in their in democratic ideal. Democratic politics no longer looked like a form of applied ethics, where principles and rules of action could strictly govern the engagement required. Faced with the demands of the Depression, even convinced followers of Dewey found themselves accepting Clarence Case's charge that "we again have to face the inability of absolutist theories of conduct to solve the concrete problems of daily life in the actual, striving, rough-and-tumble world."[104]

What was needed, then, was flexibility and sound judgment. No one should rush to criticize the efforts of unions or parties to attain a greater say; strategies and tactics should be evaluated according to their likely contributions to the battle for democratic equality. It was this sense that allowed different sorts of radicals to work alongside each other in organizations such as LIPA and the League for Industrial Democracy, on behalf of the CIO, and in related institutions like the Brookwood Labor College and Highlander Folk School that hoped to train a new generation of activists and to equip them with the knowledge they would need to succeed.[105]

That did not mean, however, that all radical thinkers gave up on the idea of a profound democratic transformation in the longer term. Lippmann and Niebuhr might have believed that it would never be possible to construct a politics that focused primarily on the common good—one where sectional interest was relegated as both an outcome and as a means of po-

[104] Clarence Case, *Non-Violent Coercion: A Study in the Methods of Social Pressure* (London: George Allen and Unwin, 1923): 413.

[105] See Richard J. Altenbaugh, *Education for Struggle: The American Labor Colleges of the 1920s and 1930s* (Philadelphia: Temple University Press, 1990); Robert Morss Lovett, "Politics and Ethics," *New Republic*, January 18, 1933, 273; and Daniel F. Rice, *Reinhold Niebuhr and John Dewey: An American Odyssey* (Albany: State University of New York Press, 1993).

litical life—but Chase, Soule, Lovett, Dewey, and many others were not so essentially pessimistic. They were certain that the Depression would abate and that political, social, and economic conditions would therefore one day be more conducive to a more thoroughgoing transformation. What this meant was that whilst American democratic political theory going into the Second World War was largely a celebration of the politics of struggle, for many it remained infused with similar principled commitments to those of the Progressive generation, including the hope that one day American democracy would see citizens participate actively and openly in dialogue with each other and in pursuit of a common good.

The demands on those seeking democracy were, therefore, still far-reaching as the interwar years ended. Citizens would need to play their part in building a new democratic order but would do so by taking innovative and dramatic action focused on overcoming the evils of political and economic inequality in the short term, even as they also drew on the best elements of the pre-existing American political tradition. By the end of the 1930s, therefore, radical democratic thought in the United States was neither fully deliberative nor solely realist. It still cleaved to the possibility of a better future when cross-national conversation would characterize citizens' political interactions, even though few strategies were to be fully barred in the struggle to create the necessary social, political, and economic order out of the chaos of the present.

"What can I do?," *Common Sense* asked at the height of the Depression. "Organize and learn," was the answer. Citizens must "prepare for the big battle ahead, when we the people will rise against the stupid and selfish and the crooked who now sit in the seats of power. Then we will build a new constitution and a new commonwealth, a community where there is no longer the same . . . poverty in the midst of wealth. Then Americans will be able to hold their heads up again."[106] Then, too, it might have added, they would be able to draw upon the core values of the American citizenry and begin to build a new democracy.

[106] Editorial, "What Can I Do?," *Common Sense* 1 (1933): 2.

CHAPTER FOUR

Doubt and the American Creed

The radical democratic thought of the late Depression Era was character-ized by aggression, assertiveness, and uncompromising confidence in the essential rightness of the cause. Although American radicals generally re-sisted the siren call of Communism and sought constantly to wrap their demands in American symbols and American values, they nonetheless de-fended and advocated a host of intense, disruptive, and potentially coercive political practices. Depression-Era radicals insisted that it was only through a forthright politics—a politics of strikes, sit-downs, and demonstrations—that Americans could hope to redress the injustices and exclusions faced by many citizens. In the Depression Era, a new democracy was to be forged through contest, and even conflict, not through deliberation and commu-nication across a disparate nation. A spirit of struggle pervaded the radical movement, unifying thinkers as otherwise dissimilar as John Dewey and Reinhold Niebuhr and flowing through the unions of the CIO and cam-paigning organizations like LIPA and LID.

Powerful as this spirit was in the late 1930s, it did not long survive the United States' entry into the Second World War. Three forces dampened it. First, there was a widely heeded wartime call for national unity following the attack on Pearl Harbor on December 7, 1941, which was sharply at odds with the sectarian assertiveness of the late 1930s, especially with regard to labor relations.[1] The war years witnessed the flourishing of "no-strike" deals and the development of a politics that prioritized consultation over con-frontation.[2] When the CIO's John L. Lewis refused to change his message, he quickly lost support both in the union movement and amongst those radical thinkers who had been most vocal in his defense only a few years earlier. As the war progressed, his influence waned until he was eventually

[1] See Robert Divine, *The Reluctant Belligerent: American Entry into World War II* (New York: John Wiley, 1979), and David Kennedy, *Freedom from Fear: The American People in Depression and War* (New York: Oxford University Press, 1999).

[2] See Fay Calkins, *The CIO and the Democratic Party* (Chicago: University of Chicago Press, 1952), and Robert Zieger, *The CIO, 1935–1955* (Chapel Hill: University of North Carolina Press, 1995), 141–90.

replaced at the head of the CIO by more moderate leaders, among them Sidney Hillman and Philip Murray.[3] "Lewis is just about the most irritating man on the public scene today," the *New Republic* insisted, in the face of the former CIO leader's refusal to condemn an illegal miners strike in 1943.[4] The CIO's own Reid Robinson put it more starkly still: Lewis, he said, is the "Number One enemy against all labor."[5]

Second, as news spread of the atrocities committed by the Nazis, the political distinction between "means" and "ends" so crucial to radicals was quickly discredited by the violence that had been committed in the name of social progress elsewhere in the world. As Lewis's own time as the actual and symbolic leader of American labor came to an end, so, too, did explicit justifications of the form of combative politics that he had championed so effectively.[6] The CIO itself replaced the imagery of the "brawny superman" with that of the "ordinary citizen" and moved to insist that its politics were no longer "raw" and "class-conscious" but "respectable" and "orderly."[7] Such moves reflected a grave concern about the politics of aggression. The end of the Second World War witnessed, in Arthur M. Schlesinger Jr.'s memorable phrase, a "revolt against revolt."[8]

Third, both of these other trends were reinforced by a more general conservative drift in American politics and society at the beginning of the Cold War. The social and economic reforms of the New Deal had become part of the institutional fabric of the United States in the early 1940s as the Depression lifted. Many moderate Republicans had also declared their acceptance of the basic outline of a form of welfare capitalism that did relatively little to challenge the basic assumptions of the market order.[9] The decade that followed the war was thus paradoxically characterized both by a sense of satisfaction at what had been achieved through the New Deal and by an anxiety that all that was good was potentially at risk from destructive

[3] See Willard Shelton, "The CIO's Own Revolution," *New Republic*, January 3, 1949, 7–8. For a critical take on the new direction, see C. Peter Magrath, "Democracy in Overalls: The Futile Quest for Union Democracy," *Industrial and Labor Relations Review* 12 (1959): 503–25.

[4] Editorial, "The Miners Have a Case," *New Republic*, June 14, 1943, 780.

[5] Reid Robinson, cited in Zieger, *CIO*, 139.

[6] See the editorial "New Leaders for Labor," *New Republic*, December 1, 1952, 6, and C. Wright Mills, *The New Men of Power: America's Labor Leaders* (New York: Harcourt Brace and Co., 1948).

[7] See Zieger, *CIO*, 186.

[8] Arthur M. Schlesinger Jr., *The American as Reformer* (Cambridge, Mass.: Harvard University Press, 1950), 65. See, too, the thorough discussion in David Ciepley, *Liberalism in the Shadow of Totalitarianism* (Cambridge, Mass.: Harvard University Press, 2006).

[9] This built upon a trend already begun before the war. See Alan Brinkley, *The End of Reform: New Deal Liberalism in Depression and War* (New York: Alfred Knopf, 1995), and Gary Gerstle, *American Crucible: Race and Nation in the Twentieth Century* (Princeton: Princeton University Press, 2002), 156–62.

forces from within and without the United States. The politics of the late 1940s and early 1950s reflected this duality, with the consensual centrism of Dwight Eisenhower's presidency symbolizing the satisfaction, and the persecutions of Senator Joe McCarthy and the House Committee on Un-American Activities capturing the anxiety.[10]

The single most important question facing all radical democratic thinkers and activists in the late 1940s and early 1950s was how to respond to these challenges. Much of the combativeness of the past had been discredited—of that there was no doubt—but the apparently all-pervading conservatism did not seem to provide a full or stable solution either.[11] It was necessary, then, to find a way of abandoning several of the crucial commitments of the past without simply giving in to the limitations of the present. When in 1954 *Dissent*, a new journal of radical opinion, appeared under the editorship of Irving Howe, its stated purpose was to break free "from the bleak atmosphere of conformism that pervades the political and intellectual life of the United States" but to do so by rethinking rather than reasserting the radical democratic politics of the interwar years.[12]

Radical democratic theorists thus began to explore once again the foundations of their own thought. As *Dissent's* opening editorial put it, they needed to separate out what needs to "remain alive" from "what needs to be discarded or modified" in the American radical democratic tradition.[13] It was a process that required a sometimes ferocious critique of the arguments of their predecessors, and one that would have crucial implications for the remainder of the twentieth century.

Democracy and Doubt

The call for a far-ranging reconsideration of radical democratic thought was widely heeded in the immediate postwar years. There emerged a new generation of varied thinkers— including Daniel Bell, Robert Dahl, Louis Hartz, Irving Howe, Hans Morgenthau, Arthur M. Schlesinger Jr., and Judith Shklar—all of whom shared both a deep skepticism of the radical optimism that had characterized the thought of much of the preceding decade and

---

[10] See Walter Goodman, *The Committee: The Extraordinary Career of the House Committee on Un-American Activities* (New York: Farrar, Straus, and Giroux, 1968), and Ellen Schrecker, *Many Are the Crimes: McCarthyism in America* (Boston: Little, Brown, 1998).

[11] See Steve Fraser and Gary Gerstle, eds., *The Fall of the New Deal Order, 1930–1960* (Princeton: Princeton University Press, 1989).

[12] Editorial, "A Word to Our Readers," *Dissent* 1 (1954): 3.

[13] Ibid.

a great desire to craft an alternative vision.[14] They were joined by many of the thinkers who had previously endorsed the prewar perspective, including the League for Industrial Democracy's Abraham J. Muste, the Socialist Party presidential candidate Norman Thomas, even Reinhold Niebuhr and the elderly John Dewey.[15]

To all of these thinkers, the most profound necessity of political thought in the immediate postwar age was a thoroughgoing reconsideration of democratic ideals built upon a rejection of the bellicose ideas and actions of the recent past. Postwar radicals were insistent that there had been far too much certainty in the politics of the Depression Era. As Robert Booth Fowler perceptively argues, the "mood" of postwar radical thinking was primarily set by "skepticism about absolute answers in politics" and an insistence on the grave dangers of "being too sure."[16] It was the certainty of totalizing visions such as Fascism and Communism that were most easily dismissed, but the troubles of "doubt-free politics" went much deeper than totalitarian ideologies alone. These issues infected any kind of political action in which the protagonists were excessively committed to the rightness of their cause and were willing to push the boundaries of acceptable political strategy to their very limits in pursuit of that cause. The politics of the Depression-Era CIO and its allies clearly fell into that category too.

To the postwar critics, the causes of political certainty of all sorts lay in the terrors of modern industrialism. American and European citizens had understandably despaired in the Depression, the argument went, as they either lost everything themselves or were terrified by the horrific injustices that surrounded them. Such citizens became deeply confused as to the possibilities of the future, the postwar argument went, and thus turned to leaders and movements that offered clear and definite political answers. "How

[14] See Daniel Bell, *The End of Ideology: On the Exhaustion of Political Ideas in the Fifties* (Glencoe, Ill.: Free Press, 1960); Robert Dahl, *A Preface to Democratic Theory* (Chicago: University of Chicago Press, 1956), and idem, *Who Governs? Democracy and Power in an American City* (New Haven: Yale University Press, 1961); Louis Hartz, *The Liberal Tradition in America: An Interpretation of American Political Thought since the Revolution* (New York: Harcourt Brace, 1955); Irving Howe, *A Margin of Hope: An Intellectual Autobiography* (San Diego: Harcourt, Brace, 1993); Hans Morgenthau, *Scientific Man versus Power Politics* (Chicago: University of Chicago Press, 1946); Arthur M. Schlesinger Jr., *The Vital Center: The Politics of Freedom* (Boston: Houghton Mifflin, 1949); and Judith Shklar, *After Utopia: The Decline of Political Faith* (Princeton: Princeton University Press, 1957).

[15] See "John Dewey: An Appraisal," special edition of the *New Republic*, October 17, 1949; Abraham J. Muste, *Where Are We Now?* (New York: Liberation, 1956); Harry Fleischman, *Norman Thomas: A Biography* (New York: W. W. Norton, 1967), esp. 250–66.

[16] Robert Booth Fowler, *Believing Skeptics: American Political Intellectuals, 1945–1964* (Westport, Conn.: Greenwood, 1978), 4–5. For contemporary observations and an almost lone critical voice, see David Riesman, "Neighbors in Utopia," *New Republic*, April 30, 1951, 21.

does it happen that the masses sell their souls to leaders and follow them blindly?," Franz Neumann asked in *Dissent*.[17] The answer was that modern citizens were blighted with "anxieties" regarding their future in an increasingly unequal and complex industrial order and those anxieties made them particularly vulnerable to the appeals of demagogues and manipulators. Citizens' feelings of alienation, loss, and confusion in the face of devastating economic circumstances made them easy consumers for those selling false certainties in politics. Theodor W. Adorno, Else Frenkel-Brunswick, Daniel Levinson, and R. Nevitt Sanford provided the most widely cited instance of this argument in their *The Authoritarian Personality*, which aimed to "develop and promote an understanding of the social-psychological factors which have made it possible for an authoritarian type of men to threaten to replace the individualistic and democratic type prevalent in the past century and a half of our civilization."[18] But theirs was far from the only study. Harold Metz and Charles Thompson's *Authoritarianism and the Individual* pursued a strikingly similar agenda in 1950, and Franz Alexander's *Our Age of Unreason* offered an even more pessimistic take on the same theme a year later.[19]

The most evocative, subtle, and psychologically perceptive description of both the causes and the consequences of a doubt-free politics was not an academic treatise, however, but a novel: Ralph Waldo Ellison's sublime *Invisible Man*, published to great critical acclaim in 1952.[20] In *Invisible Man*, Ellison told the story of an unnamed African American protagonist whose rhetorical and organizational gifts lead to him being recruited by a political organization in Depression-Era Harlem known as "the Brotherhood." Within the Brotherhood, the protagonist finds that all is planned and organized by a well-established leadership, all of whom insist that the social, political, and economic future of the United States can be clearly predicted and understood if only one theorizes carefully enough and commits to taking the necessary political action. Such clarity has immediate attractions to the protagonist, living as he does in a time in which chaos and injustice appears to reign, and when both economic and psychic insecurity are the central aspect of most working people's lives. "I was dominated by the all-embracing idea of Brotherhood," Ellison has his protagonist recall. "The

---

[17] Franz Neumann, "Anxiety in Politics," *Dissent* 2 (1955): 133, 143.

[18] Theodor W. Adorno, Else Frenkel-Brunswik, Daniel J. Levinson, and R. Nevitt Sanford, *The Authoritarian Personality* (New York: Harper and Row, 1950), x.

[19] Harold Metz and Charles Thompson, *Authoritarianism and the Individual* (Washington D.C.: Brookings Institution, 1950), and Franz Alexander, *Our Age of Unreason: A Study of Irrational Forces in Social Life* (Philadelphia: Lippincott, 1951).

[20] Ralph W. Ellison, *Invisible Man* (New York: Vintage, 1995 [1952]).

organization had given the world a new shape, and me a vital role. We recognized no loose ends, everything could be controlled by our science. Life was all pattern and discipline."[21]

The protagonist quickly discovers, however, that the socio-economic "science" on which the Brotherhood bases their certainty is almost entirely empty. The community of Harlem is dissected by far more complex social trends and individual characteristics than the Brotherhood is capable of appreciating and the organization's understandings and predictions are thus fatally undermined by this overly simplistic model of community life. The Brotherhood is shown to fall into the trap, common to all totalizing ideologies, of confusing its "own tidy models with the vast, turbulent, unpredictable, and untidy reality which is the stuff of human experience."[22] As such, it (and by implication all of the many organizations like it) overlook what one of Ellison's contemporaries called the "tragic complexities of human existence."[23] The fundamental failure of movements such as the fictional Brotherhood is shown to be their neglect of the fact that "society is too complex and human knowledge forever insufficient to allow men to alter their social environment with any degree of success."[24]

Ellison also depicted the vast political dangers that flow from such an oversight. The most obvious of those dangers lay in the justification of elitist and hierarchical forms of political organization. The leadership of the Brotherhood are shown toiling under the delusion that it possesses answers to fundamental political, social, and economic questions that are unavailable to average citizens, duped as they are by illusions perpetuated by the powerful. "We do not shape our policies to the mistaken and infantile notions of the man in the street," Ellison's protagonist is instructed by a leading member of the Brotherhood when he joins the organization. "Our job is not to *ask* them what they think but to *tell* them."[25] It is a conviction that infuses the Brotherhood's political elite, leading them to disregard the sensitivities, feelings, and insights of those in whose interests they claimed to struggle.

Ellison took pains to insist that these traits were not restricted to the Brotherhood (often understood as a stand-in for the Communist Party) but were shared across a range of social and political organizations in prewar

---

[21] Ibid., 382.

[22] Arthur M. Schlesinger, Jr., "The One against the Many," in Arthur M. Schlesinger Jr. and Morton White, eds., *Paths of American Thought* (Boston: Houghton Muffin, 1963), 535.

[23] Morgenthau, *Scientific Man*, 202.

[24] Shklar, *After Utopia*, 238.

[25] Ellison, *Invisible Man*, 473.

America, and were especially prevalent in the trade union movement.[26] His protagonist encounters a CIO-style union in a paint manufacturing plant in which he finds temporary work. As he tries to engage the union members in discussion, the protagonist is dismissed as a potentially untrustworthy infiltrator. The union's leaders even insist that he should be removed from his job as soon as possible lest he dilute the solidarity of the union in the workplace—all, of course, without him having a chance to put forth his point of view. "They had made their decision without giving me a chance to speak for myself," Ellison's protagonist complains. "I felt that every man present looked upon me with hostility; and though I had lived with hostility for all my life, for the first time it seemed to reach me, as though I expected more of these men than of others."[27]

It was not, however, just the excessive, exclusionary, and judgmental hier-archy involved in this kind of politics that Ellison cautions against. He also describes the potentially appalling political consequences that flow from its "means"-and-"ends" approach to political rationality. Toward the end of the novel, Ellison dwells on the Brotherhood's utter political ruthlessness. When the organization begins to lose its influence in Harlem, partly as a result of its inability to appreciate the community's own sensitivities, it turns directly to violence as a method of political change, plotting a terrible riot in the streets in a desperate attempt to shore up its position. A scene of terrible carnage unfolds and all the protagonist can do is to seek shelter from the wreckage and the destruction. As he hides by the roadside, he begins to feel acute guilt. By aiding the Brotherhood in the past, he realizes, he has enabled the vio-lence that now falls upon his own people. "By pretending to agree" with the Brotherhood in the past, "I *had* agreed," Ellison's protagonist reflects. "I had made myself responsible [for the] flame and gunfire in the street." Whether intentionally or otherwise, the protagonist had let down his friends and "all the others whom now the night was making ripe for death."[28]

This idea that guilt lies both with the direct perpetrators of political evil and with those who directly or indirectly assist those perpetrators coursed throughout the powerful restatements of democratic thought in the imme-diate postwar period. It was especially strikingly presented in the work of

---

[26] There is considerable debate as to whether the Brotherhood was intended to represent the Communist Party of the United States or was intended to represent democratic politics in the Depression Era more broadly. See Danielle Allen, *Talking to Strangers: Anxieties of Citizenship since Brown versus Board of Education* (Chicago: University of Chicago Press, 2004), 101–16; Barbara Foley, "The Rhetoric of AntiCommunism in Invisible Man," *College English* 59 (1997): 530–47; Jesse Wolfe, "Ambivalent Man: Ellison's Rejection of Communism," *African American Review* 34 (2000): 621–37.

[27] Ellison, *Invisible Man*, 223.

[28] Ibid., 553.

the most notable of the postwar converts to a politics of doubt: Reinhold Niebuhr.[29]

Niebuhr produced his second masterpiece just before the war's end: *The Children of Light and the Children of Darkness*. There, he argued that it was necessary once again "to distinguish what is false in democratic theory from what is true in democratic life."[30] The radical politics of the interwar years, he summarized, had been characterized by two sorts of political actors—"the children of light" and "the children of darkness"—both of whom were dangerous in their own distinctive ways. The "children of darkness," he outlined, included those like the fictional Brotherhood or the real John L. Lewis who were prepared to use almost any sort of political means in pursuit of their own ends, however undesirable either means or ends should be to their fellow citizens. Thinkers and actors like these were, he continued, essentially "moral cynics, who know no law beyond their will and interest" and who are willing to manipulate or coerce others in whatever way might be necessary for the achievement of their own purposes. They wished only to achieve what they wanted to achieve, and understood no obstacle as legitimate or deserving of serious moral or political consideration. These actors spoke about "democracy" but all they were really looking for was an excuse to legitimize actions that they pursued in their own interest. It was striking, Niebuhr concluded, how successful "the forces of darkness" had been in making "covert use of the [democratic] creed" during the Depression in the attempt to justify their self-serving actions.[31]

The response was not, however, simply to turn away from the "darkness" and toward the "light," away from those who acted from their own interest to those who far more sincerely desired a better world for all and who conducted their politics according to strict rules of applied ehtics. Just as Ellison had his protagonist realize, Niebuhr argued that it was not only the explicit manipulators and coercers—the "children of darkness"—in need of condemnation but also the naivete and excessive timidity of the "children of light." Those who believe that it is possible to transform American democracy, to make it somehow *right*, are also often led to behave badly.

---

[29] For comparisons and commentary, see Harry R. Davis and Robert C. Good, eds., *Reinhold Niebuhr on Politics* (New York: Charles Scribner's Sons, 1960); Richard Fox, "Reinhold Niebuhr and the Emergence of the Liberal Realist Faith, 1930–1945," *Review of Politics* 38 (1976): 244–65; H. Gordon Harland, *The Thought of Reinhold Niebuhr* (New York: Oxford University Press, 1960); Arthur M. Schlesinger Jr., "Reinhold Niebuhr's Role in American Political Thought and Life," in Charles Kefley and Robert W. Bertall, eds., *Reinhold Niebuhr: His Religious, Social, and Political Thought* (New York: MacMillan, 1956).

[30] Reinhold Niebuhr, *The Children of Light and the Children of Darkness: A Vindication of Democracy and A Critique of Its Traditional Defenders* (New York: Charles Sribner's Sons, 1944), 40.

[31] Niebuhr, *Children of Light*, 10, 24.

Thinkers and activists of this kind possessed both a dangerously misguided conception of how far-reaching political change was ever capable of being. They possessed a woefully utopian sense of what might be achieved in the future.

Such "children of light" were thus "sentimental rather than cynical," and although their optimism was undeniably attractive to some, it actually meant that they possessed a "fatuous and superficial view" of what was possible in politics, a view that was itself gravely dangerous. Citizens who wrongheadedly believed that a wholesale transformation of the democratic order was possible and/or convinced that the deep injustices of the here-and-now were somehow transient provided the cannon-fodder for the worst political manipulators. The "children of light," therefore, all too easily became the servants of the "children of darkness," in so far as they failed to recognize the horrific evils that were frequently and inevitably conducted in the pursuit of political goals of all sorts.[32]

The essence of Niebuhr's argument informed a host of postwar works. The historian and social critic Arthur M. Schlesinger Jr. employed Niebuhr's "light" and "dark" distinctions with exceptional acuity in his popular commentary on postwar politics, *The Vital Center*, of 1949. The excessive "optimism" generated by a "soft and shallow conception of human nature" had led earlier generations of radicals in terrible directions as they sought to recreate the American democratic order. "With the aggressive and sinister impulses eliminated from the equation, the problem of social change assumed too simple a form," Schlesinger continued. "The corruption of power—the desire to exercise it, the desire to increase it, the desire for prostration before it—had no place" in the Depression-Era vision of the future order, and such an order was plainly and emptily utopian as a result.[33]

The international relations scholar Hans Morgenthau offered an even more powerful endorsement of this view in his *Scientific Man vs. Power Politics*. "[M]an as an actor on the political scene does certain things in violation of ethical principles, which he does not do, or at least not so frequently and habitually, when he acts in a private capacity," he outlined. In politics, he continued, man "lies, deceives, and betrays; and he does so quite often."[34] "There is no escape from the evil of power, regardless of what one does." "Whenever we act" in a political cause "we must sin," and that will

---

[32] Ibid., 11.

[33] Schlesinger, *Vital Center*, 40. For more on Schlesinger's debt to Niebuhr, see Fox, "Niebuhr and the Emergence of the Liberal Realist Faith," esp. 264–65.

[34] Morgenthau, *Scientific Man*, 179. See, too, Fox, "Niebuhr and the Emergence of the Liberal Realist Faith," 244–45.

continue to be the case in the future, even in a much improved political order.[35]

All of these thinkers agreed that there were two great dangers of the inability of the "children of light" to recognize this fact about the political world. The first, and most straightforward, was that it made them peculiarly vulnerable to domination by others. It was because Ellison's protagonist failed to see how exploitative, manipulative, and delusional the Brotherhood was that *he* found himself exploited and manipulated by it.[36] But second, and probably more importantly, the inability or unwillingness to acknowledge the ineradicable nature of the least desirable political impulses was also said to lead citizens themselves to seek to dominate others. It was because Ellison's protagonist trusted the Brotherhood too much and believed in its vision of a new order that he helped set the conditions for the riot in Harlem. Citing Pascal, Schlesinger similarly concluded that all too often it was "he who would act the angel" who ends up acting "the brute."[37]

This second theme was particularly important for Morgenthau and Schelsinger. It was the unawareness of (or unwillingness to admit to) the essential corruption of politics that most often led citizens to act in terrible ways as they were led like sheep by the leaders who they had foolishly chosen to follow in the name of supposedly noble causes. "It is only the awareness of the tragic presence of evil in *all* political action" that can "enable man to choose the lesser evil and to be as good as he can be in an evil world," Morgenthau explained.[38] Without such knowledge, the temptation to act in terrible ways in the name of some putative good was simply too strong. It was only a "consistent pessimism," Schlesinger concurred, that could "inoculate" American democracy against the dangers of excessively utopian political thinking.

The Revival of American Radicalism

It often appeared that all that the new generation was left with was doubt: doubt about the place of certainty in politics, doubt about the possibilities of political action, and doubt about the capabilities of American citizens. And

---

[35] Morgenthau, *Scientific Man*, 202.

[36] Schlesinger, *Vital Center*, 40. See, too, James Nuechterlein, "Arthur M. Schlesinger Jr. and the Discontents of Postwar American Liberalism," *Review of Politics* 39 (1977): 3–40.

[37] Schlesinger, *Vital Center*, 170, 156. See, too, Reinhold Niebuhr, *The Irony of American History* (New York: Scribner's Sons, 1951). For rare contemporary criticism, see Morton White, "Of Moral Predicaments," *New Republic*, May 5, 1952, 18–19.

[38] Morgenthau, *Scientific Man*, 203.

this doubt threatened the whole purpose of radicalism. As Judith Shklar put it, "radicalism is the belief that people can control and improve themselves and, collectively, their social environment" but one that "at present . . . even those who regard themselves [as radicals] seem to lack."[39] No one, it seemed, was prepared to predict the future with any certainty or to insist that desirable political outcomes would necessarily follow from particular political strategies. Indeed, some commentators even expressed uncertainty as to whether American democracy as it currently existed could survive in the late twentieth century. The Soviet threat, the unsettling demands for ever greater economic prosperity, the ongoing war between capital and labor, the tensions between different ethnic groups, and the decreasing faith in the psychological capacities of citizens—all were considered potential causes of the unraveling of the American political order.[40]

All of this doubt provided deeply unpromising material for the shaping of a new radical democratic theory, yet that was the task that this generation set for themselves. However daunting they looked, these multiple expressions of doubt were not intended to obstruct but rather to assist with what Arthur Schlesinger called "the revival of American radicalism."[41] Having accepted that all efforts to understand the social and political world were flawed, noted that politics was always likely to be corrupted by those "intoxicated by power," and rid themselves of the belief that citizens were in any serious way "perfectible," it was now necessary for self-identified radicals to build their theory up again by outlining a series of key principled commitments and concrete political practices that could survive such an onslaught. For all their pessimism, they had no intention of giving up entirely on the "images of hope, human fraternity, and individual self-realization" that had characterized the greatest moments of previous generations.[42] After all of the "heartbreak" it was now time for radical democrats to return "to the basic principles of democracy."[43]

The Cold War itself provided the backdrop for the first of those basic principles, which Schlesinger described as "the affirmation of a belief in free society and an absolute repudiation of totalitarianism."[44] It was not just anti-

---

[39] Shklar, *After Utopia*, 219.

[40] See Robert A. Dahl, "A Brief Intellectual Autobiography," in Hans Daadler, *Comparative European Politics: The Story of a Profession* (London: Pinter, 1997), esp. 69.

[41] Schlesinger, *Vital Centrer*, 157. See, too, A. J. Taylor, "Up From Utopia: How Two Generations Have Survived Their Wars," *New Republic*, October 30, 1950, 15–18.

[42] Ralph Ellison, "Brave Words for a Startling Occasion," in John F. Callahan, ed., *The Collected Essays of Ralph Ellison* (New York: Random House, 2003 [1953]), 151–54. See, too, Schlesinger, *Vital Center*, 160–62, 156.

[43] Schlesinger, *Vital Center*, 142.

[44] Ibid., 146.

Communism that justified this claim, however. The new generation of radical democrats were full-blown Pluralists whose primary commitment was to the inevitable diversity of human experience. Intellectually reared on the works of Harold Laski, Walter Lippmann, and Mary Follett, they shared the basic pluralist conviction that it was impossible to fully and accurately identify a substantial common good that bound all of America's citizens together.[45] We must "accept a pluralistic destiny for mankind," Schlesinger insisted. "Free men know many truths," he continued, but no "mortal man knows The Truth," both because the human intellect is too limited and because the truths of some individuals necessarily conflict with those of others.[46] But where many radicals in the past had seen such plurality as a problem—especially as an obstacle to national solidarity—it was now to be celebrated. "Whence all this passion toward conformity anyway?" Ellison had his protagonist ask at the very end of *Invisible Man*. "Diversity is the word. Let man keep his many parts and you'll have no tyrant states. . . . America is woven of many strands; I would recognize them and let it so remain."[47]

Although this demand for greater freedom was ubiquitous amongst postwar radicals, there was nonetheless something distinctly novel to it. For most of the twentieth century, after all, self-described radicals had been deeply skeptical about the insistence on personal freedom. Early-twentieth-century Progressives had generally sought to transcend the individualism of what they saw as conservative appeals to freedom, seeking instead a new form of national solidarity. Many interwar pluralists, similarly, had decried celebrations of personal freedom, largely because they believed some form of coercion was essential to the transformation of a deeply unjust political order. In the postwar age, though, radicals continually demanded that all American citizens be given the space to live their lives "without boundaries." Too often in the past, Ralph Ellison explained, well-meaning reformers had sought to put "the world in a strait jacket." But a new radicalism would now be based on the presumption that the only good human life is one full to the brim with "possibility." Individuals were able genuinely to flourish only in "a vast seething, hot world of fluidity."[48]

This celebration of difference, then, led directly to a call for greater protection of the private sphere of individual and social action. What Americans needed, then, was freedom: social and economic freedom from excessive state control, personal freedom from the bullying and coercive interference of powerful sectional interests, and intellectual freedom from the totalizing

[45] See Dahl, "Intellectual Autobiography," 71.
[46] Schlesinger, "One against the Many," 537, 538.
[47] Ellison, *Invisible Man*, 577.
[48] Ibid., 489. See, too, Niebuhr, *Children of Light*, 124.

systems of thought that characterized the prewar ideologists. So central was this demand that when Stuart Hampshire summarized developments in postwar American radicalism in 1955, he concluded that the movement had only one fundamental commitment. "For a radical," he insisted, "the right of each man to choose for himself his own manner of life, as long as he does not disregard the equal right of others to do the same, is the *sole criterion* in political decision."[49]

The most straightforward consequence of this new agenda was a sharp rejection of the more excessive ambitions of the New Deal, and especially of the ideas of those like George Soule and Stuart Chase who had wished to push the direct planning and state control of economic life much further than had Roosevelt. "If the distinguishing moral commitment of the new radicalism is its faith in freedom," Schlesinger explained, then "the distinguishing political commitment is its belief in the limited state."[50]

That was not to say that these postwar radicals endorsed the kind of Hayekian neo-liberalism then beginning to enjoy a vogue on the right of American politics.[51] They still recognized the need for the regulation of the market and even for Keynesian economic demand-management in order to ensure that the poorest could enjoy the "freedom from want" that had been so central to the interwar agenda. The difference now, though, was that the ambitions and expectations of such reform had to be dramatically scaled back. Radicals had to be aware that excessive state power was just as dangerous as the plutocratic power that they had raged against in the Depression years.[52] Such was the lesson of the Soviet Union, where the taking of all private property into state hands may have appeared to have removed the perils of want but only at the cost of creating a state machine that posed a far more serious threat to the lives and liberties of the average citizen. It was clear, Arthur Schlesinger concluded, that anyone who truly cared about freedom should seek to ensure that the state aimed "at establishing conditions for economic decisions, not at making all the decisions itself."[53]

Crucially, though, it was not just the extent of state intervention that needed to be rethought. Just as much attention was paid to the means by which political life was conducted—that is to say, to the methods of political

---

[49] Stuart Hampshire, "In Defence of Radicalism," *Dissent* 3 (1956): 172.

[50] Schlesinger, *Vital Center*, 150.

[51] See the discussion in O. H. Taylor, "The Economics of a Free Society: Four Essays," *Quarterly Journal of Economics* 62 (1948): 641–70.

[52] See Shelton, "The CIO's Own Revolution," 7–8. For commentary see the excellent Harold Brick, *Daniel Bell and the Decline of Intellectual Radicalism: Social Theory and Reconciliation in the 1940s* (Madison: University of Wisconsin Press, 1986), esp. 80–100.

[53] Schlesinger, *Vital Center*, 182. See, too, Niebuhr, *Children of Light*, 110, and Dahl, "Brief Intellectual Autobiography," 69–70.

action. The ways in which the case for reform was to be made was as crucially important as the substantive nature of that reform itself. From this perspective, Depression-Era radicals were dismissed for their willingness to employ distinctively adversarial forms of political action. They had championed the use of strikes, sit-downs, and other potentially coercive forms of political engagement. Indeed, the young Reinhold Niebuhr had told them that they would never reach their goals unless they did so. In the immediate postwar world, however, such efforts were widely condemned, in part because they appeared to threaten the very individual liberties that the new generation had placed at center stage. Now it was necessary to ensure that whenever political changes were sought all efforts were made to ensure that they were "brought about in a way which will not disrupt the fabric of custom, law and mutual confidence, upon which personal rights depend." Such efforts at "transition" must be "piecemeal" rather than dramatic. Political action "must be parliamentary," Schlesinger insisted, borrowing a popular British idiom. "It must respect civil liberties and due process of law," for "only in this way can it preserve free society."[54] Democratic politics in an era of doubt had turned its back on the possibility of securing ideals by whatever means might be necessary and had become, instead, "a method of finding proximate solutions for insoluble problems."[55]

As drama and adversarialism were removed from the radical's strategic toolbox, therefore, compromise and conciliation were intended to take their place. Depression-Era activists had cleaved to the purity of their ideological vision, certain in the knowledge that their ideals were preferable to the injustices imposed by the prevailing order.[56] Postwar radicals were skeptical of just such certainty, however, and that skepticism encouraged them to concentrate on the task of finding common ground with potential opponents. Thus compromise, conciliation, and even reasonable persuasion had to become the tools of political movements. This search for a politics of compromise rather than confrontation was thought to be both intrinsically and instrumentally valuable. First of all, it would prevent any one group from dominating the others in the United States. Postwar radicals were insistent that "no special group of the people is more perfect" than any other and that meant that it was constantly necessary to prevent any one group from achieving its ends through the use of brute force or positional advantage. Second, it would prevent the sort of excessive infighting in the United States that threatened to inflict irreparable damage on the political

[54] Schlesinger, *Vital Center*, 154.
[55] Niebuhr, *Children of Light*, 118.
[56] See previous chapter.

system itself, presenting the serious risk that America would fail in its competition with authoritarian rivals. Some sort of "conflict" between differing economic, social, and political groups was inevitable in a diverse society, Arthur Schlesinger noted, but such "conflict must be kept within bounds, if freedom itself is to survive."[57]

The spirit of compromise would not come easy, however. After all, movements on all sides of American politics had emerged from the Depression with an adversarial character, a sense that their values were superior to those of their rivals and that it was worth employing contentious political means in order to realize them. And although the national unity of wartime had papered over some of these divisions it had not eliminated them entirely. "People who know they alone are right find it hard to compromise[,] and compromise is the strategy of democracy," Arthur Schlesinger bemoaned, noting in particular that relations between industrial labor and employers remained strained even after the achievements of the New Deal.[58]

The former Depression-Era firebrand Stuart Chase was so acutely conscious of this difficulty that he addressed the last book of his career directly to it. In the tellingly entitled *Roads to Agreement*, Chase offered a blow-by-blow guide to how competing groups could compromise with each other in difficult social and economic situations.[59] Most commentators, though, believed that far more was required than guidance from guilty intellectuals. A new spirit of compromise would have to take root amongst the American citizenry themselves. Americans would need to develop "a positive and continuing commitment" to a moderate form of political action, concentrating on give-and-take, and recognizing the essential place of self-doubt in a free political order. Only then would they be able to maintain their freedom and protect themselves either from domination by powerful private interests within the United States or from authoritarian challenges originating overseas.[60]

The difficulty that remained, of course, was explaining how this spirit could be built. To answer this, many postwar thinkers ironically turned to a popular refrain of the Depression Era. Politics, they insisted, was at least partly an emotional business.[61] Citizens chose how to act, and how not to act, as much on the basis of irrational impulse as self-interested calculation. Any political vision that was to have a chance of success must, therefore, have "a living emotional content." It was citizen feelings that would lead

---

[57] Schlesinger, *Vital Center*, 170, 173. See, too, Taylor, "Up From Utopia," esp. 18.

[58] Schlesinger, *Vital Center*, 174.

[59] Stuart Chase, *Roads to Agreement* (New York: Harper and Row, 1951).

[60] Schlesinger, *Vital Center*, 189.

[61] See n. 23, above.

to citizen actions. Those feelings, moreover, were frequently generated by myths and popular stories that made sense of the complex political world and provided powerful motives, whether rational or irrational, for action.[62] What the vision of moderate political action required, therefore, was a story that was psychologically and emotionally "rich enough" to replace its alternatives. It was vital to draw upon political stories that were "deep enough to rally [citizens] to battle for freedom" when that freedom was threatened either from within or without. "The death pallor will indeed come over free society, unless it can recharge the deepest sources of its moral energy," Arthur Schlesinger intoned.[63]

Paradoxically, this meant that for all their worries about totalizing visions, unrealistic ideological utopias, and their insistence on pluralism and diversity, the postwar radicals held that it was nonetheless crucial for Americans to find a kind of emotional unity. If it was going to be possible to "buttress" the "democratic culture" of compromise and conciliation, that is, American citizens would have to feel the force of a particularly unifying political myth, one that emphasized the necessity of individual freedom, that was skeptical of both state power and of sectional interest, and that recognized the need for all citizens to engage in politics in a spirit of mutual tolerance and with limited aspirations.[64] Only if citizens truly appreciated the necessity of all of that—*felt* it in their hearts as much as they understood in their minds—could a democracy suited for an age of doubt appear.

Fortunately this sort of unifying story already existed in the United States, claimed the postwar radicals. Indeed, that story was integral to the very sense of national identity. The root of this idea lay, of course, in the arguments of Depression-Era radicals who had been convinced that the vast majority of Americans shared, and could be led passionately to feel, commitments to key political ideals, including freedom and democracy, as encapsulated in a distinctive American political story. These ideals, shaped by the experience of the nation since its struggle for independence, were immanent in the American condition, waiting only on radical political actors to awaken, and then to employ, them in the construction of a new political order.[65]

---

[62] See Alexander, *Our Age of Unreason*, 232–41.

[63] Schlesinger, *Vital Center*, 245–46. See, too, the editorial "Democracy Is a Weapon," *New Republic*, October 9, 1950, 247.

[64] See Fox, "Niebuhr and the Emergence of the Liberal Realist Faith," 247.

[65] For continuities and contrasts in the pre- and postwar versions of this account, see Wendy L. Wall, *Inventing the "American Way": The Politics of Consensus From the New Deal to the Civil Rights Movement* (Oxford: Oxford University Press, 2008).

A New American Creed

For all of its apparent similarity with the Depression-Era story, though, postwar radicals shaped the idea of an American creed in a very different way than did their predecessors in the 1930s. This American creed was not intended to motivate resistance or insurrection; nor was it designed to mobilize a skeptical citizenry behind radical plans for far-reaching change. Instead, the creed was now celebrated for almost diametrically opposed reasons. It was imagined differently in two crucial ways, both of which sharply differentiated the postwar version from its interwar equivalent.

First, while Depression-Era radicals argued that the American political story was one of conflict and struggle, with the political heroes of the past celebrated as revolutionaries and Civil War warriors, the postwar theorists emphasized instead an American proclivity to openness, toleration, conciliation, and political compromise. There is a "beautiful absurdity" to "American identity," Ralph Ellison had his protagonist eulogize at the close of *Invisible Man*, and that lies in the fact that it is at once an identity of singularity and one of difference, one grounded in communality and in individuality. American political identity, on this account, was said to consist in a deeply held belief that it is necessary for Americans to live happily together without eroding the differences that central to their individual lives. While Americans feel passionate about their nation, they also remain deeply loyal to the distinct choices that have shaped their own lives. The core political values of "Americanism," according to this postwar account, thus lie not in citizens' potential for campaigning zeal and for endless courage in the pursuit of justice, as the Depression-Era radicals suggested, but in a series of distinctly "liberal" values and attributes, including generosity of spirit, open-mindedness, and skepticism with regard to overbearing authority of any kind.[66] American political identity was characterized not by a belief in the country's capacity to build an ever better future, but by its love of liberty and acceptance of diversity.

The second difference drew out the temporal suggestions implicit in the first. Depression-Era radicals had suggested that this American political identity was a latent phenomenon. It consisted in a lurking possibility that political values grounded in American history and political experience might be brought forth at any time by determined campaigners. Postwar thinkers, on the other hand, insisted that it was an already-existing reality that shaped American political experience in the present. According to the postwar radicals, then, living, breathing, and voting American citizens

---

[66] Ellison, *Invisible Man*, 559.

already identified themselves with key American political values and drew sustenance from the American political story. Citizens already felt the emotional pull of American political liberty: they did not need to be forced to appreciate it by campaigning activists. Indeed, it was precisely because they already appreciated the importance of freedom and the ideals of tolerance and limited authority that underpinned it that they might be expected to rally to the cause of its protection in times of trouble. Whatever the psychic attractions of factionalism, adversarialism, and authoritarianism to troubled citizens across the world, the living reality of a liberal American political identity enabled American citizens to withstand their siren calls in ways the peoples of other countries could not.

Although this American ideal was presented as an enduring truth, appreciated since the Revolution itself, this interpretation of American political identity was actually consciously crafted during the Second World War, at a time when all manner of sociologists, anthropologists, and cultural critics had generated a story of American identity well-suited to the struggle against Fascism. Whereas interwar scholars had concentrated on examining distinctive group loyalties and explaining the conflicts inherent in American pluralism, the social scientists of wartime instead turned their attention to tracing an already-existent American political identity that might see the nation through its battle with Fascism.[67]

Many of these accounts were striking in their simplicity. The anthropologist Margaret Mead offered the earliest example of this sort in her *And Keep Your Powder Dry* of 1942. Her purpose there was "to measure the nation's character." As she did so she claimed to have discovered that Americans had a strong collective allegiance to a particular "way of life." Americans stood "for a number of things," she concluded, from a desire for material goods "such as refrigerators and automobiles" to a deep dedication to personal freedom. Americans shared a conviction that it was vital to be allowed to continue "marrying whom you like and working for whom you like and not having to be regimented and wrapped up in yards of governmental red tape."[68] It was a message echoed in remarkably similar works written during the war and in the few years immediately after. Even the titles were all but indistinguishable. Geoffrey Gorer's *The American*

---

[67] See the superb study of Andrew Abbott and James T. Sparrow, "Hot War, Cold War: The Structures of Sociological Action, 1940–1955," in Charles Calhoun, ed., *Sociology in America* (Chicago: Chicago University Press, 2007), 281–313.

[68] Margaret Mead, *And Keep Your Powder Dry* (New York: William Morrow and Co., 1942), 17, 201. I thank Andrew Abbott for bringing this to my attention.

People surprisingly offered almost no disagreement with Gerald Johnson's *This American People*.[69]

Ironically, the most celebrated and influential of all of these studies was not written by an American social commentator but by the Swedish economist Gunnar Myrdal. Commissioned by the Carnegie Corporation before the war to examine "all of America from the outside," Myrdal's aim was to cast light on the distinctive features of American race relations.[70] His eventual study, *An American Dilemma: The Negro Problem and Democracy*, placed the idea of a shared "American creed" at the very heart of its analysis. Although it "is a commonplace to point out the heterogeneity of the American nation," Myrdal thus explained, "there is evidently a strong unity in this nation and a basic homogeneity and stability in its valuations." "Americans of all national origins, classes, regions, creeds, and colors, have something in common," he continued, and that was "a social ethos, a political creed."

That creed, in turn, consisted in the support of the very values of freedom, toleration, and political moderation that were central to the postwar generation's political vision. Moreover, this creed was not just a shared set of political values. It also provided the basis for a peculiar form of emotional nationalism. "The American creed" was thus not just "the implicit background of the nation's political and judicial order," but was instead the "cement in the structure of this great and disparate nation," providing a lived experience that was more deeply felt, "widely understood[,] and appreciated than similar ideals are anywhere else" in the world.[71]

It is almost impossible to exaggerate the hold that this idea had on the radical American political imagination in the decade immediately following the Second World War. For a while, at least, it appeared all but impossible to dispute the notion.[72] Almost every serious commentator on American politics agreed that the citizens of the United States were characterized by a widespread consensus on core liberal democratic ideals and this consensus provided the crucial emotional glue that kept a diverse nation together, preventing it from lapsing into authoritarianism or intemperate adversarialism. Nor was this argument, which quickly became known

---

[69] See Geoffrey Gorer, *The American People* (New York: W. W. Norton and Co, 1948), and Gerald Johnson, *This American People* (New York: Harper and Row, 1951).

[70] Gunnar Myrdal, with Richard Sterner and Arnold Rose, *An American Dilemma: The Negro Problem and Modern Democracy* (New York: Harper and Brothers, 1944), l.

[71] Myrdal, *American Dilemma*, 3.

[72] See the discussion in Rogers M. Smith, "Beyond Tocqeuville, Myrdal, and Hartz: The Multiple Traditions in America," *American Political Science Review* 87 (1993): 549–66.

as the "liberal tradition thesis" or the "story of the American creed," restricted to radical commentators. Literary commentators such as Lionel Trilling noted that "liberalism is not only the dominant but even the sole intellectual tradition" in the United States.[73] Historians also adopted the argument as their own: both Louis Hartz and Richard Hofstadter employed it in their efforts to explain the course of American reform, demonstrating that reform movements that were capable of framing their ideals in terms of this American creed had a chance of succeeding and those that could not inevitably failed.[74] Political scientists, too, submitted to it. Even those who called themselves pluralists invoked this self-same consensus in their explanations of the apparent political stability of the United States. In sharp contrast to Lippmann's pluralism of two decades earlier, Robert Dahl's classics, *A Preface to Democratic Theory* and *Who Governs?*, both written during the 1950s, took for granted "wide agreement on the democratic creed" amongst American citizens. Indeed, Dahl even seemed to push it further than Myrdal or Hartz, contending that "to reject the democratic creed is in effect to refuse to be an American."[75]

The advantages of this argument were clear to see. If the American creed was already a reality, then free and democratic politics could find the emotional engagement that it required without any hint either of the manipulative coercion characteristic of the "children of darkness" or the overly optimistic plans associated with the "children of light." There was no need here for any vanguard political agency to seek to force consensus upon an unwilling citizenry or for any utopian political vision full of empty hope about what the future might be. Instead, an already existing American political identity was all that was required to shore up a decent, democratic, and free political system that was threatened by adversarialism and authoritarianism. Freedom and democracy could be maintained in the United States, then, because the emotional hold of the American creed would enable citizens to withstand the most powerful of authoritarian challenges and resist the most alluring of anti-American temptations. It, and it alone, Schlesinger concluded, should persuade political thinkers of all allegiances that the United States possessed citizens of the "high courage and faith" necessary to "preserve freedom."[76]

---

[73] Lionel Trilling, *The Liberal Imagination* (New York: Viking, 1950): 1.

[74] See Hartz, *Liberal Tradition*, and Richard Hofstadter, *The Age of Reform: From Byran to FDR* (New York: Alfred A. Knopf, 1955).

[75] See Dahl, *Preface to Democratic Theory* and *Who Governs?*, 318. See, too, Darryl Baskin, "Pluralism: Theory, Practice, and Ideology," *Journal of Politics* 32 (1970): 71–95.

[76] Schlesinger, *Vital Center*, 256.

So appealing was this new description of the American creed taken to be that the most conspicuous political efforts of the years immediately following the Second World War concerned its protection. The late 1940s and early 1950s were thus full of attempts to further entrench the creed in the psyche of the American people.[77] Most of these efforts involved small-scale local programs rooted in school curricula, in community-action programs, or in the activities of professional associations like the American Political Science Association, and that concentrated on the propagation of American values and the skills of "good citizenship."[78] Some efforts, though, were more spectacular. Most famously of all, in 1948 President Truman agreed to support a "Freedom train" that would track across the entire country displaying documents from the history of American liberty, including the Declaration of Independence and the Bill of Rights, and stimulating local festivities on the subject of freedom and the American creed. Visitors to the train were asked to recite "nine promises of a good citizen" committing them to do all they could to uphold the American creed. Irving Berlin even wrote a song underscoring its promotion of both toleration and patriotism. The train's motto summed up the whole movement perfectly—"freedom is everybody's job!"[79]

There was, though, an irony in all of this. For it was often the very same thinkers and activists who argued that the American creed already provided the vital emotional "cement" keeping Americans free who also insisted that the creed was so fragile that it required continual efforts to maintain and enhance it. To Louis Hartz, these two commitments were straightforwardly inconsistent. His *The Liberal Tradition in America* thus presented the creed as almost entirely immune to challenge in the postwar United States. It was only an irrational "national hysteria" that could explain why anyone would doubt the solidity of the creed or question its place in the "hearts and minds" of Americans. The creed was set, Hartz insisted. It was, after all, the creed that made America the country it is.

---

[77] See Sparrow and Abbott, "Hot War, Cold War," 302; Robert Griffith, "The Selling of America: The Advertising Council and American Politics, 1942–1960," *Business History Review* 57 (1986): 388–412; Richard M. Fried, *The Russians are Coming! The Russians are Coming! Pageantry and Patriotism in Cold-War America* (New York: Oxford University Press, 1998).

[78] See Louis Hartz et al., "Goals for Political Science: A Discussion," *American Political Science Review* 45 (1951): 1001–15.

[79] "The Nine Promises of a Good Citizen," Port Huron Museum Collection, Freedom Train Visit to Port Huron, Michigan, August 27, 1948. The lyrics to Berlin's song included the memorable lines: "Here comes the Freedom Train / You better hurry down / Just like a Paul Revere / It's comin' into your home town / Inside the Freedom Train / You'll find a precious freight / Those words of liberty / The documents that made us great." See http://www.lyricstime.com/irving-berlin-the-freedom-train-lyrics.html

Hartz did not just believe that efforts to reinforce and entrench the creed were wasteful, though. He also insisted that the "hysteria" that provoked them could easily lead American politicians to pursue policies that were paradoxically incompatible with the core ideas of the creed itself. Most obviously, the worry about Communist threats to liberal freedoms had encouraged a ferocious and dogmatic anti-leftism, which in turn had legitimized the surveillance, inquisition, and black-listing encouraged by Joseph McCarthy and conducted by the CIA, all of which stood in stark opposition to the actual liberal values of the creed itself. Even more worryingly, Hartz argued, misplaced anxieties about the creed's stability also had profound psychological and intellectual consequences for prospective radicals. It led, in particular, to "a new and unprecedented caution" in political imagination that had generated "an unwillingness to play with [supposedly] dangerous ideas." Such caution even threatened to become a "paralysis of mind when certain questions appear," even though such paralysis presented a serious obstacle not only to Communism but to any kind of political and social innovation, including those that citizens genuinely loyal to the American creed should actually demand.[80]

Hartz's concern shot right to the heart of the central difficulty for all radical thinkers in the postwar period. The faith in the existence of the American creed had reassured them that both freedom and democracy had a future in the United States, but it was far less clear how the creed could also provide the basis for a more constructive politics—for, in other words, an actual politics of reform. This was a question that could not be dodged. For all of their skepticism of transformative politics, none of the postwar radicals suggested that the prevailing American order was *entirely* satisfactory. There were simply too many immediate difficulties for even the most skeptical of radicals to overlook, especially in two areas of the national life.

The first of those areas concerned the continuing problem of poverty and the status of industrial labor. While almost everyone accepted that the combined impact of the New Deal and the war had ameliorated the worst aspects of the Depression, few contended that they had rid the United States of the evils of poverty and exploitation forever.[81] The *New Republic* under

---

[80] Hartz, "Goals for Political Science," 1005. See, too, Louis Hartz, *Liberal Tradition*, esp. 11–13, and Louis Hartz, "American Political Thought and the American Revolution," *American Political Science Review* 46 (1952): 321–42. For commentary see John Patrick Diggins, "Knowledge and Sorrow: Louis Hartz's Quarrel with American History," *Political Theory* 16 (1988): 355–76; Desmond King and Marc Stears, "The Missing State in Hartz's America," in Mark Hulliung, ed., *The Liberal Tradition Reconsidered* (forthcoming); and Murray Levin, *Political Hysteria in America: The Democratic Capacity for Repression* (New York: Basic, 1971).

[81] Myrdal, *American Dilemma*, 21.

the editorship of Bruce Bliven and Michael Straight was especially exercised by the continuing inadequacies of the American welfare state, producing an annual special edition called "The State of the Union" throughout the early 1950s in order to highlight the persistence of poverty and inequalities of opportunity in the United States, a theme that was later given even more prominence by Michael Harrington's *The Other America*.[82] Industrial relations also continued to occupy radical attention. Although in hindsight the postwar years appear as the zenith of American labor's power, especially after the CIO merged with the AFL in 1955, most radicals remained concerned that this position could be quickly eroded and many wished to see plans for the democratization of industry pushed still further.[83]

The second area was destined to occupy an even more central place in radical thought and action: the continuing injustice and democratic exclusion faced by African Americans across the country, and especially in the South. "The subordinate position of Negroes is . . . the greatest unsolved task for America," Gunnar Myrdal noted, demonstrating an awareness of the unbearable conditions that shaped the lives of African Americans that had been all-too infrequent in white radical political thought for most of the twentieth century. It was an awareness that was still rare amongst even radical intellectuals in the late 1940s and early 1950s. Louis Hartz failed entirely to comment on the discrepancy between racial injustice and American political identity in *The American Liberal Tradition*, for example, as did Arthur Schlesinger in *The Vital Center*, and Reinhold Niebuhr in *The Children of Light and Children of Darkness*. But undeniably the tide was turning. President Truman's Committee on Civil Rights issued its findings in 1947, just as the Supreme Court began to reconsider the constitutional legality of the doctrine of "separate but equal," opening with *Henderson versus United States*, which declared the segregation of railway dining carriages illegal, and leading eventually to the landmark *Brown versus Board of Education* decision of 1954.[84] By the end of the decade following the cessation of the war, the question of how the political status of African Americans could be transformed was therefore unavoidable, even for those who had previously seemed determine to ignore it.

[82] See Michael Harrington, *The Other America: Poverty in the United States* (New York: MacMillan, 1962).

[83] See Maurice Neufeld, "The Persistence of Ideas in the American Labor Movements," *Industrial and Labor Relations Review* 35 (1982): 207–20, and Judith Steppan-Nottis and Maurice Zeitlan, "Insurgency, Radicalism and Democracy in America's Industrial Unions," *Social Forces* 75 (1996): 1–32.

[84] See William Berman, *The Politics of Civil Rights in the Truman Administration* (Columbus: Ohio State University Press, 1970), and Michael Klarman, *From Jim Crow to Civil Rights: The Supreme Court and the Struggle for Racial Equality* (New York: Oxford University Press, 2004).

Democratic Change and the American Creed

The chief question facing radicals like Ralph Ellison, Louis Hartz, Irving Howe, Reinhold Niebuhr, and Arthur Schlesinger in the early 1950s was not whether the American creed was able to provide the resources necessary to keep America stable, free, and socially harmonious. All of them thought that it quite clearly could. Instead, they had to ask whether it was also able to generate a response to the severe problems that remained in American society, including deep economic inequality and vast racial injustice. Here the task was far harder, for what was required was an approach to the politics of reform compatible with all of the restrictive conditions that theorists had placed upon political action in this new era of doubt. The creed would somehow have to explain how it was possible to strive for potentially far-reaching change while also avoiding excessive ideological certainty, accepting the need for compromise and conciliation between diverse groups, and being "realistic" rather than optimistic about the behavior of political actors.

Daunting as this might have appeared, these radicals were convinced that the American creed was indeed able to rise to the challenge. The great advantage of the creed in this regard, they insisted, was that it did not just provide the social glue necessary to hold America together, but it also provided a clear standard against which the nation's politics could be judged. After all, the American creed bound Americans through core principles and not through the irrational patriotism or myth making that characterized other nations. It was a common faith in freedom, diversity, and social equality that unified Americans and constituted the creed. Whenever a sector of society or a political movement made a complaint about some aspect of the nation's political, social, or economic life, the values of the creed were there to provide a crucial litmus test. The key question to ask in all instances was, "Are the principles of the creed at stake?" When the core values of freedom, diversity, and equality were compromised, then Americans could be certain that action was required to put things right. When they were not, then the call for protest could be written off as an undesirable expression of private interest or a naive, even dangerously misconceived, aspiration.

Paradoxically given how long the issue had been ignored by twentieth-century white radicals, it was racial injustice that was said to provide the perfect example of this advantage. As Gunnar Myrdal and his colleagues were at pains to point out, it was the values of the creed that demonstrated beyond doubt that African Americans had a cast-iron political cause at the beginning of the postwar age. The American creed promises a "system of freedom," it was suggested, but such freedom "can not be erected on a system of caste." Racial hierarchies and ethnic inequalities were therefore essentially "un-American," not because they did not exist in the United States—they clearly did—but because they stood in direct opposition to the ideals and principles that held Americans together and of which they were so rightly proud. "Segregation is a monster" that brings "shame and disgrace upon the United States' flag," the early civil rights campaigner Paul Murray thus insisted, because it directly clashes with the very values of freedom, diversity, and equality that make Americans who they are. "Discrimination and democracy are absolutely antithetical terms," Murray's colleague William Shepard concurred, and in so far as democracy was essential to American national identity, the cause of anti-discrimination had to be as well.[85]

The creed was not just to be used to identify the right causes for political action, however. It was also said to provide the specific means by which political rectification of the evils of racial injustice could be achieved. Neither Ellison, Hartz, Howe, Schlesinger, nor Niebuhr wished to return to the confrontational politics of the 1930s, even in pursuit of the values of the American creed itself. By the mid-1950s, they had longed insisted that it was simply unacceptable to tackle injustices and undemocratic exclusions "by any means necessary," as they thought the interwar radicals had been wont to do. "Force is not the way," Paul Murray thus summarized. No matter how grave the evil or extensive the exclusion, "bloodshed is not the answer."[86] Instead, these injustices were to be overcome by rhetorical appeals to the creed itself. As Myrdal explained, the disjuncture between America's professed ideals and its actual racial practices could be effectively overcome not by dramatic and disruptive politics but rather by a sustained, peaceable, and essentially "moral" appeal to "the hearts of Americans."[87] "There is no question whatsoever that the great majority of the American people accept these ideals," and all reformers had to do was to demonstrate clearly and convincingly that those ideals would be served better by racial justice than by injustice, inclusion rather than exclusion.[88] "[T]he status accorded to the Negro in America represents nothing more [than]a century-long lag of public morals," Myrdal concluded, and therefore what the cause of its rectification required was an appeal to those morals. An appeal, if you like, to the conscience of the nation.[89]

[85] William Shepard, "The Tools for Ethnic Democracy," *Common Ground* 4 (1944): 4.

[86] Paul Murray, "An American Credo," *Common Ground* 5 (1945): 23.

[87] As described by John Dryzek in *Deliberative Democracy and Beyond: Liberals, Critics, Contestations* (Oxford: Oxford University Press, 2000), 51–52.

[88] William Shepard, "The Tools for Ethnic Democracy," *Common Ground* 4 (1944): 11.

[89] Myrdal, *American Dilemma*, 21, 24; italics added.

This argument was widely posited in the 1940s and early 1950s. Change will come to the United States when reformers learn how to "draw on the inner power of the story of this country," Myrdal's protégé Louis Adamic argued.[90] If the "common beliefs in democracy and the ideals of liberty" were invoked by reformers in the right way, then they could build a society in which every citizen is "an equal partner" regardless of their "national or racial origins."[91] America's "high tradition of idealism, decency, and fair play, and our heritage of faith in government of the people, by the people, for the people," provides both the necessary reassurance and the necessary means for action, William Shepard similarly concluded. The cause of the "black American," Ralph Ellison more forcefully noted, could be advanced by reformers putting "pressure upon the nation to live [up] to its ideals," or by striving to convince citizens of the need for a "closer correlation between the meaning of words and reality, between ideal and conduct, between our assertions and our actions."[92]

What all of this meant for the postwar generation was that the American creed not only guaranteed a stable American future or a future free from authoritarian terror; it also provided reformers with the full range of political strategies they needed to pursue their goals. The grave evils that still blighted the United States could be put right without the dangers of discord or domination that came with the more dramatic and disruptive strategies of interwar radicalism if they were pursued through rhetorical and moral appeals to the values of the American creed itself. American radicals "have never regarded democracy as a finished product" but rather as "something to keep on building," Arthur Schlesinger rightly summarized.[93] That much had not changed. The crucial difference from the prewar age, though, was that radicals believed they had discovered a method by which they could continue to build that democracy without relying on the disruption, adversarialism, conflict, or coercion that had characterized the efforts of prewar radicals. This marked a fundamental shift in the American radical democratic tradition and one that would have major consequences for the direction of postwar American democratic thought and practice. Or, at least, so they thought.

---

[90] Louis Adamic, "The Crisis is an Opportunity," *Common Ground* 1 (1940): 63.

[91] Ibid., 69.

[92] Ralph Ellison, "What America Would Be Like Without Blacks," in Callahan, *Collected Essays of Ralph Ellison*, 587.

[93] Schlesinger, *American as Reformer*, 96.

CHAPTER FIVE

The Explosive Enclave

On February 1, 1960, four African American students—Ezell Blair Jr., David Richmond, Joseph McNeil, and Franklin McCain—sat down at the lunch counter in F. W. Woolworth's store in downtown Greensboro, North Carolina, and refused to move until they were served by staff instructed to adhere to a "whites-only" policy. They were refused all afternoon. But the next day they returned, along with twenty-five others. A week later there were three hundred students participating in the protest. Within two months similar demonstrations had spread to fifty-three cities across nine states. Soon after, the "sit-in" protest was being employed in campaigns against segregated facilities and differentiated democratic rights across the southern United States. Images of these sit-ins became the icons of a new movement for democratic reform, one that would capture the imagination not just of America but of the world: the movement for civil rights.

Despite the excitement, the sit-in tactic itself was, of course, not new. It had been employed by trade unionists fighting for recognition in the General Motors plants in Flint, Michigan, twenty-three years earlier, through a series of sit-down strikes that had captured national attention in the same way the Greensboro protest did. In Flint, just as in Greensboro, activists peacefully yet forcefully occupied space in order both to dramatically draw attention to an injustice that would otherwise be ignored and to demand immediate redress. This was a politics where the firm insistence on swift and far-reaching change was embodied in the unmovable persons of the protesters themselves.[1]

For many radical democratic theorists in the early 1960s, however, the shared tactics of the civil rights movement and the trade union protests of the 1930s were misleading. To these thinkers, the civil rights movement was grounded in the new account of the methods of democratic change shaped in the late 1940s and 1950s, one that rejected the sectionalism, adversarialism, and explicit coerciveness of most Depression-Era thought and

---

[1] See Staughton Lynd, "Introduction," in Staughton Lynd, ed., *Non-Violence in America: A Documentary History* (New York: Bobbs Merrill, 1966), esp. xxxvii.

argued instead that change should be brought about by a moral appeal to core American values alone. On this account the sit-in at Greensboro was not a forceful attempt to be served a meal but rather was part of a broader appeal to the moral conscience of the nation.[2]

This interpretation was widely shared at the time, endorsed not only by the original proponents of the idea like Gunnar Myrdal and Arthur Schlesinger Jr., but also by a new generation that included Michael Walzer and John Rawls. It has also remained influential ever since, even becoming the subject matter of a small subdiscipline, civil disobedience studies.[3] Most recently, deliberative democrats have called the movement their own, celebrating it for demonstrating the possibility of a noncoercive, persuasive politics even in the hardest of circumstances. The civil rights movement, and especially that part of it led by Martin Luther King Jr., is thus said to have offered a form of political action that incorporated egalitarian and democratic values even in the face of grave injustices and that emphasized the importance of creating inclusive dialogue across disagreement in the hope of forging an ever more thoroughgoing spirit of political community. As Amy Gutmann and Dennis Thompson paradigmatically put it, "Martin Luther King Jr.'s leadership of the civil rights movement exemplifies a politics of deliberative engagement. He mobilized African Americans around a moral cause that he publicly justified in reciprocal terms. . . . He furthered the cause of civic integrity by calling on American citizens to live up to their professed principles, and he appealed to American leaders to live up to their constitutional commitments." Here, it seemed, was the politics of the American creed at its best.[4]

Pervasive though this interpretation is, however, it is seriously misguided. For although there were important differences between the democratic theory and practice of the civil rights movement and that of the Depression-Era CIO and its supporters, there were also crucial continuities. Despite the rhetoric of King, James Farmer, and others, civil rights theorists and activists did not understand the causes of democratic exclusion to be exclusively "moral" in character, nor did they believe that the only legitimate and effective way to overcome such exclusions was

---

[2] Editorial, "We Are Not Afraid," *New Republic*, March 14, 1960, 3–4, and Helen Fuler, "Southern Students Take Over: The Creation of the Beloved Community," *New Republic*, May 2, 1960, 14–16.

[3] For an account of this trend and insightful critical commentary, see Mark Philp, *Political Conduct* (Cambridge, Mass.: Harvard University Press, 2007), 169–84. See, too, David Spitz, "Democracy and the Problem of Civil Disobedience," *American Political Science Review* 48 (1954): 386–403.

[4] Amy Gutmann and Dennis Thompson, "Reply to Critics," in Stephen Macedo, ed., *Deliberative Politics: Essays on* Democracy and Disagreement (Oxford: Oxford University Press, 1999), 254.

through an appeal to the conscience of American citizens as represented by the values of the American creed. Instead, the movement approached the question of democratic transformation in much the same way as had radical democratic movements of the earlier part of the century. Its task was to build a more ideal political order out of a less ideal one and that involved recourse to a wide range of political strategies and behaviors, most of which would be considered undesirable, even illegitimate, in an improved future state.

Whatever outside observers might have hoped, therefore, the primary difference between the movement for civil rights and earlier efforts did not lie in any dedication to pursuing democratic change exclusively through moral and rhetorical reference to the American creed. It lay, instead, in a more subtle disagreement as to the precise types of behaviors and practices that could engender democratic transformation and in the argument about the role that the sufferers of injustice themselves could and should play in that transformation. This was far from a minor change. Indeed, it would reshape the radical democratic tradition for generations to come. But it was not the change that many of the movement's admirers—including latter-day deliberative democrats—believed they had detected.

The Redemptive Community

There are many reasons why both contemporary commentators and deliberative democrats of the present day misinterpret the theory and practice of the civil rights movement as grounded in a moral appeal to the values of the American creed. Perhaps primary amongst them, though, is the story of the movement's origins. The movement as we now know it initially emerged when the one-time League for Industrial Democracy (LID) chairman and disgruntled former CIO campaigner Abraham J. Muste joined forces with a group of young radical thinkers and activists, black and white, including David Dellinger, Bayard Rustin, James Peck, and James Lawson, in the explicitly pacifist organization The Fellowship of Reconciliation (FOR). The FOR was the most ambitious of all the myriad postwar organizations in its insistence that the values of the American creed provided the basis for a radical transformation of the social, political, and economic order of the United States. It was not surprising that it did so, for Muste's own life story was characteristic of the argument. Having once supported the coercive pluralism of the CIO, he had grown skeptical of its adversarial posture even earlier than most. The "corrupting influence of the whole end justifies the means business is repeatedly seen," he insisted as early as 1937. Such an approach "poisons, corrupts and thwarts the struggle for justice," leading only to a dangerous factionalism that possesses all the evil potential of authoritarianism.[5] Those committed to wide-ranging change had instead to craft a strategy of transformation that worked in "the realm of standards and values, the realm in which moral judgment is pronounced, the realm in which ethical and spiritual appeals are made."[6] And the American creed provided the basis for just such an appeal.

Muste and FOR's contribution to the genesis of the civil rights struggle came when Muste agreed, if rather reluctantly, to support an initiative of a young African American FOR member, James Farmer. Farmer's idea was to counter the increasing racial segregation of public facilities in Chicago through a method of nonviolent direct action. Such action, Farmer argued, would dramatically alert Americans to the contradiction between the state ideals of wartime America celebrating individual liberty and equality and the social reality in which African Americans were forced to live. By drawing attention to this disjuncture and by appealing to the moral values at the heart of the American creed, Farmer suggested, the acquiescence of American citizens to racial injustice, which formed the very basis of segregation, could be effectively challenged.

Although Muste was openly skeptical as to the program's chance of success, he encouraged Farmer to experiment and permitted him to use FOR resources in any trial actions.[7] The results were almost instantly impressive. There had, of course, been efforts earlier in the twentieth century from within the African American community to overcome exclusions, most notably those of A. Philip Randolph, W.E.B. Du Bois, Booker T. Washington, and the National Association for the Advancement of Colored People (NAACP), but nothing quite of this scale or effectiveness had been seen before.[8] Farmer and colleagues, including FOR's own Jim Peck and Bayard Rustin, managed to desegregate Chicago restaurants in very short order, and they quickly began to lead similar campaigns to desegregate other

---

[5] See Abraham J. Muste, "The Problem of Violence" *Modern Monthly* 10 (1937): 7–9.

[6] Abraham J. Muste, cited in Staughton Lynd, "Introduction," in Lynd, *Non-Violence in America*, xxxviii. See, too, David MacDonald, "Why I am No Longer a Socialist," *Liberation* 3 (1957): 4–6, and William Heseltine, "Coercion in American Life," *Liberation* 2 (1957): 12–19.

[7] Muste was not alone in his skepticism. Norman Thomas argued that "it would be a mistake to embark on such a campaign, not because I do not believe in the principle, but because I do not believe that it is well enough understood among Negroes or that it could be sufficiently well carried out to be effective." See Norman Thomas's contribution to Reinhold Niebuhr, ed., *Civil Disobedience: Is it the Answer to Jim Crow?* (New York: Non-Violent Action Committee, 1947), esp. 21.

[8] See the discussion in Herbert Shapiro, *White Violence and Black Response: From Reconstruction to Montgomery* (Amherst, Mass.: University of Massachusetts Press, 1988), 428–54.

facilities, including municipal buildings, libraries, swimming pools, and roller skating rinks, across multiple states, including California, Maryland, Missouri, New Jersey, New York, and Pennsylvania, always employing the same tactics of peaceful yet determined noncompliance with segregationist rules.[9] As they progressed, Farmer persuaded FOR to provide further financial support for the endeavor, eventually breaking with Muste to create an organization of his own, which eventually became known as the Congress of Racial Equality (CORE).[10]

By the middle of the 1950s, this new form of protest against segregation and other forms of racial exclusion was indelibly associated with the campaign for civil rights for African Americans and was no longer solely related to CORE. The determining moment of that broader association came, of course, in December 1955 when Rosa Parks returned to Montgomery, Alabama, from a Highlander Folk School course in trade union politics, refused to move to a segregated black section on a municipal bus, and was duly arrested. The mass boycott of segregated bus services that ensued captured the attention of the entire United States. It also catapulted a new, young, and charismatic preacher to a position of de facto leadership in the new struggle: Martin Luther King Jr. The radical democratic philosophy and practice that King promoted throughout the boycott closely resembled that outlined by Farmer, but, much to the latter's chagrin, it was King's fame that grew most spectacularly and it was with his name that the new political approach became most frequently linked.[11]

Within a few years other organizations had begun to follow in the wake of King's Southern Christian Leadership Conference (SCLC.). Most notably, in April of 1960 SCLC activist Ella Baker drew together all of the various groups of young people who had spontaneously engaged in action across the South, initiating the Student Nonviolent Coordinating Committee (SNCC, pronounced *snick*) and involving campaigners, like James Forman, Bob Moses, and James Lawson, many of whom had already experienced campaigns led by CORE in the North. SNCC quickly developed a life of its own and by the middle of 1960 it was involved in an often uneasy alliance with both CORE and the SCLC in an effort to lead a whole host of campaigns across the South, focusing on formal rights of democratic inclusion,

[9] For accounts of the early actions, see Jim Peck, *Cracking the Color Line: Non-Violent Direct Action Methods of Eliminating Racial Discrimination* (New York: CORE, 1962).

[10] For a detailed history, see August Meier and Elliott Rudwick, *CORE: A Study in the Civil Rights Movement, 1942–1968* (New York: Oxford University Press, 1973).

[11] See Gerstle, *American Crucible*, esp. 274–77, and James Farmer, *Lay Bare the Heart: An Autobiography of the Civil Rights Movement* (Austin: Texas Christian University Press, 1985), 186–87.

the abolition of segregationist Jim Crow laws in public and private facilities, the need for massively expanded opportunities in education, and economic empowerment.[12]

What all of these movements shared was a commitment to nonviolent direct action. Both together and separately they led events that would swiftly become the stuff of radical legend, including the Freedom Rides, which carried CORE and SNCC activists across the South in buses in an attempt desegregate transport facilities in that part of the country; the McComb voter registration drive in Mississippi, which sought to break down years of exclusion from the franchise; and the Mississippi Freedom Schools, which offered educational programs to young and old African Americans who had been abandoned by racist public schools. By the end of 1962, CORE, the SCLC, and SNCC were indisputably the most important of all of the radical movements in the United States: their actions were vibrant, their rhetoric forthright, and their demands extensive. "Thus a mass movement . . . of unprecedented proportions was born," James Farmer recalled. "There were sit-ins and there were marches and there was singing. There were arrests and bail-outs and re-arrests. In living rooms throughout the land, America sat on the edge of its seat, watching the unfolding drama."[13]

Despite the salience of direct action, the leaders of CORE, the SCLC, and SNCC constantly insisted that their politics was not a return to interwar adversarialism, and it was here that their appeal lay for supporters of the American creed. Thus the major organizations involved with the civil rights movement came to insist that the lessons of the postwar period had been well-learnt and that there would be no return to the violence of form or spirit that characterized radicalism in the late Depression years. Direct action for civil rights was thus presented as "an eloquent method of arousing the moral conscience of society," as opposed to a means by which to force others to do what they otherwise would not wish to do.[14] As Martin Luther King Jr. famously phrased it in his *Letter from Birmingham City Jail*, when SCLC activists march, demonstrate, and sit-in, "we present our very bodies as a means of laying our case before the conscience of the local and national community."[15] Such an appeal was to be made to every American and not

---

[12] For introductory overviews, see Aldon Morris, "Black Southern Student Sit-In Movement," *American Sociological Review* 46 (1981): 744–67, and Aldon Morris, "A Retrospective on the Civil Rights Movement," *Annual Review of Sociology* 25 (1999): 517–39.

[13] Farmer, *Lay Bare the Heart*, 192.

[14] Paul Kurtz, "Misuses of Civil Disobedience," *Dissent* 17 (1970): 66 -67. See, too, the editorial "Across the Editors' Desk," *Student Voice* 1 (1960): 2.

[15] Martin Luther King Jr., *Letter from Birmigham City Jail* (1963), reprinted in Bedau, *Civil Disobedience*, 74.

just to the influential and the powerful. "We can and must win the mind of the prejudiced person," King insisted, and that could be achieved by appealing to key American ideals, which were currently more frequently breached than honored by large sections of the population.[16]

To this end, the leadership of CORE, SNCC, and the SCLC laid down comprehensive behavioral demands on those who wished to participate in their actions. CORE's "Rules of Action" and SNCC's "Statement of Purpose" were the most far-reaching documents in this regard, presenting a wide and detailed range of prescriptions and proscriptions, most of which concentrated on the ways in which participants in direct action should seek to engage with their adversaries. CORE's "Rules" insisted that each "member will seek at all times to understand both the attitude of the person responsible for a policy of racial discrimination, and the social situation which engendered the attitude" and "will never use malicious slogans or labels to discredit an opponent."[17] SNCC's "Statement," similarly, required all participants to "nurture" an "atmosphere in which reconciliation and justice become actual possibilities."[18] The SCLC had no such formalized rules, but in many ways their expectations were even higher, with King continually outlining the organization's abhorrence of violence and its dedication to achieving enduring change in a way that honored norms of peaceful, democratic interaction.[19]

The argument was reinforced by the fact that many of the struggles that the movement was engaged in were in pursuit not of new laws based on abstract ideals but of effective enforcement of already existing federal legislation and judicially recognized constitutional rights. The Freedom Rides through the South were designed to ensure that the Supreme Court's judgments against segregation in transportation were upheld, not to insist that new rights be granted. The McComb voter registration drive was similarly intended to ensure that voting rights granted by the Fifteenth Amendment were actually available to all. As James Farmer put it, "civil rights workers in the south are only doing the job which the federal government ought to be doing for itself: insuring for all citizens the enjoyment of their constitutional rights."[20] In this way, therefore, the movement was able to claim that its actions "manifest[] a respect for legal procedures," even when individual

[16] Martin Luther King, "Introduction," in Peck, *Cracking the Color Line*, i.

[17] CORE, "Rules for Action," reprinted in Staughton Lynd and Alice Lynd, eds., *Nonviolence in America: A Documentary History* (New York: Orbis, 1995), 221.

[18] SNCC, "Statement of Purpose," reprinted in Lynd and Lynd, *Nonviolence in America*, 222.

[19] See Martin Luther King, Jr., "The Social Organization of Nonviolence," *Liberation* 4 (1959), 5–6.

[20] James Farmer, *Freedom — When?* (New York: Random House, 1965), 21.

protesters broke individual laws—especially state laws—in order to make its case.[21]

The clarity of this commitment itself was enhanced further still by the celebrated willingness of many civil rights campaigners to accept legal penalties that were imposed upon them for their protesting actions, even when they were of dubious legality in themselves. King was especially insistent on the importance of this. "[A]n individual who breaks a law that conscience tells him is unjust, and willingly accepts the penalty by staying in jail" both "arouse[s] the conscience of the community over its injustice" and "is in reality expressing the very highest respect for law," he explained.[22] If Americans were to understand that civil rights protest was designed to ensure equal rights under the law rather than being intended to gain a group-based advantage at the expense of other social groups, King explained, then that commitment had to be continually manifested in their actions and their willingness to accept the consequences. [23]

All of this delighted those radical scholars who had come of age reading the postwar work of Ellison, Myrdal, Niebuhr, and Schlesinger. The civil rights movement appeared to these commentators to be deeply committed to the idea that the United States was primarily characterized by its shared creed of liberal and democratic values, a creed that made it possible to call for great changes without employing coercion by couching one's demands in terms of its shared values. Writing in *Dissent*, the young Michael Walzer thus argued that the campaign for civil rights was the perfect fulfillment of the postwar reconsideration of American radical politics. "Disillusionment with the idea of revolution is one of the most interesting features of American intellectual life today," he reminded his readership. "After seeing the terror and the purge and all that goes with the revolutionary transformation of society, the brutal manipulation of human beings, the corruption of culture—after seeing all this we are none of us, I suppose, revolutionaries," Walzer insisted. "We have denounced Bolshevik 'realism,'" he concluded, and hoped instead to construct an account of democratic reform that was grounded more in moral persuasion than in winning a battle "of organizational pressures."[24] In such an interpretation, the civil rights campaigners appeared as "happy warriors," a "refreshing contrast to the revolutionaries of old." The highly moralized politics of this civil rights

---

[21] John Rawls, "The Justification of Civil Disobedience" in Hugo Bedau ed., *Civil Disobedience* (New York: Pegasus, 1968), 247.

[22] King, *Letter from Birmingham City Jail*, 78–79.

[23] Kurtz, "Misuses of Civil Disobedience," 67.

[24] Walzer, "Idea of Resistance," 370.

movement demonstrated "the possibility of communal resistance."[25] This resistance was grounded in respect toward opponents rather than in self-interested conflict or violent insurrection whilst also demanding "not that our society abdicate, but that it fulfill, its announced claims."[26]

The civil rights movement was therefore seen "as a political action which addresses the sense of justice of the majority in order to urge reconsideration of the measures protested and warn that in the opinion of the dissenters the conditions of social cooperation are not being honoured."[27] The radical imagination was thus captured in a way that it had not been since the Second World War. "SNCC moved us, seized our imaginations" in the early 1960s, the white student radical Todd Gitlin thus later recalled. Except amongst a few Leninists," Paul Goodman observed, "the mood is euphoric."[28] Even when they were subject to repression and arrest, Howard Zinn concluded admiringly (if rather naively), "they smile and wave while being taken off in the paddy wagons; they laugh and sing behind bars."[29]

The Explosive Enclave

Despite its popularity, this interpretation was always seriously flawed as a description of either the actual democratic practices of the civil rights movement or of the theoretical arguments that were used to justify those practices.[30] Even though the critiques of interwar adversarialism did have some bite, neither King nor any of the other leading players in the civil rights movement ever believed that expansive change in the United States could or should be brought about solely by means of a moralized appeal to the values of the American creed. As Adam Fairclough has argued, "there is little evidence that King ever believed that non-violent protest functioned solely, or even mainly, as a form of moral persuasion."[31] Rather, as Clyde Frazier also noticed, it was the "simultaneous appeal to both the conscience

---

[25] Irving Howe, "The Negro Revolution," *Dissent* 10 (1963): 207.

[26] Walzer, "Idea of Resistance," 373.

[27] Rawls, "Justification of Civil Disobedience," 240.

[28] Paul Goodman, "Reflections on Civil Disobedience and Lawlessness," in Robert A. Goldwin, ed., *Civil Disobedience: Five Essays* (Kenyon, Ohio: Public Affairs Conference Center, 1968): 23.

[29] Howard Zinn, *S.N.C.C.: The New Abolitionists* (Boston: Beacon, 1964), 5.

[30] For the difficulties of an overemphasis on Martin Luther King Jr., see Richard H. King, *Civil Rights and the Idea of Freedom* (Oxford: Oxford University Press, 1992).

[31] Adam Fairclough, "Martin Luther King Jr. and the Quest for Nonviolent Social Change," *Phylon* 47 (1986): 3

and the self-interest of the public" that characterized the democratic thought and action of the civil rights movement at its height in the early 1960s.[32]

The difference between the civil rights movement's understanding of its own democratic practice and the interpretation given to it by its eager admirers goes to the very heart of their analysis. The creed-centered democratic theory that commentators widely associated with civil rights activism only made sense within the context of a "nearly" or "piecewise" just social and political order, one in which appeals to political conscience grounded in core and shared political principles would be both comprehensible by all citizens and at least potentially effective at swaying their opinions on the crucial issues being addressed.[33] This meant, as Michael Walzer also insisted in 1960, that the "moralized" approach to direct action is only ever advisable in "an already constituted political community," where common standards of political justice are available to all and provide potentially effective means of resolving disputes.[34]

Very few, if any, of the major players in the civil rights movement actually saw the United States in the 1950s and 1960s in these terms. Although most of them longed to live in a society that was conducted according to the values imputed to the "creed"—to share citizenship with others in a political order that was governed in accordance with fair principles with which every reasonable citizen could agree—they understood the prevailing American order to be far removed from this ideal. In fact, and quite to the contrary, they believed that the United States was a political order characterized by domination. Its government, at both a state and a federal level, was at best only partially grounded in potentially shared principles and was often conducted with little or no relevance to such ideals. The structuring concept at the heart of the civil rights movement's analysis of American governance was not, therefore, a common idea of justice and freedom or a shared heritage of liberal democracy. Rather it was the "concept of political power" in its most straightforward sense.[35]

This fact was clear in almost all of the organizations' activities. When SNCC met to draw up syllabi for the Mississippi Freedom Schools, therefore, they agreed that the primary purpose was to "create an awareness of the power structure" of American society and to demonstrate "that some people make decisions that profoundly affect others" without any consideration

---

[32] Clyde Frazier, "Between Obedience and Revolution," *Philosophy and Public Affairs* 1 (1972): 328

[33] See John Rawls, *A Theory of Justice* (Oxford: Oxford University Press, 1972), esp. chap. 6.

[34] Walzer, "Idea of Resistance," 371.

[35] Noel Day, "Introducing the Power Structure," The Staughton Lynd Papers 4/13, Wisconsin State Historical Society, Madison, Wisconsin.

for those others' interests.[36] The movement's analysis as such owed more to the young Reinhold Niebuhr than the old, more to the philosophers of coercion than to those of consensus. Young students were thus encouraged not to think of points of principled connection between themselves and the white elite, or to consider the United States as held together by shared liberal values. They were asked instead to examine their own states, communities, schools, and families and to "construct an organizational chart of the power structure" illustrating where the possibilities for domination and control lay at each level of hierarchy. [37] The focus was constantly on the reality of the coercive power of repressive forces in American society and their effective points of control. Outside of the freedom schools, this analysis was also a commonplace. Even the most highly moralized of all the civil rights movement's leading activists placed power at the center of their understandings; it shaped their view both of the prevailing political order and the means by which to change it. At the SNCC conference of 1963, Bob Moses thus concluded that the essence of the civil rights struggle lay in two commitments: first, its sense that "the problem is with the power structure of this country" and, second, its distinctive view as to "how we can change it so that it works to our advantage."[38]

For all of the rhetorical emphasis on conscience and persuasion, then, the strategy of direct action that the movement pursued was directly dependent on this understanding of the American political order. Power was the key. For many in the movement, the primary purpose of direct action for civil rights was to reveal the fact of domination and to illustrate its locations and its mechanisms. Marches, demonstrations, and sit-ins worked best, therefore, when they provoked a violent response from officials and from the public, laying bare for all to see the nature of the power structure of the United States, demonstrating that it was only possible to maintain the prevailing order by means of violence, and robbing "the opponent of the moral conceit by which he identifies his interests with peace and order."[39] As King's advisor Bayard Rustin explained, direct-action "protest becomes an effective tactic to the degree that it elicits brutality and oppression from the power structure," because in so doing the power structure reveals itself for

---

[36] Ibid. For insightful commentary, see Daniel Perlstein, "Teaching Freedom: S.N.C.C. and the Creation of the Mississippi Freedom Schools," *History of Education Quarterly* 30 (1990): 297–324, and idem, "Minds Stayed on Freedom: Politics and Pedagogy in the African-American Freedom Struggle," *American Educational Research Journal* 39 (2002): 249–77.

[37] Day, "Power Structure."

[38] Bob Moses, "Address to S.N.C.C. Washington Conference, December 30, 1963," in The Staughton Lynd Papers 4/12.

[39] Reinhold Niebuhr, *Moral Man and Immoral Society* (New York: Continuum, 2005 [1932]), 163

what it really is.[40] The task of civil rights protest was thus to "dramatize to the American people the existence of this situation and also our determination that these conditions shall not continue to exist."[41]

This argument was strikingly similar to that made by interwar radicals such as the CIO. It also infused almost every aspect of the civil rights movement's work. It was particularly exposed in their internal communications. Almost every edition of CORE's internal newsletter the *CORE-lator* and SNCC's the *Student Voice* contained detailed, almost lurid, accounts of violent assaults on civil rights workers by the agents of the state, retelling in intricate fashion each blow that demonstrators had received and each stage of the mounting attack upon them.[42] Leaders within the movement were also lionized more for the violent attacks they had suffered than for the protests that they had led or the practical successes they had achieved. When John Lewis was elected SNCC chairman in 1963, the *Student Voice* ran a front-page story that concentrated exclusively on his experiences of violence during the civil rights struggle. Despite being only twenty-three, the *Voice* reported that Lewis "has been arrested 24 times," 17 of those in Nashville alone. He was "also savagely beaten in Montgomery, Alabama." No other talent or experience was reported. Lewis had served the movement best by revealing the oppressive power of the state, by exposing its violence and its repression for all to see.[43]

This strategy of drawing out repression from the state was, of course, at least partially compatible with the appeal to the American creed on which so many liberal admirers placed emphasis. By showing that the exclusion of African Americans was enforced by violence it was possible to reveal the extent to which the liberal values of the American creed were ignored by most citizens in the United States, and thus to build a case for far-reaching reform. But the strategy was also intended more directly to intimidate those in positions of power and those who supported them. It did that primarily by encouraging their oppressors to see the limitations of their strength, and thus to reconsider the sustainability of their position. It was also intended as a tool by which to mobilize support amongst African Americans themselves, the more conservative of whom had learnt to endure the daily repression of segregation but who could be raised to action

---

[40] Cited in Fairclough, "Quest for Nonviolent Social Change," 6. See, too, the editorial "Rebellion in Mississippi," *New Republic*, October 8, 1962, 3–4.

[41] Editorial, "Politics and the Student Movement," *Student Voice* 1 (1960): 7.

[42] For a paradigmatic example, see Carole Bradford, "Nonviolence on a New Orleans Picket Line," *CORE-lator* 88 (1961): 1–2. See, too, G. Carey, "New Freedom Task Force in the South," *CORE-lator* 99 (1963): 1–2.

[43] Editorial, "Lewis Elected as S.N.C.C. Chairman," *Student Voice* 4 (1963): 1.

when the sources of domination were continually and dramatically drawn to the surface.[44]

Beyond that, these actions were also intended to be a mechanism of power itself. There was, that is, a distinctly and explicitly coercive element to at least some of the civil rights movement's protest. Such coercion took many forms. Most straightforwardly, there was the hope that the forces of repression could be effectively exhausted through the use of protest. As Bayard Rustin explained in the *Student Voice* early in 1960, the reason for protesters to "accept the penalty" of jail time if they were arrested did not reside in any demonstration of "fidelity to the law." If that was the case then protesters should agree to pay their fines and post their bail. Instead, it rested in the hope that "there are not enough jails to accommodate the movement." "If upon arrest you pay bail or fine," Rustin continued, "you provide room for a friend. Only so many can fit into a cell; if you remain there, there can be no more arrests! This is one of the best ways to immobilize [the] police apparatus."[45] On a larger scale, such a desire to directly impact the forces of repression lay behind King's insistence that civil rights protesters should "never let them rest." Protest should be dramatic, far-reaching, and wide-ranging, King thus insisted, for if "tens of thousands" of "disciplined and sustained" actions could take place, then the energies of the repressors would be drained, and the consequences would be far more "permanent and damaging to the enemy than a few acts of organized violence."[46]

The most important contribution of such tactics resided not in any one victory but in their ability to precipitate a crisis in the power structure. Such a crisis would partly be brought about by tying up the established authorities' resources in the constant struggle to maintain order. It would also be induced by the creation of a constant state of unease amongst those who maintained and profited from racial injustice, a sense that the social order could explode at any minute. Even King himself was abundantly clear on this point. "I am not afraid of the word tension," he wrote in the *Letter from Birmingham City Jail*, because there "is a type of constructive tension that is necessary for growth." It was only when those in positions of power felt intimidated that they were likely to act. Indeed, King concluded, the very "purpose of . . . direct action is to create a situation so crisis-packed that it will inevitably open the door to negotiation."[47] The argument was far from confined to King. Indeed, it was nowhere better put than in Bob Moses's

---

[44] See Herbert Shapiro, *White Violence and Black Response: From Reconstruction to Montgomery* (Amherst, Mass.: University of Massachusetts Press, 1988), esp. 395–427.

[45] Bayard Rustin, "Jail vs Bail," *Student Voice* 1 (1960): 7.

[46] King, "Social Organization of Nonviolence," 6.

[47] King, *Letter from Birmingham City Jail*, 75.

addresses to SNCC in 1963. The direct-action protests of the civil rights movement, Moses announced, were necessary because only they could begin "[t]he annealing of the south," where "to anneal is to heat an object to white hot heat and then to mould it while it is cooling off."[48]

In their own self-understanding, the civil rights movement, therefore, was not committed to the belief that the United States was a "nearly" or even "piecewise" just, free, or democratic society in which citizens shared adherence to the key liberal principles of the American creed even if they did not live up to them, nor was it dedicated to a model of political action that always prioritized the moral desirability of persuasion over coercion. Rather, the leading activists within the movements saw themselves, as James Forman so evocatively put it, as "an explosive enclave" that would move across the United States revealing, challenging, undermining, and reshaping the prevailing power structure.[49]

Such a self-description did not please many of the movement's admirers, most of whom chose simply to ignore it. They continued to place the campaign in the categories that they had inherited from Myrdal and his colleagues in the immediate aftermath of the Second World War. But it would have impressed the scholars who had supported the Flint sit-downers, many of whom had made very similar arguments about the purpose of direct action against injustice.[50] Indeed it was Reinhold Niebuhr in his younger, prewar incarnation who had first called for the adoption of a program of direct action by African Americans, insisting as he did that it was necessary simply because it was "hopeless for the Negro to expect complete emancipation from the menial social and economic position into which the white man has forced him, merely by trusting in the moral sense of the white race."[51] It was a call almost directly echoed thirty-three years later, when forty-eight African American clergymen tired of the Myrdal-style analysis so popular in the white intelligentsia and wrote to the *New York Times* in protest. It is time, they demanded, to "reject the assumption that white people are justified in getting what they want through the use of power, but that Negro Americans must, either by nature or circumstance, make their appeal only through conscience."[52]

---

[48] Moses, "Address to S.N.C.C."

[49] See James Forman, *United States, 1967: High Tide of Black Resistance* (New York: Students for a Democratic Society, 1967), 3.

[50] Editorial, "Flint and a New Social Order," *Common Sense* 6 (1937): 3.

[51] Niebuhr, *Moral Man and Immoral Society*, 165.

[52] Cited in Claybourne Carson, *In Struggle: S.N.C.C. and the Black Awakening of the 1960s* (Cambridge, Mass.: Harvard University Press, 1981), 223.

At its height, between 1960 and 1964, the civil rights movement strove to create a better democratic order in the United States, one that would make good the promise of American liberal democracy and that would include every citizen blind to racial background in ongoing political participation aimed at uncovering an American common good, but in so doing, they recognized the necessity of fighting power with power. They thus outlined a host of approaches to political protest that did not shy away from the occasional use of coercion. A fundamental "means/ends" distinction was reasserted in the movement's approach to democratic politics. CORE, SNCC, and even the SCLC saw themselves more as "explosive enclaves" than as a collection of ideal deliberators, even as they longed for the day when such explosiveness would no longer be required. As King put it, it was vital to appreciate the need "for non-violent gadflies to create the kind of tension in society that will help men to rise from the dark depths of prejudice and racism," even though the long-run goal remained the creation of a democratic political order capable of reaching "the majestic heights of understanding and brotherhood."[53] As with the radical democrats of the prewar era, theirs was a theory designed to explain how the democratic order of the United States was to be radically reformed, a theory that continually stressed the need to create a more ideal democracy out of the non-ideal material of the prevailing social and political world.

The Virtuous Politics of Democratic Transformation

The civil rights movement did, nonetheless, understand the precise relationship between "means" and "ends" differently than had many of their predecessors. Unlike the Depression-Era CIO, it combined its emphasis on the need to fight power with power with a highly moralized commitment to specific sorts of protesting behavior, including nonviolence and the need to treat opponents with some semblance of democratic respect, as prescribed by CORE's "Rules of Action" and SNCC's "Statement of Purpose." It is this change that marks the most important contribution of the movement to the radical democratic tradition itself.

The relationship between the civil rights movement's chosen means and their desired ends had two specific dimensions. The first was not new to CORE, SNCC, or the SCLC but involved a clear sense that the means employed at least partially determined the ends that could be reached. Just as Ellison, Niebuhr, and Schlesinger had argued in the immediate postwar

---

[53] King, *Letter from Birmingham City Jail*, 75.

years, so the leading players in the civil rights movement were convinced that it would be hard to build an inclusive, democratic order out of a violent transition, partly because the memories of violence take too long to pass, obscuring shared ideals and hindering the democratic pursuit of any postconflict common good.[54] CORE, SNCC, and the SCLC's commitment to nonviolence was, then, most frequently explained not in terms of the moral duties owed to fellow citizens in the present but in terms of the sort of social and political order that it would contribute to creating in the future. "Nonviolent resistance is the sword that heals," the movement's leading activists explained. Such a sword would "cut[ ] without wounding," establishing a real break with the present unjust order with some force if necessary but doing so in a way that did not generate ineradicable tensions for the future.[55] As Andrew Sabl has perceptively argued, the civil rights movement was concerned with the "conditions for future cooperation" and it often contended that "violence causes an escalation of tit-for-tat retributions and increasing hatred, while non-violent civil disobedience leaves open the possibility of a just harmony in a scale of years rather than generations."[56]

But it was not this interest in the general, long-term consequences alone that led the civil rights movement to moralize its political behavior. For unlike most of those who had argued for democratic transformation in the 1930s, CORE, SNCC, and the SCLC were also committed to the virtuous negotiation of the challenges posed by the need to transform the political order for its own sake. Or, putting that another way, those who led the movement believed that those who engaged in the often dangerous, ferocious, and demanding campaigns for civil rights must immediately benefit from that participation themselves, not in a material or even in a political sense, but in the sense of actually being able to lead a good life in the here-and-now, despite the difficulties posed both by racial injustice itself and by the need coercively to respond to that injustice. The campaigns had to be conducted, therefore, in a way that would politically empower African Americans in the long term but could also uplift their personal experiences, and the experiences of their allies, before the fight was won. As Moses explained, this meant for all participants that "we are not only involved in a political struggle; we're also involved in a more personal struggle, that is, within ourselves."[57]

[54] Niebuhr also made a similar argument. See *Moral Man and Immoral Society*, 166–67.

[55] Herbert Storing, "The Case Against Civil Disobedience" in Goldwin, *Civil Disobedience*, 5–6.

[56] Andrew Sabl, "Looking Forward to Justice: Rawlsian Civil Disobedience and its Non-Rawlsian Lessons," *Journal of Political Philosophy* 9 (2001): 315.

[57] Moses, "Address to S.N.C.C."

This commitment to providing an experience of virtuous action in the struggle for civil rights occasionally took on Gandhian proportions of spiritual uplift. King's rhetoric of *agape*, of redemptive suffering, and of the possibility of reaching personal salvation through love of one's enemies certainly soared to those heights.[58] But the justification for nonviolence did not generally take such a dramatically religious or idealized form.[59] Much more frequently, the virtuous experiences that participants were said to enjoy in nonviolent direct action were those more frequently associated with participation in struggles for democracy: those of solidarity, courage, consideration, and good judgment.[60] As James Farmer put it, joining a march or a demonstration or a Freedom Ride allowed "individual apprehensions" to be transformed by "collective determination."[61]

The commitment to fostering such virtues amongst all of the participants in the movement led directly to the movement's astonishingly strong dedication to an egalitarian and inclusive understanding of the struggle itself. Unlike the Depression-Era CIO, which approached its direct-action campaigns as almost military-like exercises, complete with rigid discipline and top-down control, there was nothing elitist or exclusive about the politics of sit-ins, mass demonstrations, or Freedom Rides. Rather, each form of direct action was said to present opportunities for every interested citizen directly to engage in the process of political transformation in a way that would enable them to improve their personal strength and character through their experiences on the front lines of the battle for change.

The idea of providing a large number of citizen activists with the experience of "moral witness, sacrifice, commitment, and community" was thus of the very essence of direct action for civil rights. This was also an advantage that was widely noted, especially in the context of the 1950s and early 1960s, when apathy and disengagement were generally thought to characterize American politics.[62] Indeed, even commentators like Michael Walzer understood the concept's importance. "The students in Greensboro called

---

[58] On *agape*, see King, *Civil Rights and the Idea of Freedom*, 99–100, and Paul. F. Power, "Morphologies of Nonviolent Action," *Journal of Conflict Resolution* 12 (1968): 381–85.

[59] As Farmer explained, "the Machiavellian thrust of black church politics would make Democratic and Republican Party shenanigans look like a Boy Scout jamboree." Farmer, *Lay Bare the Heart*, 34.

[60] In her influential discussion of ideas of courage in the civil rights movement, Holloway Sparks suggests that this virtue belongs in *both* the struggle for democracy and in more stable democratic orders. See Holloway Sparks, "Dissident Citizenship: Democratic Theory, Political Courage, and Activist Women," *Hypatia* 12 (1997): 74–110. An alternative is George Kateb, *Patriotism, and Other Mistakes* (New Haven: Yale University Press, 2006), 169–95.

[61] Farmer, *Lay Bare the Heart*, 1.

[62] Calvert, *Democracy from the Heart*, 69.

their demonstration a passive sit-down demand," he reported for *Dissent*, but "what was most impressive about it . . . was the number of students it involved in *activity*." "Each new sit-down, each day of picketing, each disciplined march, each mass meeting," Walzer continued, "was cause for pride and exhilaration" amongst those taking part because it helped them develop a clear sense of their own potential political importance and left them feeling dramatically uplifted as a result; each time an individual struggle began, those involved believed that their actions mattered for the future of democracy.[63]

The participatory element of the civil rights movement's approach was not just confined to the actual protests themselves. Both SNCC and CORE were committed to organizational structures that placed the rights and responsibilities of decision making directly with the participants themselves. Theirs was a vision that would soon become known as "participatory democracy," or what they called at the time "direct-action democracy from the bottom up."[64] There were still leaders and rules within CORE and SNCC, of course, but they saw their role as "channelling and structuring the energy for change that was releasing itself" amongst the participants in the struggle, rather than in directing from the top.[65]

Such participatory decision making was particularly important to Ella Baker, James Lawson, and Bob Moses, all of whom were committed to what they called "group-centered leadership," which would enable every single participant to play a full role in the decision making in the organization. On such an account, the task of the full-time staff of CORE and SNCC was to facilitate and organize already-existing struggles and grass-roots campaigns and occasionally to inspire citizens to take up the cause where they had not already done so. It was distinctly not to instruct participants in what they should be thinking and doing, not to provide the kind of dramatic, charismatic leadership that King symbolized, not even to guide them in their considerations. The crucial decisions had always to emerge directly from the people themselves.[66]

Despite the excitement about participatory politics within CORE and SNCC, it is vital to note that the civil rights movement was not intended to be a "prefigurative" democratic community where the ideals of the future democratic order were somehow "mimicked" or approximated in the

[63] Michael Walzer, "A Cup of Coffee and a Seat," *Dissent* 7 (1960): 116.

[64] Calvert, *Democracy from the Heart*, 70.

[65] James Laue, "The Changing Character of Negro Protest," *Annals of the American Academy of Political and Social Science* 357 (1965): 120. See, too, King, *Civil Rights and the Idea of Freedom*, 150.

[66] For a detailed account of this commitment, see Francesca Polletta, *Freedom Is an Endless Meeting: Democracy in American Social Movements* (Chicago: University of Chicago Press, 2002).

present, as Wini Breines has influentially argued.[67] At times, civil rights campaigners did speak of having provided participants with a glimpse of the future, of having enabled them to experience life as it would be in a racially just, inclusive democracy, or, as Staughton Lynd put it, of "building a brotherly way of life even in the jaws of the Leviathan."[68] The Freedom Schools, in particular, were often described in this way: as a "microcosm [in which] we begin to live a brotherhood that we dream some day will expand into society."[69] But generally the argument was not that it was necessary, or even desirable, precisely to model the behaviors and underlying virtues of the future democratic order during the period of struggle. Rather, it was vital to create virtuous and uplifting experiences that were suitable for a time of conflict.

The movements thus valued the virtues of democratic transformation not of normalized democratic life itself. Some of those virtues were, no doubt, the same; there would always be a call for intellectual insight, political judgment, and empathetic understanding, for example. But others would be different, or at least would be needed to different degrees. The call for courage, hope, steadfastness, and solidarity, to take just four examples, is far greater when one is building a democracy than when one is living quietly, at peace, within one.[70]

At its height, then, the civil rights movement offered an approach to democratic politics in the non-ideal present that emphasized the importance of transforming the American political order and the lives, experiences, and characters of those who were to be the agents of that change. That meant engaging with coercive power and using it, but doing so in a way that would both lay the foundations for a better order and draw out the best from those involved. That did not provide precise guidance as to how participants should behave at all times and in all places: there were constant disputes as to how the "Rules for Action" should be interpreted, as debates within the *CORE-lator* and the *Student Voice* demonstrate.[71] There were also frequent arguments as to how far nonviolence could be stretched. But it did provide a justification for the basic approach to political action and,

---

[67] See Wini Breines, *Community and Organization in the New Left, 1962–1968: The Great Refusal* (New York: Praeger, 1982). For a different critique of the idea of "prefiguration," see Polletta, *Freedom Is an Endless Meeting*, 205–33.

[68] Staughton Lynd, "The New Radicals and Participatory Democracy," *Dissent* 12 (1965): 333.

[69] Letter from "Dan," The Staughton Lynd Papers 4/14.

[70] For a subtle account of the sorts of political virtues shaped by civil rights campaigning, see Andrew Sabl, "Community Organizing as Tocquevillian Politics: The Art, Practices, and Ethos of Association," *American Journal of Political Science* 46 (2002): 1–19.

[71] See, for example, Gordon R. Carey, "New Freedom Task Force in the south," *CORE-lator* 99 (1963): 1–2.

perhaps more importantly, it appeared to capture the feelings, enthusiasms, fears, and opportunities that participants in the campaign experienced. "Not one of the men and women who shared the Freedom Ride could ever be the same," James Farmer thus explained. "Nothing would ever again be routine. . . . A Promethean spark had been infused into the soul of each of us. The younger ones had left a little of their youth in the prison cells" but "the older were surely younger now, more enthralled with freedom, imbued with its quest."[72]

Black Power and the Return to Pluralism

Underpinning all of the civil rights movement's actions, from the founding of CORE in wartime Chicago to the nationwide campaign of the mid-1960s, was the view that the democratic order of the United States could only be transformed by the consistent application of nonviolent direct action targeting both individual instances of racial injustice—such as segregated transport and educational and recreational facilities—and elite and public opinion at large. By 1964 an enormous amount had been achieved, culminating in the Civil Rights Act of that year, and the legacy of the movement appeared established forever.

Yet in the same year, many influential players in the movement began for the first time to doubt the efficacy of the strategy that CORE, SNCC, and the SCLC had pursued. These doubts were first brought to the surface when the Democratic Party's annual convention of 1964 chose to seat delegates from the official Democratic Party of Mississippi rather than from the Mississippi Freedom Democratic Party, despite the fact that the former had been chosen in elections that illegally excluded African Americans.[73] Those concerns were exacerbated still further when protesters across the South began to be more ferociously repressed both by state officials and civilian militias than they had been in the late 1950s and early 1960s. In the face of an explosion of violence in 1965, even the passage of the Voting Rights Act was not enough to detract attention from the deaths of campaigners like Jimmy Lee Jackson and James Rebb in Selma, Alabama. As Greg Calvert recalls, the "faith that held the civil rights movement together from the sit-ins of 1960 to the Democratic Party Convention of 1964 was that somehow politics and morality could be brought back together through non-violence and grassroots organizing," but by 1965 that faith had been shaken to its

---

[72] Farmer, *Lay Bare the Heart*, 30.
[73] Editorial, "Mississippi Democrats," *New Republic*, September 5, 1964, 4.

core.[74] As James Farmer so evocatively put it, "we are learning that freedom will not be now."[75]

The anxieties crossed all barriers within the movement.[76] But they were felt especially keenly in CORE and SNCC, reliant as they were on the youngest and most enthusiastic of campaigners. SNCC, in particular, fell into almost constant emergency session in 1964 and 1965, with Jim Forman insisting that "the nature of SNCC has to change and we have to realize this."[77] Such rethinking brought with it a new set of issues, a new collection of answers, and a new generation of leaders. The years between 1964 and 1967 thus saw the rapid rise to prominence of more radical voices, including Stokely Carmichael, who captured the chairmanship of SNCC in 1966, Carmichael confidant and dazzling rhetorician H. Rap Brown, and the new head of CORE, Floyd McKissick. These years also witnessed the withdrawal of other previously prominent figures, including some like Bob Moses and Jim Peck who had been with CORE and SNCC since the very beginning, the ideological radicalization of others, including Jim Forman and James Farmer, and a further fracturing of the alliance with King's more cautious SCLC.[78]

As the reconsideration began it was not immediately clear what the search for a new direction would involve. Initially, it appeared that it might involve a switch in focus from the civil rights of African Americans in the South to the socio-economic destitution faced by those in cities in the North, a constituency previously courted almost exclusively by Malcolm X and the Nation of Islam. James Farmer's personal correspondence was more concerned with the economic standing of African Americans than with any other issue in the mid-1960s.[79] Even King, who was never entirely comfortable outside his southern Christian base, attempted to respond to the issue by moving into a run-down apartment in Chicago in 1966 to draw national attention to conditions in the urban ghetto.[80] For some in the movement the potential switch to a concentration on economic rather than social and democratic exclusion opened up a host of exciting new possibilities. Chief amongst them was the possibility of building a new interracial coalition of

---

[74] Calvert, *Democracy from the Heart*, 86.

[75] Farmer, *Freedom—When?*, x.

[76] See Arnold Aronson, Memo 45 to Leadership Conference on Civil Rights, The CORE Papers 5/25/1, Wisconsin State Historical Society, Madison, Wisconsin.

[77] James Forman, S.N.C.C. Executive Committee Meeting, 1965, The CORE Papers. See, too, Staughton Lynd, "S.N.C.C.: Beginning of an Ideology," *Activist* 5 (1965): 12.

[78] See the extended discussion in Carson, *In Struggle*, 215–29.

[79] See the CORE Papers 1/5/1–5, and Marvin Rich, "The Congress of Racial Quality and its Strategy," *Annals of the American Academy of Political and Social Science* 357 (1965): 113–18.

[80] See Peter Ling, *Martin Luther King, Jr.* (London: Routledge, 2002), 208–41.

the poor. Such a "labor coalition," Casey Hayden and Staughton Lynd argued, could even generate a third political party to challenge both Democrats and Republicans on the model of previous generations, thus transforming the civil rights movement from a single-issue, direct-action movement to a force capable of challenging for control of the political mainstream.[81]

This interracial political response to the disillusionment of the mid-1960s was not shared by all, however. Most of the new generation of black leaders took an almost entirely opposite tack. Indeed, the new leadership of Carmichael, Brown, and McKissick was chiefly characterized by their vigorous attack on the interracial methods and the integrationist expectations of the earlier years. The apparent failures of the movement were thus almost entirely blamed on the movement's reliance on untrustworthy allies within the white establishment and within the white community at large. "Can whites, particularly liberal whites, condemn themselves?" Carmichael asked. "[A]re they capable of the shame which might become a revolutionary emotion?"[82] His answer, of course, was that they were not. The life-experiences of blacks and whites across the United States, both in the South and in the urban North, were so different as to make cross-racial understanding, let alone political sympathy, all but impossible.

The result was straightforward. From now on, Carmichael continued, African Americans "are just going to work, in the way *we* see fit, and on goals *we* define."[83] The demand was for a movement that was racially pure, that focused on the immediate needs of African Americans, and that did not seek advice or support from a white community that had proved to be incapable of grasping the political challenge it had laid down for well over a decade.[84]

Within the movement, of course, this marked a dramatic practical and philosophical break. Practically, it entailed the withdrawal or expulsion of whites such as Jim Peck and Casey Hayden, many of whom had been central to the movement's initial development. By 1968 Farmer could thus openly ask whether "white liberals" are "obsolete in the black struggle?" and both CORE and SNCC had become effectively all-black organizations.[85]

---

[81] See Casey Hayden, "Notes on Organizing Poor Southern Whites," *ERAP Newsletter*, August 27, 1965, 11; Lynd, "New Radicals," 332; Paul Feldman, "The Pathos of Black Power," *Dissent* 14 (1967): 72.

[82] Stokely Carmichael, *Power and Racism* (Nashville: Southern Student Organising Committee, 1966), 9.

[83] Ibid.

[84] For a detailed overview, see Floyd D. Barbour, ed., *The Black Power Revolt* (New York: Porter Sargent, 1968).

[85] See "Underdogs and Upperdogs," the James Peck Papers, Wisconsin State Historical Society, Madison, Wisconsin; James Farmer, "Are White Liberals Obsolete in the Black Struggle?," the Pamphlet Collection 84/345, Wisconsin State Historical Society, Madison, Wisconsin.

Philosophically, it required an even more profound change. While the movement had never been dedicated to the idea that the United States was a "nearly just" interracial political order, as Myrdal and his admirers had wished, it had been committed to an integrationist political future, one that focused on the possibility of creating an egalitarian, inclusive, democratic politics capable of identifying or generating a cross-race common good. From the mid-1960s onward, both CORE and SNCC explicitly rejected such an ideal, at least in the short-to-medium term. Now they were convinced that justice and democracy demanded not efforts to create a political mechanism that concentrated on the "common ground" but action that could bring attention to the particular needs of a particular group: African Americans.

Although this position was new to the civil rights movement, it marked a return to the philosophical arguments of an earlier generation in the American radical tradition, and especially to those of the Depression Era. As the sympathetic commentators Jane and Wilson Record noted in 1965, "in the 1930s, liberals gravitated toward pluralism, which sees the public interest best served in urban industrial society not by the national collective will of ethical men but by the competition and compromise of group interests," and it was essentially that view that underpinned Carmichael, Brown, and McKissick's reformulation of the democratic theory of civil rights. As the Records put it, it was thus this "pluralism"—with its emphasis on the impossibility of divining a "common good" in a society that even approximately resembled the present order—that enabled "Negro protest" to move from being "interracial" to "exclusively Negro."[86]

Just as in the 1930s, this move to a more explicit pluralism was accompanied by the contention that politics in the United States depended far more on coercive power than on the balance of opinion. The implications of the new position, Stokely Carmichael explained, was that African Americans will have "to work for power" because "this country does not function by morality, love, and non-violence, but by power."[87] Even former moderates like James Farmer concurred, arguing that the disappointments of the early to mid-1960s had demonstrated once and for all that in American politics

---

[86] Jane Record and Wilson Record, "Ideological Forces and the Negro Protest," *Annals of the American Academy of Political and Social Science* 357 (1965): 93–94. The relationship of "black power" to Depression-Era Pluralism was also noted, if far more critically, by Hannah Arendt. See her "On Violence," in Arendt, *Crises of the Republic* (New York: Harcourt, Brace, and Co., 1972), esp. 121.

[87] Carmichael, *Power and Racism*, 1.

"what men feel and believe matters much less than what, under various kinds of external pressures, they can be made to *do*."[88]

To those who knew their history of political thought this might have appeared to be a wholesale return to the arguments of the younger Reinhold Niebuhr, who had contended, especially with regard to racial exclusion, that protest "will hardly result in justice as long as the disproportion of power remains."[89] In fact, though, the argument went even further than Niebuhr's had. For whilst the pluralists of the 1930s had always stopped short of endorsing violent rebellion, many of the new generation of civil rights campaigners were not so shy, with the dispute between nonviolence and what was called "self-defense" becoming one of the most vociferous within the movement. "The [white] man does not want any more Harlems, Watts, Newarks, Detroits," Jim Forman ominously asserted, referring to the race riots of 1965. But he better get ready because "he ain't seen nothing yet!"[90] "For too many years, black Americans marched and had their heads broken and got shot," Stokely Carmichael added, but "[w]e cannot be expected any longer to march and have our heads broken in order to say to whites; come on, you're nice guys. For you are not nice guys. We have found you out."[91]

By the late 1960s, Stokely Carmichael, James Forman, Floyd McKissick, and others had reshaped the democratic theory and practice of the civil rights movement in a way that embraced the pluralism and coerciveness of the 1930s, reworked it for the cause of racial justice, and injected into it a concern for the development of a virtuous life during struggle. "Black power," Carmichael explained, "does not mean merely putting black faces into office"; it means developing the power "of a community" and allowing it to "emanate from there."[92]

Both this pluralism and the more open coerciveness that accompanied it were, of course, captured best in that slogan first coined by a relatively obscure activist, Willie Ricks: "black power." The slogan was popularized by Carmichael in June of 1966 on a march in memory of the assassinated activist James Meredith and it rapidly became synonymous with the new movement as a whole.[93] The significance of "black power as a slogan," Carmichael explained, was essentially straightforward. It meant that "for once black

---

[88] Farmer, *Freedom—When?*, 17.

[89] Niebuhr, *Moral Man and Immoral Society*, xv.

[90] Forman, *United States, 1967*, 3.

[91] Carmichael, *Power and Racism*, 1.

[92] Ibid., 3.

[93] On the background of the slogan, see Carson, *In Struggle*, 215–26.

people are going to use the words they want to use—not just the words whites want to hear."[94]

"Black power" was more than a slogan and it was also more than an abstract social and political philosophy. It also entailed a radical reorganization of the structure and political methods of both SNCC and CORE. Previously SNCC and CORE had stood somewhere in the middle ground between the peaceable, creed-centered politics of the postwar years and the disruptive adversarialism of the Depression Era. Now, they moved squarely back to the older position. Most importantly, "black power" led to the rejection of the open, discursive, and participatory structure of old. For whereas the emphasis of the movement in the early 1960s had been on bringing about a relatively rapid democratic transformation in the United States and doing so in a way that enriched the lives of those involved in the struggle, the emphasis from 1965 onwards was on effective challenges to ingrained racial injustice, where "power" was all and persuasion counted for naught. What this new agenda required, therefore, was not the inclusive decision making of old, but a form of central control and effective direction. Just as the movement returned to the pluralist, coercive political philosophy of the 1930s, then, it also returned to the military-style discipline that had structured the politics of the CIO in the Depression Era.[95] All of this generated a sort of plebiscitary rather than participatory democracy within SNCC and CORE, a form that celebrated powerful leadership capable of imposing unity and discipline on an unruly movement.[96]

This did not mean, however, that the movement ceased to be interested in enhancing the "virtuous" experience of those involved in the struggle. Indeed, if anything, that interest increased in the late 1960s. The difference now, however, was that attention was even more clearly focused on the virtues of struggle against domination than it was on the virtues of democratic life. In this regard, Carmichael, Forman, Brown, and McKissick were enrapt by arguments emerging from the anticolonial campaigns in Africa, especially as described by Frantz Fanon in *The Wretched of the Earth*. Fanon's book first appeared in the United States in 1965, just as the movement began its rebirth. It explained how violent campaigns against colonial forces across the continent were not only appropriate responses to centuries of

[94] Carmichael, *Power and Reason*, 1.

[95] It is important to note that it was not strategic rethinking that led to ideological change but ideological change that led to strategic rethinking. Contrast my argument here with Polletta, *Freedom Is an Endless Meeting*, 55–115. See, too, Akinyele O. Umoja, "The Ballot and the Buller: A Comparative Analysis of Armed Resistance in the Civil Rights Movement," *Journal of Black Studies* 29 (1999): 558–78.

[96] See King, *Civil Rights and the Idea of Freedom*, 152.

colonization but also provided manifold opportunities for the personal development of the participants. Insurrection, rebellion, and revolution, he argued, had all enabled individual Africans to transform themselves from "spectators crushed with their inessentiality" into "privileged actors," enabling "the "thing" that has been colonized" to "become man during the same process by which it frees itself."[97]

No single idea excited more attention in SNCC and CORE in the late 1960s. Here was a promise of an improved life for participants, even in the face of a ferocious struggle against tremendous odds. For the new generation of SNCC and CORE leaders, this was precisely the combination that was desired. It offered a virtuous circle whereby preparation for coercive struggle generated an enriched spirit within the black community that in turn enabled the struggle to be executed all the more effectively.[98] The "psychological equality" that comes from an all-black, coercive engagement with the bases of white power, Carmichael outlined, "is the reason why SNCC today believes that blacks must organize in the black community." "Only black people can convey the revolutionary idea that black people are able to do things themselves," he continued. "Only they can help create in the community an aroused and continuing black consciousness that will provide the basis for political strength."[99]

All of this seemed extraordinary to the remaining advocates of the original approach to civil rights protest, and especially to those that remembered the anti-authoritarian theorizing of the immediate postwar years. Indeed, many of these former activists simply could not understand the new era. Jim Peck, whose career had started in the Fellowship of Reconciliation back in the 1940s, insisted that "black people must realize that in adopting the enemy's tactics of racism and violence, they will become just like the enemy. The ideals of brotherhood and equality are inevitably lost in the process."[100]

Old allies from outside the movement similarly turned away. Few were more critical than the commentators of *Dissent*, who had welcomed the movement so warmly back in 1960, believing it to be the perfect instantiation of their approach to democratic change, an approach grounded, of course, in moral appeals to the values of the American creed. Now, of course, they could no longer believe their own myth. By the beginning of the 1970s, *Dissent* was warning of "black militants" launching an "assault [on] democratic institutions" and encouraging the Left to take its stand

---

[97] Frantz Fanon, *The Wretched of the Earth* (London: Penguin, 2001 [1965]), 28.
[98] Forman, *United States, 1967*, 8.
[99] Carmichael, *Power and Racism*, 8.
[100] Peck, "Underdog and Upperdog," 98.

against their separatist demands.[101] Hannah Arendt, who had long been wary of the "sectionalism" of the civil rights movement, went further still, dismissing the entire "black power" movement, with more than a hint of racism herself, as both "silly and outrageous."[102]

Black Power and the American Radical Tradition

In many ways, this critical response was warranted. Some of the arguments for "black power" were ill-considered philosophically and none of the movement's leaders appear to have given much thought to the ways in which an openly coercive, even violent, struggle against racial injustice could actually be won in the United States, given the effective monopoly of the instruments of physical power held by both the federal and state governments. Most importantly, these leaders also seem to have overlooked that their pluralist, separatist aspirations did not reflect the will of the black community. They were shocked almost into submission when membership in and support of CORE and SNCC amongst African Americans themselves dwindled at the very moment that they claimed to speak more directly for the people.[103] As Clayborne Carson argues, "talk about black power" ironically "left SNCC militants more powerless than ever."[104]

Whatever the difficulties, however, there is some cause for pause here. The advocates of "black power" actually had more in common with both their predecessors in the civil rights movement and in the American radical tradition at large than is generally accepted. Contrary to the ever repeated orthodoxy that insists that the civil rights movement moved in a volte-face from "peaceful confrontation" conducted in the terms of the American creed to a "black nationalism" that rejected it, the activists for civil rights had never argued that the United States possessed a "nearly just" political order, within which a continuous appeal to conscience or to the values of the creed could effectively transform the system and provide free, fair, and open democratic opportunities for all.[105] Rather, they believed, just as most of their predecessors earlier in the twentieth century had, that a new democratic order would have to be wrought from the material of the non-

---

[101] Kurtz, "Misuses of Civil Disobedience," 66.

[102] Arendt, "On Violence," 121.

[103] See Cornel West, "The Paradox of Afro-American Rebellion," *Social Text* 9 (1984): 44–58.

[104] Carson, *In Struggle*, 257. See, too, the indictment of the "black power" movement in West, "Paradox of Afro-American Rebellion," 44–58.

[105] James Morone, *The Democratic Wish: Popular Participation and the Limits of American Government* (New Haven: Yale University Press, 1998), 198.

ideal present. Some of that material was promising—including the fact the some Americans upheld the key tenets of the so-called American creed—but some of it was not, not least the racism entrenched at almost all levels of American society.

What really changed in 1964, then, were the judgments about the extent of the challenge and the time that it would possibly take to meet it.[106] The early civil rights movement did not believe that democratic transformation was either immanent or imminent—as their liberal supporters claimed to believe—but they did generally believe that something approximating a fair democratic order could be achieved in their lifetime, and that the struggle should be conducted with that in mind. After the disappointments of 1964 and 1965, though, that optimism disappeared. Now, most in SNCC and CORE, and even many in the SCLC, held that the struggle was going to be much more protracted, that allies in the establishment could not be trusted, and that even white members of the civil rights organizations themselves could not understand the struggle of their black counterparts. It was in response to that judgment that the coerciveness of CORE and SNCC's politics became more explicit, that hope for realizing the benefits of a cross-racial American creed in the near future dropped away, and that the account of the virtues necessary to meet the needs of the movement shifted accordingly.

Some continuity remained, however, even at the very end of the 1960s. For all his provocative talk of "black power," even the much reviled Stokely Carmichael always also hoped that a "community of love" could be built one day, where all citizens, black and white, could enjoy the same rights and be included in the same processes of "self-determination."[107] As the 1960s ended, James Farmer similarly insisted on the need to see the struggle for "black power" in these terms. "If black people can bring into the nation's life the new ingredient of popular participation, the wielding of levers of real decision-making and power by the hitherto excluded, they will have transformed America," he argued. "They will have made a significant contribution to the extension and perfection of democracy—as significant as the revolution of labor through trade unions and the revolution of females through women's suffrage."[108]

This was a call for action that resonated across the ages and that would continue to find supporters, even in the face of the sometimes disastrous strategic decisions of CORE and SNCC in the late 1960s. As one such group

---

[106] On which see Donald Von Eschen, Jermoe Kirk, and Maurice Pinard, "The Disintegration of the Negro Non-Violent Movement," *Journal of Peace Research* 6 (1969): 215–34.

[107] Carmichael, *Power and Racism*, 6.

[108] Farmer, "Civil Disobedience and Beyond," 25.

of allies explained, "[w]e doubt critics would find themselves so upset if SNCC sought to accept the major premises of American life" but it is precisely "because it is trying to bring about a fundamental rearrangement of power in America, that they shrink in horror."[109] The question of how a truly inclusive and fully just democracy could really be built remained unanswered.

---

[109] Editorial, "SDS Statement on S.N.C.C.," *New Left Notes* 1 (1966): 2.

CHAPTER SIX

"We Are Beginning to Move Again"

On March 6, 1970, almost exactly ten years after the Greensboro sit-in, three young political activists—Ted Gold, Diana Oughton, and Terry Robbins—blew themselves up in a townhouse in New York's Greenwich Village whilst preparing an explosive device for a terror campaign that they were about to unleash on an unexpecting United States. The three were members of the Weather Underground, a group of radicals named after a line in a song by Bob Dylan that had broken away from the largest American radical student organization of the twentieth century, Students for a Democratic Society (SDS), just a few months earlier. It was not the only time those with connections to SDS, and the so-called New Left of which it was a part, would be involved in deadly incidents that year. Just two months later four other young Americans were killed. This time they were students gunned down at Kent State University, Ohio, as the National Guard dispersed a protest against university-sponsored recruitment for the Vietnam War.[1] These deaths, coming as they did shortly after the assassination of Martin Luther King Jr., the rise of the Black Power movement, and the intensification of the Vietnam War, marked the end of the optimism of the earlier 1960s and ushered in a period of despair for radical politics in the United States.

To many looking on, there was a deep irony that SDS and the New Left movement ended in this way. It had been celebrated only a few years previously for offering a new conception of democratic politics. Just like the early civil rights movement, it was said to have abandoned the adversarialism associated with radicalism in the Depression years, advancing a politics grounded in an inclusive idea of the common good, underpinned by structures of considerate, democratic participation, and even by a commitment to an ideal of deliberation.[2] Of all the American movements to end in violence and despair, then, many observers found it shocking that it was this one, whose activists were renowned for their commitment to conflict

---

[1] For a full account, see Kirkpatrick Sale, *SDS* (New York: Vintage, 1974), 600–658.

[2] For an introduction to the era, see Todd Gitlin, *The Sixties: Years of Hope, Days of Rage* (New York: Bantam, 1987).

resolution and were drawn from the generation that joined with the Beatles in claiming that "all you need is love."

The surprise is lessened when the New Left is placed within the American radical democratic tradition, of course. As this book has demonstrated throughout, radical democratic movements had long been convinced of the necessity of a dual dedication. They were committed, that is, both to an ideal of democratic life that celebrated openness, inclusivity, and deliberation, and to a political strategy that recognized the necessity of political struggle in the distinctly non-ideal present. SDS and the New Left clearly acted within the established patterns of this tradition. They were even so described by Saul Alinsky, who noted that the New Left's "young protagonists [were] at one time reminiscent of the idealistic early young Christians"— heavily moralized, obsessed with fairness and inclusiveness, focused on obtaining a utopian "heaven on earth"—yet they were also uncompromising critics of the prevailing order who would not yield to prevailing opinion or seek allies in the political mainstream. They were willing to alienate, even bully, large sections of society, and often to be found crying, "[b]urn the system down!"[3] The difference between ideal vision and non-ideal political strategy was as stark as it had ever been.

SDS and the New Left did, however, contribute two new characteristics of their own to that tradition's development. First, they helped reshape the ideal of democracy itself by offering an understanding often dubbed "participatory democracy" that reinvigorated a way of thinking that had lain effectively moribund at least since John Dewey's work of the 1920s. SDS and the New Left thus aspired to create a democratic order that would involve a deep commitment to citizen participation, to the use of reason in political decision making, and to the development of a spirit of the common good. Second, they further emphasized the possibility that the struggle for democratic reform could transform the immediate lives of those who were involved in it, even if the ultimate democratic prize was always expected to elude them. The thinkers and agitators associated with SDS and other New Left organizations therefore insisted that citizens could change their own lives through the campaign for a better, more inclusive democratic future. It was these contributions for which the New Left should be remembered, as well as for the fact that it was to be effectively the last iteration of the twentieth century's radical democratic tradition.

[3] Saul D. Alinsky, *Rules for Radicals: A Pragmatic Primer for Realistic Radicals* (New York: Vintage, 1971), xiii. Alinsky's own movement shared some similarities with the New Left and SDS but did not endorse their broader transformative vision. SDS activists used this difference to describe Alinsky as "downright reactionary." For details of this rivalry, see Harvery Molotch, "Radicals in Urban Politics," *Contemporary Sociology* 4 (1974): 434–35.

The Origins of the New Left

The New Left was born out of a reaction against the moderation, skepticism, and pessimism of the immediate postwar generation. To the theorists of the late 1940s and early 1950s, the tasks facing American radicals were, first, to protect American freedom, resisting the threats of both totalitarianism abroad and excessive adversarialism at home, and, second, to bring about slow and incremental reform in American society by drawing on the widely shared values of the American creed. To a new generation, those born during the war or immediately after it, however, this politics appeared far less desirable. It seemed, in particular, far too accepting of materialist affluence, including spiritual apathy, and far too easily persuaded by an obsessive and doctrinal anti-Communism that effectively served the interests of the Right. To the thinkers who would become the inspirations of the New Left, then, the 1950s were characterized not by the dominance of the American creed but by the peculiar combination of the apparently consensual centrism of Dwight Eisenhower's presidency and the closed conformity enforced by the antiradicalism of Senator Joe McCarthy and the red-baiting House of Un-American Activities Committee. It was a time when American culture was captured by a combination of consensus and repression.[4]

Seen from the perspective of later decades, of course, the 1950s were the uneasy calm before a storm. Broader American culture at the time certainly suggested that it was so. The cold solitude in the paintings of Andrew Wyeth and Edward Hopper challenged viewers to ask what forces really lay behind the quietude of the American scenes that they depicted so eerily: satisfaction or anxiety?[5] A host of plays and films, including most famously Arthur Miller's *View from the Bridge* and Nicholas Ray's *Rebel without a Cause*, both of 1955, posed similar questions by depicting rage effectively repressed by social expectations but constantly bubbling to the surface.[6] Thomas Pynchon's haunting short-story "Entropy" perhaps captured it best of all, telling of a fantastical moment when the failure of the temperature to change topples the United States into an age of emptiness, characterized by "the final absence of all motion."[7]

[4] See the discussion in chapter 4, above.

[5] See Ralph Bogardus and Fred Schroeder, "Andrew Wyeth and the Transcendental Tradition," *American Quarterly* 17 (1965): 559–67, and J. A. Ward, *Unspeakable Silences: The Realism of James Agee, Walker Evans, and Edward Hopper* (Baton Rouge: Louisiana State University Press, 1985).

[6] See J. David Scolum, *Rebel Without a Cause: Approaches to a Maverick Masterwork* (Albany: State University of New York Press, 2005); Arthur Miller, *A View from the Bridge* (New York: Viking, 1955); Delmore Schwartz, "Films," *New Republic*, April 25, 1955, 22.

[7] See Thomas Pynchon, "Entropy," in Pynchon, *Slow Learner* (London: Vintage, 2000 [1960]), 98.

But to young and impatient white radicals at the decade's close, it was hard to see from what the political opportunities for dramatic change were going to arise. To them, the immediate postwar United States appeared to be "beyond ideology" and "after utopia," as Daniel Bell and Judith Shklar famously described it—that is, in a period when the vaulting political ambitions of the past appeared consigned to history, dismissed as dangerous illusions and precursors of totalitarianism.[8] Even the CIO had drifted away from the radicalism of the past, reuniting with the AFL and decisively turning its back on the adversarialism of its founding.[9] What stirrings there were in the 1950s emanated from the fringes of the American political scene. The LID, in particular, remained a meeting point for disaffected radicals. Although the League's leadership steered well clear of class conflict and anything that could be tainted with the accusations of Communism in the postwar period, it continued to offer resources to less formal groupings of more discontented radicals, including many associated with CORE and SNCC. It was unsurprising, therefore, that it was out of the League that the first real organization of the New Left emerged:[10] the Student League for Industrial Democracy (SLID), also tellingly known as the John Dewey Discussion Club.

In 1960 SLID became Students for a Democratic Society, almost always known simply as SDS. Provided with generous funding from its parent organization, SDS opened a central office in New York, and was directed by Al Haber, who employed a young Masters student, Tom Hayden, as a roving organizer to travel across the country making connections with student networks and establishing new ones where none existed. By the mid-1960s, SDS had chapters in almost all of the major universities, enjoyed a membership of over 25,000, and published a weekly journal *New Left Notes*, which although written almost entirely by students rivaled more established outlets such as *Dissent* and the *New Republic* as the major voice of American radicalism.[11]

Haber and Hayden were precocious political talents, both of whom shared an interest in the emergent critique of the idea of the American creed so popular amongst the elders of the LID at that time. That critique

---

[8] See Daniel Bell, *The End of Ideology: On the Exhaustion of Political Ideas in the Fifties* (Cambridge, Mass.: Harvard University Press, 1960), and Judith Shklar, *After Utopia: The Decline of Political Faith* (Princeton: Princeton University Press, 1957).

[9] See Arthur J. Goldberg, *AFL-CIO Labor United* (New York: McGraw-Hill, 1957).

[10] See Tom Good, "Ideology and SDS," *New Left Notes* 1, no. 29 (1966): 5.

[11] For a thorough overview, see Sale, *SDS*. For a more skeptical take, see Allen Smith, "Present at the Creation and Other Myths: The Port Huron Statement and the Origins of the New Left," *Peace and Change* 25 (2000): 339–62.

was initiated by the activists in CORE and SNCC, as demonstrated in the last chapter, but it also found increasing intellectual respectability in the mainstream through the work of the Berkeley political theorist Sheldon Wolin and, even more notably, the Columbia sociologist C. Wright Mills. Wolin and Mills captured the attention of this new, increasingly skeptical generation by dismissing the prevailing sense that the cause of a crusading American radicalism had come to a close and been replaced by a stable, prosperous, and open political order, and by an incremental approach to political change grounded essentially in moral suasion and appeals to the American creed.

Mills insisted that all of this talk of the American creed and the related "end-of-ideology perspective" was disingenuous. Indeed, it was itself an ideology, Mills insisted, just "one supportive of American institutions."[12] "It is an ideology of political complacency," a simple way "for many writers to acquiesce in or to justify the *status quo*."[13] The American creed was itself at best an "ambiguous ideal" that, insofar as it existed at all, consisted largely "in the rhetoric of expectation," Mills argued. Its values were rarely either substantiated in institutional reality or even felt deeply in the hearts of many American citizens. In "substance and in practice" the United States, then, "is very often non-democratic, and in many institutional arenas it is quite clearly so."[14]

Mills's most celebrated contribution to this argument was, of course, his masterpiece *The Power Elite*, of 1956, which set out to demonstrate that the widespread view that American government was permeable and responsive to popular opinion was mistaken, and to show instead that the primary decisions that shaped American lives were, in fact, made by a small and self-perpetuating elite.[15] It was the task of a "New Left," Mills thus concluded, to rekindle the enthusiasm of previous generations for radical reform and to ensure that radicals in America were no longer rendered "powerless, distracted, and confused" by the illusions of the "American creed."[16]

---

[12] Tom Hayden, *Radical Nomad: C. Wright Mills and his Times* (Boulder: Paradigm, 2006), 177. *Radical Nomad* was Hayden's master's thesis, completed in 1961 shortly after he drafted *The Port Huron Statement*. For commentary, see David M. Potter, "The End of Ideology," *New Republic*, May 23, 1960, 17–18.

[13] C. Wright Mills, "A Letter to the New Left," in Irving Horowitz, ed., *Power, Politics, and People: The Collected Essays of C. Wright Mills* (New York: Ballantine, 1964 [1960]), 251.

[14] C. Wright Mills, *The Sociological Imagination* (Oxford: Oxford University Press, 1959), 188.

[15] C. Wright Mills, *The Power Elite* (New York: Oxford University Press, 1956). See, too, Daniel Bell, "The Power Elite Reconsidered," *American Journal of Sociology* 64 (1958): 238–50, and J. L. Simich and Rick Tilman, "Radicalism vs. Liberalism: C Wright Mills' Critique of John Dewey's Ideas," *American Journal of Economics and Sociology* 37 (1978): 413–30.

[16] Mills, quoted in Hayden, *Radical Nomad*, 77.

In their efforts to meet the challenge of building such a "New Left," Haber and Hayden were swiftly joined by a small group of extraordinarily able, eager, young, and largely white male activists, including Greg Calvert, Todd Gitlin, and James Miller, many of whom had first engaged in political action through the early civil rights campaigns of CORE and SNCC. Together, they helped SDS set about establishing its own ideological identity and its own political program. Their initial efforts came to a head at a meeting held—appropriately enough—at an abandoned CIO training camp in Port Huron, Michigan, in February 1962. There Tom Hayden drafted a manifesto for an organization he hoped would capture the spirit of an age and shape radical democratic argument for at least the next decade. The document that emerged, known thereafter as *The Port Huron Statement*, did just that.

Participatory Democracy

As Haber and Hayden's debt to Mills would suggest, the primary subject of the *Port Huron Statement* concerned the parlous state of American democracy in the middle of the twentieth century and the prospects for its improvement. Democracy, Al Haber argued, borrowing freely from SNCC literature as he did so, was "a basically moral proposition that people should have the opportunity to participate in shaping the decisions and the conditions of economic, political, and cultural existence which affect their lives and destinies" and the United States, of course, was said currently to fall far short of that ideal.[17] As the *Statement* put it, "the American political system is not the democratic model of which its glorifiers speak. In actuality it frustrates democracy by confusing the individual citizen, paralyzing policy discussion, and consolidating the irresponsible power of military and business interests."[18]

The task of SDS, and the generation that it represented, was to put that right. "We seek the establishment of a democracy of individual participation governed by two central aims," the *Statement* explained, "that the individual share in those decisions determining the quality and direction of his life; that society be organized to encourage independence in men and provide the media for their common participation."[19] It was an ideal that came to be known as "participatory democracy," a phrase that had been coined just two years before by the philosopher Arnold Kaufman.[20]

[17] Al Haber, "Radical Education Project," *New Left Notes* 1, no. 10 (1964): 2.

[18] *The Port Huron Statement* (New York: Thunder's Mouth, 2005 [1962]), 67.

[19] Ibid., 53.

[20] See Greg Calvert, *Democracy Is from the Heart: Spiritual Values, Decentralism, and Democratic Idealism in the Movement of the 1960s* (Eugene, Ore.: Communitas, 1991), 68.

This dedication to democratic transformation was far from new, of course, but the idea of "participatory democracy" did include elements that were crucially at odds with the theories that preceded it.[21] There was, in particular, no return to the Progressives' call for enhanced national control of social lives, or to their demands for an enhanced state backed up by an informed, unified national public, as formulated in SDS's statement. Quite to the contrary, whereas the generations of Herbert Croly and George Soule had struggled to build an ever larger government machine in the United States, SDS's chief target of attack was the growing power of the state and especially the excessive bureaucratization that had accompanied the creation of a new machinery of government in the Second World War. SDS thus railed against the "corporate state," the new "American Leviathan" that, they charged, was staffed with unaccountable "experts" who made decisions without directly consulting the people.[22]

Drawing on both Mills and Wolin, SDS activists at Port Huron thus insisted that for all the talk of pluralism and open political access in the United States, the enormous mechanisms of government in fact ensured that politics "still operates for and by a small group of powerful men who control the quality of the daily lives of millions of people, not only in America but around the world."[23] Political systems that "operate top-down are inadequate whatever their nature," *New Left Notes* later reported, because they always mask exclusions, illegitimately enhancing the power of some groups over others, and ensuring that the voices of minorities, of the dispossessed, the innovative, and the unpopular go unheeded in decision making.[24] Everywhere citizens look in such a political order, there "is organization; everywhere bureaucratization." As Wolin had so evocatively put it, Americans in such an age did not live in a real democracy, they lived within "the castles of Kafka."[25]

This rejection of big government did not, however, imply that SDS endorsed straightforward competitive and coercive social pluralism either. For although most in SDS shared concerns about the untrustworthiness of the overbearing state, such as those that had first emerged in Lippmann's and Niebuhr's pluralist critique of Progressivism, they raged against the general pessimism that had accompanied this perspective in the early

---

[21] Haber, "Radical Education Project," 2.

[22] Ibid.

[23] See Hayden, *Radical Nomad*, 104, 190–92. See, too, James Miller, *Democracy Is in the Streets: From Port Huron to the Siege of Chicago* (Cambridge, Mass.: Harvard University Press, 1987), 87.

[24] M. Goldfield, "What is a Radical Perspective?," *New Left Notes* 2, no. 5 (1967): 3.

[25] Sheldon Wolin, *Politics and Vision: Continuity and Vision in Western Political Thought* (Princeton: Princeton University Press, 1960), 354.

postwar years. Rather, they insisted wholeheartedly on the possibility of a democratic transformation and the construction of a new kind of politics based neither on adversarialism nor on the dominance of the state but on the direct and reasoned involvement of citizens in political decision making. As the *Statement* again put it, SDS rejected "the dominant conception" of the citizen that he is "a thing to be manipulated and that he is inherently incapable of directing his own affairs." Instead, they wished to build a democratic theory and practice that regarded each citizen "as infinitely precious and possessed of unfulfillled capacities for reason, freedom, and love."[26]

The *Statement* also insisted on the continual possibility of a democratically discovered sense of trans-American community. The overbearing state was to be rejected for its illegitimate exclusions, rather than because it was premised on the possibility of a singular "public."[27] A properly democratic politics, SDS activists insisted, had always to "be seen . . . as the art of collectively creating an acceptable pattern of social relations," a process whereby citizens would be brought "out of isolation and into community."[28]

In the self-understanding of SDS's leaders, therefore, the primary task of radical politics in 1960s America was to rekindle the democratic enthusiasm amongst the entire citizenry and to help construct new democratic mechanisms that would allow each and every citizen to play an active role in political life. Once you do that, Hayden and colleagues continued, you will see that "men have unrealized potential for self-cultivation, self-direction, self-understanding and creativity." Democratic renewal thus demanded that the social and political order of the United States be reconstructed so that those capacities be fully realized.[29] It required, in particular, that Americans "break down the administrative top-down apparatus," ensure that "political control would be decentralized," and create decision-making structures at all levels of political life that could "include all men and women for their inherent value."[30] The pessimists of the postwar years had always insisted that "men can't always be political heroes," C. Wright Mills once bemoaned. "But keep looking around you and why not search out the conditions of such heroism as men do and might display."[31]

This ideal was put into practice immediately within SDS itself. Just as at the level of the ideal, participatory democracy broke with state-centrism

---

[26] *Port Huron Statement*, 51.

[27] See Gitlin, *The Sixties*, 258.

[28] *Port Huron Statement*, 53. See, too, Tom Hayden, "The Politics of The Movement," *Dissent* 13 (1966): 75–87.

[29] *Port Huron Statement*, 52.

[30] Paul Booth, "Facing the American Leviathan," *New Left Notes* 1, no. 33 (1966): 8.

[31] Mills, "Letter to the New Left," 253.

and combative adversarialism, so when it came to the methods of political organization, SDS followed CORE and SNCC's lead in breaking from the prewar CIO-style organization of discipline, structure, order, and control. SDS thus emphasized the importance of involving all members in a process of internal decision making, a process that would be grounded not on authority or hierarchy but on "deliberativeness, honesty, reflection." SDS therefore not only asked young people to sign up to the ideal of participatory democracy for the long-term future of the United States, but they offered them a chance to work within an organization that featured many of the most stimulating and enjoyable elements of such a future in the here and now. As Greg Calvert argued at the time, it was "participatory democracy as an *organizational style*" as well as an abstract ideal that "appealed to the deep anti-authoritarianism of the new generation," making possible the opportunity to experience "the values of openness, honesty and community in human relationships which they so desperately desire."[32]

The organization's first major statement of practice, *Politics, the Individual and SDS*, published a year after *The Port Huron Statement*, explained the practical ramifications of the commitment. SDS was going to provide all of its members an actual opportunity to practice democracy in a whole new way; participatory democracy was to be both an idealized objective and a practiced democratic form.[33] This ensured that continual emphasis was placed on the value of democratic equality within the movement itself. SDS thus strove to "assume that everyone was equal in their potential understanding and contribution" and to ensure that all decision-making processes within the organization should, as far as possible, involve the active contribution of everyone who would be affected by the resulting decision.[34]

Such a commitment entailed that SDS had to go to considerable efforts to accommodate the differential styles and capacities of all of their members, helping them overcome any obstacles to effective communication.[35] Gender was of particular concern here, even though in later years many feminists would be severely critical of SDS's attitudes to women. Many in SDS were conscious that a loud, extroverted style of political argument often

---

[32] Greg Calvert, "Participatory Democracy, Collective Leadership and Political Responsibility," *New Left Notes* 2, no. 45 (1967): 1.

[33] See *Politics, the Individual and SDS*, in The SDS Papers, The Tamiment Institute Library, New York University, 2. See, too, Martin Oppenheimer, "Alienation or Participation: The Sociology of Participatory Democracy," *New Left Notes* 1, no. 45 (1966): 4.

[34] Wini Breines, *Community and Organization in the New Left: 1962–1968: The Great Refusal* (New York: Praeger, 1982), 57, and Haber, "Radical Education Project," 2.

[35] See Francesca Polletta, *Freedom Is an Endless Meeting: Democracy in American Social Movements* (Chicago: University of Chicago Press, 2002), 130–40, and Bob Rogers, "Referendum Democracy: A Proposal," *New Left Notes* 1, no. 29 (1966): 8–9.

associated with student movements might discourage the contributions of women. Various techniques of inclusion were suggested. Chairs were often arranged in a circle rather than in potentially intimidating rows and women were "invited and encouraged to write papers" before meetings, rather than to make speeches at them.[36] Race, too, emerged as a concern. Aware that membership of the organization was overwhelmingly white, SDS activists made considerable efforts to reach out to civil rights organizations that catered to a young radical audience, especially CORE and SNCC, in an effort to train its own workers in how to conduct effective race-blind decision making within the organization itself.[37]

Beyond these efforts at inclusion, anyone involved in decision making within SDS was expected to treat fellow members with the respect that their equal status demanded, which in effect meant pursuing common rather than individualistic or sectarian goals and doing so in ways that engendered a spirit of cooperation. Thus equality and inclusion were not enough. Rather, SDS should not be run like a normal adversarial democracy but as a community of "friends" pursuing a shared agenda. "Democracy becomes meaningful only in a non-manipulative context," SDS activist Miles Goldfield argued. It is by its nature the work of "persuaders" rather than "manipulators or coercers."[38] Debate and discussion in the movement, it was thus insisted, "should serve to clarify problems in a way instrumental to their solution. . . . [O]pposing views should be organized so as to illuminate choices and facilitate the attainment of goals; channels should be commonly available" so "that private problems . . . are formulated as general issues."[39]

This in turn entailed that there be no factions within the organization, no "parties" or "caucuses," and that discussions should always be held in a spirit of comradeship rather than in a spirit of competition. Many of the normal tools of political organizing—including rhetoric, bargaining, mobilization, and even leadership—were thus openly scorned.[40] As Francesca Polletta reports, when members of SDS debated within the organization they "expected each other to provide legitimate reasons for preferring one option to another" and they "strove to recognize the merits of each other's reasons for favoring a particular option." As a result, theirs "was a particular kind of

---

[36] Editorial, "On Roles in SDS," *New Left Notes* 1, no. 2 (1966): 4.

[37] See Max Gordon, "Radicalism: Old and New," *New Left Notes* 1, no. 29 (1966): 1–10.

[38] Mike Goldfield, "What is a Radical Perspective?," *New Left Notes* 2, no. 5 (1967): 6, and Mills, *Sociological Imagination*, 194.

[39] *Port Huron Statement*, 55.

[40] See Sidney Lens, "Participatory Democracy," *New Left Notes* 1, no. 3 (1966): 3, and Henry Haslach, "Thoughts on Leadership," *New Left Notes* 2, no. 24 (1967): 4–5.

discourse, governed by norms of openness and mutual respect": a discourse that was intended to "generate new bases for legitimate authority."[41]

Such commitments did not, of course, always achieve their desired goals. Efforts to construct an ideal democracy within the organization were often taken to justify organizational structures that were ineffective at best and almost entirely anarchic at worst. There was, for example, hardly any administrative continuity from year to year within SDS because suspicion of leaders entailed that those holding offices were subject to strict term-limits. There was also often little opportunity for serious discussion about day-to-day practical affairs because almost every meeting presented an opportunity for some members to vent their feelings or open up discussion on issues of more foundational interest. There was little that was predictable about the schedule of decision making either, as organization was thought to prohibit spontaneity.[42] For all their good intentions, then, the results of such practices were often profoundly difficult for the organization, leading either to administrative paralysis or, as Greg Calvert put it, to "elitist manipulation by individuals or cliques which can operate freely" in the absence of structure and organization, controlling the proceedings without others even noticing.[43]

Despite these problems, the participatory elements of internal decision making remained crucial to the self-identity of SDS. They provided a vitality, openness, and congeniality toward innovation that no other political organizations in midcentury America, with the exceptions of CORE and SNCC, could offer. They were also thought to provide an insight into the advantages of the participatory democratic future that the movement was striving for in America at large. Some even said that activity in SDS enabled participants to "constitute in here-and-now community" a version of "the future commonweal itself."[44] Whatever the hyperbole, it was clear that political life was intended to be both principled and fun within SDS.

The Politics of Democratic Transformation

Many commentators sympathetic to SDS and the New Left in its early years believed that, with CORE and SNCC, the movement had achieved something that many considered impossible. It had revitalized the American

---

[41] Polletta, *Freedom Is an Endless Meeting*, 7–8.

[42] See the excellent discussion of this trend in Jane Mansbridge, "The Limits of Friendship," *Nomos* 16 (1975): 248–51.

[43] Calvert, "Participatory Democracy," 7. See, too, the excellent discussion in Polletta, *Freedom Is an Endless Meeting*, 120–48.

[44] Gitlin, *The Sixties*, 84.

radical democratic tradition, freeing it from the hold of arguments about the American creed without recourse to the adversarial politics that had characterized the Depression Era. By rejecting the failed "consensus" of midcentury America while at the same time emphasizing the crucial importance of participation and the possibility of attaining a new common good, the student movement had, as Hannah Arendt put it, sought to demonstrate that it was possible to put the pursuit of "common opinion" ahead of the competition of brute "interest" in democratic politics.[45] Seen in this way, SDS was acting almost as if, by creating a movement that celebrated the possibility of discovering shared goods and that placed enormous faith in the democratic capacities of the average American citizen, it intended to refute the skeptics and pessimists of the late 1940s and the 1950s.[46]

Swept up in such enthusiasm, many commentators contended that, along with CORE and SNCC, SDS entirely eschewed the "strategic politics" of the sort associated with the interwar CIO and embraced an alternative form of political action instead. Wini Breines has thus particularly influentially argued that the insistence upon ambitious internal participatory structures demonstrates that SDS engaged in a "prefigurative politics," one that did not seek confront the established order on its own terms but attempted to engender widespread change instead by "creat[ing] and sustain[ing] within the live practice of the movement relationships and political forms that "prefigured" and embodied the desired society."[47]

A "prefigurative politics" of this sort is best understood as a politics of democratic transformation by example, one in which the efforts of the movement to live up to the ideals that it sets society at large is thought to inspire others to adopt those same ideals. Change would come through the experience of lived participation, the argument goes, and not from a traditional struggle against established power, conducted, as Niebuhr and his colleagues would have recommended, with strategic sense and tough-minded "realism." Seen in this way, life within SDS was itself "a search for democratic community;" its adoption of strict rules of participatory democracy within the movement demonstrating that it "rejected the criteria of narrow efficiency, efficacy, compromise, discipline, and the rules of the game as they are played in politics today." The group sought to lead the way to a new political order through the lived experience of a better example.[48]

[45] Hannah Arendt, "Civil Disobedience," in Arendt, *Crises of the Republic* (San Diego: Harcourt, Brace, and Co., 1972), 56.

[46] Miller, *Democracy Is In the Streets*, 149.

[47] Breines, *Community and Organization*, 6.

[48] Ibid., 151.

Such an interpretation of the action of SDS is not entirely misguided. Many SDS activists argued that the New Left had to stay true to participatory ideals within the movement itself if it was ever to expect those principles to be adopted by society at large. As Henry Haslach summarized, SDS aimed to "create within our own movement a non-authoritarian society" partly in order to "prove by example that it can work."[49] It was also sometimes argued that a large movement constructed on participatory grounds would have a destabilizing effect on the established order merely by virtue of its existence. As Staughton Lynd suggested, "the building of a brotherly way of life even in the jaws of the Leviathan" was intended to upset the expectations of skeptics so severely as to disorient them, enabling alternative structures to be constructed almost by default.[50]

There was also a constant emphasis on the need to recruit young members into the movement, not solely for purposes of growth but also because in doing so the experience of a life lived in a participatory democracy could be diffused among the population at large. Almost nothing was celebrated more in New Left circles than when a child of the suburbs ran away from a conservative family home to join an open, communal, participatory house of SDS supporters.[51]

But despite all of this, it is a very serious mistake to think that the New Left in general, or SDS in particular, ever thought that "prefiguration" was an effective method for transforming the American political order. Moreover, it is deeply misleading to suggest that SDS's approach to interactions with those outside of the movement was ever shaped by the norms of participatory democracy. In fact, quite to the contrary, almost everyone within SDS was certain that the battle to establish a new and better democratic order for all American citizens to enjoy would require much more than a "good example" or a mimicking of ideal democratic standards in the non-ideal democratic present. "The goals we have set are not realizable next month, or even next election," *The Port Huron Statement* admitted.[52] Instead, SDS was "determined to attempt to transform the American power structure" and it was also certain that it would take more than a "moral gesture" to do so.[53]

[49] Haslach, "Thoughts on Leadership," 8.

[50] Staughton Lynd, "The New Radicals and Participatory Democracy," *Dissent* 12, no. 3 (1965): 333. See, too, Hayden, "Politics of the Movement," 87.

[51] See Jonathan Eisen and David Steinberg, "The Student Revolt Against Liberalism," *Annals of the American Academy of Political and Social Science* 382 (1969): 83–94.

[52] *Port Huron Statement*, 151.

[53] Lynd, "New Radicals," 333.

As such, SDS was convinced that the participatory, deliberative, and open style of politics that it deemed necessary within the movement was entirely inappropriate in relations with the outside world. For all of their excessive commitment to idealized norms of democratic behavior within the organization, therefore, SDS openly and continuously rejected such norms when it came to relating to other groups, and especially to political opponents on whom they blamed the injustices and exclusions of American society at large. In other words, the contest to construct a new democratic order did not demand democratic behaviors, it demanded something else altogether.

SDS activists believed that there were two essential reasons why the democratic transformation of the United States could not be brought about by a moralized politics of democratic "example setting," each of which they owed to a key intellectual influence. The first was derived from C. Wright Mills and relied especially on his concept of the "power elite." Following Mills, the New Left contended that real political and economic power in the United States was held by a relatively small group and that that group was, unsurprisingly, deeply resistant to significant political change. The elite, moreover, was thought to control most of the key mechanisms of political change in the United States. Party politics, for example, was dominated by the elite, ensuring that all mainstream "elections are a hoax." "It is clear," *New Left Notes* explained in this regard, "that the money interests—the giant corporations, the military, the universit[ies]—make the important decisions about people's lives" and partisan "candidates are always people who clearly represent the interests of those who control America."[54]

The elite's stranglehold also extended to most established social movements, including the trade unions, which Mills suggested had put aside their almost revolutionary fervor in exchange for a share of the elite's political and economic spoils.[55] What this meant, of course, was that SDS rejected almost all established efforts at political reform. People "who recognize the political process as perverted will not seek change through the institutions that process has created," *New Left Notes* argued. "A diseased structure cannot create a healthy solution."[56] "[W]e are dealing with a colossus that does not want to be changed," one-time SDS President Carl Oglesby similarly concluded, and that demanded the adoption of a far more dramatic and contestatory form of political action than the argument from "prefiguration" suggests.[57]

---

[54] Editorial, "Can"t Get No Satisfaction," *New Left Notes* 3, no. 33 (1968): 3.

[55] See C. Wright Mills, *The New Men of Power: America's Labor Leaders* (New York: Harcourt, Brace, and Co., 1948).

[56] Steve Halliwell, "Personal Liberation and Social Change," *New Left Notes* 2, no. 30 (1967): 1.

[57] Carl Oglesby, "Liberalism and the Corporate State," *New Left Notes* 1, no. 1 (1966): 3.

The second reason why a moralized politics of example would not be enough also owed something to Mills, but its primary source was the French existentialist novelist Albert Camus, who was widely read in New Left circles throughout the 1960s.[58] This argument suggested that the vast majority of American citizens were blind both to the existence of the power elite and to the extent of the injustices and democratic exclusions that the elite perpetuated.

In this regard, Tom Hayden recalled being especially struck by the analogy Camus provided in *The Plague*. There, Camus told of a French-Algerian town, Oran, where a deadly illness decimated the population but the citizens were unable—and unwilling—to appreciate what was actually going on around them and thus to fight back.[59] Oran's citizens were blinded by many forces but most of all by narrow-minded individualism. Such individualism initially meant that they were unable to transcend the banality of their own, closely circumscribed private lives and to grasp the enormity of the crisis that was besetting them. Later, it meant that even when they did begin to appreciate that their community was falling apart, each maintained an irrationally exaggerated sense of his own ability to survive in the face of both the illness and the social disintegration that it engendered.[60]

For the generation of the New Left and of SDS, the analogy with the postwar United States was stark and clear. Most citizens of the United States in the 1950s and early 1960s existed in a state of "apathy." Bought off by self-congratulatory stories of the American creed, they lived almost entirely in "a privately-constructed universe, a place of systematic study schedules, two nights each week for beer, a girl or two, and early marriage."[61] Just as in the plague-ravaged city of the novel, such citizens were unable to understand what was going on around them, unable to grasp the true and horrific extent of the injustices and exclusions in their own society.

Even when they did fleetingly grasp the realities, they were unable to reach the heights of emotional intensity required for effective action. Just as Camus had described, it seemed to the New Left that of American citizens, "no-one among them experiences any great feelings any more. . . . [E]veryone had banal feelings."[62] You could not expect people in that state—

[58] See Staughton Lynd, "The New Left," *Annals of the American Academy of Political and Social Science* 382 (1969): 71–72.

[59] See Tom Hayden, *Reunion: A Memoir* (New York: Random House, 1988), 76, and Albert Camus, *The Plague* (London: Penguin, 2002 [1947]).

[60] See Camus, *The Plague*, 30.

[61] *Port Huron Statement*, 58.

[62] Camus, *The Plague*, 139.

people who were stuck in what Mills described as a "private milieu"[63]—to initiate drastic change. *New Left Notes* thus argued that "for the most part" Americans are "docile accepters" of "regimentation [and] control." The combination of excessive individualism, self-congratulatory Americanism, and simple emotional and intellectual inadequacies allowed Americans to be disciplined by an ever prevalent bureaucracy, whose standardized rules, practices, and expectations tended "to implant attitudes and [an] out-look conducive to the maintenance of the [prevailing] structure and its authoritarian nature."[64]

It was this process, increasingly connected with the sociological theory of "alienation" in the early 1960s, that Tom Hayden and others claimed was at the root of American citizens' inability to challenge the power elite and the injustices it perpetuated. As *The Port Huron Statement* put it, the "isolation of the individual" meant that "the vital democratic connection" between the American people "has been so wrenched and perverted" that "disastrous policies" are able to "go unchallenged time and again."[65] According to the New Left's analysis, most Americans in the 1960s were left, at best, with a bemused sensation of powerlessness. At worst, they were turned, in Mills's deeply disconcerting phrase, into "cheerful robots."[66] The majority of American citizens was thus extremely unlikely to be effected simply by a politics of good example. Indeed, most of them could not even be reasoned with to any significant extent.

The very same paradox of politics that had challenged radical democrats in the Progressive and Depression Eras thus re-presented itself to the New Left. On the one hand, the activists of SDS were passionate democrats. In contrast to their immediate postwar predecessors, they wanted to believe in the possibility of a new democracy, one grounded in the reasoning powers of the public and the possibility of a common good, where the proud dedication could be "let the people speak." On the other hand, they were hugely skeptical of the ability of the American public to commit to the struggle that was required. Contemporary American citizens, on this account, were little better than the citizens of Camus' Oran, who had they been allowed to continue running their own lives, would all have perished in the plague. Mills

---

[63] Mills, *Sociological Imagination*, 174.

[64] Pat Hensen and Ken McEldowney, "A Statement of Values," *New Left Notes* 1, no. 42 (1966): 5, and John Pennington, "RYM Walks Out," *New Left Notes* 5, no. 1 (1969): 7. See, too, William Spinrad, "Assessing the 1960s," *Sociological Forum* 5, no. 3 (1990): 511–16; Gitlin, *The Sixties*, 121; Tom Hayden, *Revolution in Mississippi: A Special Report* (New York: Students for a Democratic Society, 1960), 1; and Wolin, *Politics and Vision*, 353.

[65] *Port Huron Statement*, 58.

[66] Mills, *Sociological Imagination*, 175.

put the challenge most clearly in his deeply unsettling essay on democracy *The Sociological Imagination*. "If we take the simple democratic view that what men are interested in is all that concerns us," he argued, "then we are accepting the values that have been inculcated, often accidentally and often deliberately by vested interests." But if we rejected that simple view and endorsed instead a revolutionary politics that suggested that change should be led by an informed vanguard working against the preferences of the population at large as Communists had always wished, then we stood in danger of descending into a group of "manipulators" and "coercers," potentially no better than the power elite against which we claimed to struggle, just as the Bolsheviks had in the Soviet Union.[67]

It was a dilemma to which Mills offered no solution. Grasping the enormity of this challenge, SDS activist Bob Ross vividly recalls his first response to reading Mills. "I walked the streets weeping," he describes. "What can we do?," he asked. "Is this our fate?"[68]

Transformation Through Confrontation

The combination of Mills and Camus might have been too much even for the optimists of the New Left. But despite *The Power Elite*'s latter-day association with such pessimism, and with the bleak vision of a "liberalism of fear" that often follows from it, both Mills himself and his followers in SDS did not take such a dim view.[69] Rather, they believed that radical democratic change was still possible in the United States, however hard it might be to realize. The intellectuals and activists of SDS thus aimed to problematize American citizens' complacent response to the entrenched power of the elite and to discover an alternative form of political action that might kick start the process of democratic renewal.[70]

The first act of such a movement for change was to bring awareness of the power elite and the injustices and exclusions it perpetuated to an ever wider audience. As Camus had argued, real "evil in the world comes almost always from ignorance."[71] In this regard, there was still initially some place for the politics of reason, deliberation, and persuasion. Conversations,

[67] Ibid., 194.

[68] Bob Ross, cited in Miller, *Democracy Is in the Streets*, 87.

[69] For the pessimistic reading of Mills, see Miller, *Democracy Is in the Streets*, esp. 88–90, and Ira Katznelson, "At the Court of Chaos: Political Science in an Age of Perpetual Fear," *Perspectives on Politics* 5 (2007): 3–15.

[70] This, indeed, was the central theme of *Radical Nomad*.

[71] Camus, *The Plague*, 100.

discussion groups, and "teach-ins" were thus crucially important to the efforts of SDS. Ideally, sessions were organized where individuals from diverse backgrounds could share their stories of repression and injustice and respond to the tales of others in order to reveal a previously hidden pattern of exclusion: to show, in other words, "that the power elites were to blame" for all their "seemingly individual troubles."[72] "Our task" in such meetings "was to penetrate that isolated web and replace it with a social one," Tom Hayden later recalled. In SDS discussion meetings, Hayden continued, "we would encourage one person after another . . . to talk about specific problems until they were all shaking their heads in agreement and a system of collective abuse had become apparent." Such meetings offered the possibility of helping citizens recognize the reality of the power elite, without any form of coercion. It would just take an extended conversation to allow citizens to reach an "understanding of the ways nature and society *really* work."[73]

On the surface, this emphasis on discussion and discovery can appear reminiscent of the ideal of participatory democracy itself. But for all the discursiveness of these forums, the emphasis was neither on consensus building nor the sharing of multiple perspectives in any sort of deliberative way. Rather, SDS and the broader New Left were convinced that if individuals were encouraged simply "to tell it as it is" then they were bound to concur with the analysis of Mills and his followers.[74] Discussion with people outside of SDS was not aimed, therefore, at pursuing new ideas or searching for alternative "truths." It was instead about explaining the "who, how and why of power on the campus and in the community" to those who were not currently aware of it and encouraging them therefore to see the world as SDS already did.[75]

This was particularly true of the initiatives that SDS led in working class neighbourhoods, such as the Economic Research and Action Project (ERAP) that it ran in the summer of 1964. There student organizers brought members of disparate poor communities together in urban centers across America and encouraged them to identify common objects of hostility through discussion. The stated aim of ERAP was "participatory" but its outlook was hardly "democratic" in any fully fledged sense. This was dis-

---

[72] Hayden, *Reunion*, 81.

[73] Paul Booth, "Facing the American Leviathan," *New Left Notes* 1, no. 33 (1966): 8; emphasis added.

[74] See, for example, Hayden, *Revolution in Mississippi*.

[75] Editorial, "Program Skills," *New Left Notes* 1, no. 9 (1966): 4. See, too, the editorial "Radical Education Project Programs," *New Left Notes* 1, no. 17 (1966): 2–3, and Hayden, *Reunion*, esp. 81, 131.

cussion as "consciousness raising," not as consensus building or discovering the common good.[76]

As so often in the past, though, the radical democrats of SDS discovered that the sharing of "knowledge" was not sufficient to mobilize radical political action. ERAP disintegrated without much significant effect in 1964, largely because few of the urban poor wanted to come together to be lectured by student activists on the causes of their discontent when they had more familiar channels of assistance and action to which to turn. And no other large-scale endeavor to popularize the New Left's analysis of the "power elite" met with any more significant success.[77]

This failure, though, embarrassed few involved with SDS. Instead, it only reinforced the widespread sense that Mills and Camus had been right all along, showing that even the very poorest Americans were caught in a vicious circle whereby an isolated, apathetic, and helpless citizenry cedes decision-making power to some centralized elite only thereby to become still more isolated, apathetic, and helpless. It would take more than discussion circles to enable citizens to free themselves of the illusions perpetuated by the elite and its apologists. More than "knowledge" was needed to enable the democratically excluded to wake up to the weaknesses that flowed from their apathetic isolation and to engage in collective action against injustice as they had at crucial moments in the past.

What was required, SDS's most prominent theoreticians therefore concluded, was a more dramatic form of politics, one that would allow a large number of people fully to experience an alternative way of being, thinking, and feeling rather than merely suggesting it intellectually. American citizens were now held to be so emotionally and psychologically dulled to the possibilities of politics that even rational self-interest would not be enough to draw them back into the political fold. They would need to be given the opportunity to share for the first time a real sensation of solidaristic commitment and to sense injustice and exclusion in a direct way. Only such a politics would allow citizens to replace the feelings of apathetic individualism with a new set of emotions, ones that were characteristic of passion rather than apathy, action rather than inaction, solidarity rather than individualism. SDS was thus committed to allowing those inside and outside of its ranks directly to experience a new "kind of independence," one that "does not mean egoistic individualism" but rather draws people together once again.[78] Putting that in the terms of the times, before American citizens

---

[76] See ERAP files in SDS Papers.

[77] See Richard Flacks, "On the Uses of Participatory Democracy," *Dissent* 8 (1966): 701–9.

[78] *Port Huron Statement*, 4.

would be capable of building a new democracy, the movement would have to engender "an altered consciousness of reality."[79] It was time, in Mills's provocative phrase, to get "moving again."[80]

SDS's distinctive approach to political action emerged directly from this idea. It was an approach that can fairly be described as "the politics of confrontation." Initially borrowed from the civil rights movement, it consisted chiefly in confrontational activities, including sit-ins and occupations, demonstrations, and other forms of nonviolent direct action. For Hayden and colleagues, such tactics of confrontation had implications for participants, their enemies, and onlookers. From SDS's perspective, it was the impact on participants themselves that seemed to matter most, with the experience and accompanying sensations of actually pitting oneself against a recognized injustice—of putting one's "body on the line," as the saying went—providing profound transformational opportunities for all of those involved. In particular, anyone having engaged in a direct conflict with injustice could begin to feel the emotional power of acting "authentically in concert with others" in a way that loosened the grip of the psychology of powerlessness and isolation on which the power elite depended.[81]

This notion was again borrowed from Camus, who had breathtakingly described both the logic and the nature of the process both in *The Plague* and *The Rebel*. In the latter he sought to explain how even the most isolated of individualists can come to find a sense of communal connection through engagement in a struggle against almost any injustice, no matter how small. In "our daily trials, rebellion plays the same role as does the *cogito*," Camus suggested. Initially, forcefully being made aware of injustice "lures the individual from his solitude," making him think about its causes and perhaps investigate means of its rectification. But it was only the experience of a real campaign against such injustice that binds people together for the first time, making them feel a new sense of power, of morality, of being, and, most importantly, of solidarity with others. Such an experience, Camus concluded, brings a spirit of communality to the fore for the first time in many people's lives, potentially leading each participant to declaim "I rebel – therefore *we* are."[82]

For Camus, then, the very act of rebellion, as a result both of the revulsion against injustice and of the campaigning opportunities provided by activists, was the essential catalyst for the construction of a better, more communal, and eventually more democratic form of life in modern societies. This was an idea that intoxicated SDS. Ever SDS's intellectual, Tom

[79] See Gitlin, *The Sixties*, 197–99.
[80] Mills, "Letter to the New Left," 254.
[81] Calvert, *Democracy from the Heart*, 204.
[82] Camus, *The Rebel*, 28.

Hayden was clear about the debt: it was Camus, he recalled, who had taught Americans that it was only the "act of rebellion" that could reliably draw "the individual from solitude to solidarity."[83] But the idea was far from confined to those who had actually read Camus. It became, rather, the raison d'etre of SDS.

Solidarity-building confrontations with exclusionary authorities thus constituted the vast majority of the movement's political activities. Mass confrontations were employed on multiple fronts. They were most frequently seen in battles with campus authorities: the famous Berkeley Free Speech movement of 1964 and by SDS in the Columbia University occupation of 1968. But they also made their way onto the national political stage—as in the 1965 March on Washington and more spectacularly still at the siege of the 1968 Democratic Party Convention—and they stretched far beyond these celebrated incidents, structuring a form of politics across the nation.[84]

The transformative effect of such campaigns was said to extend far beyond the actual participants. It was not only that those who were directly involved would feel the thrill of the action and reconsider their political and social assumptions as a result. For just as SNCC and CORE believed that mass civil rights protests brought the injustices of racial segregation to the attention of the public at large, so SDS believed that the experience of witnessing campaigns against exclusion and injustice would have a similar impact on onlookers. As the social psychologist Christian Bay explained, only those who are "too neurotic, to stymied to develop a consciousness of their own humanity, their own solidarity with all men" could possibly "remain indifferent and passive when confronted with victims or perpetrators of injustice" as they would be when SDS took to the streets and the mechanisms of repression met them there.[85]

Even Hannah Arendt, usually highly suspicious of the divisiveness involved in a politics of confrontation, understood the movement's actions in this way, suggesting that "reasonable behavior" alone would never bring the experience of injustice directly to the consciousness of the mass of the American people. "To tear the mask of hypocrisy from the enemy, to

---

[83] Hayden, *Reunion*, 77.

[84] See, amongst an enormous literature, Allen Barton, "The Columbia Crisis," *Public Opinion Quarterly* 32 (1968): 333–51; David Farber, *Chicago '68* (Chicago: University of Chicago Press, 1988); Mark Kitchell, *Berkeley in the Sixties* (Berkeley: Kitchell Films, 1990); and W. J. Rorabaugh, *Berkeley at War* (New York: Oxford University Press, 1989).

[85] Christian Bay, "Civil Disobedience: Prerequisite for Democracy in Mass Society," in David Spitz, ed., *Political Theory and Social Change* (New York: Atherton, 1967), 179. See, too, Gitlin, *The Sixties*, 84.

unmask him and the devious machinations and manipulations that permit him to rule," Arendt argued, was the single most important motive behind the confrontational politics of the student New Left, and only by doing so, by bringing not just the issue but the *feelings* of injustice to bear, could the New Left hope to "provoke action" to overcome the power elite.[86]

All of this led, therefore, to a politics not only of confrontation but of exhibition as well. There was a carnivalesque character to the activities of SDS and related organizations, stretching from the celebration of alternative lifestyles on the streets of Haight-Asbury in San Francisco and Greenwich Village in New York to mass artistic celebrations of the sort run by the Bread and Puppet collective in the Vermont countryside. There were few better places to witness challenges to the orthodox or to enjoy the euphoric feelings of political contestation.[87]

At its crudest, the movement's activists suggested that protest "*is* good when it *feels* good—not only at the point of disruption, but when one looks back after the euphoria and the crowds have dispersed."[88] But the idea went deeper than this indulgent expression would imply.[89] Indeed, it was not even entirely new, but drew instead on a tradition of American democratic ritual that stretched at least back to the end of the nineteenth century, a time when Walt Whitman had celebrated the emotional power drawn from people pouring collectively onto the streets, waving banners and singing songs in celebration of their equality and their communality, leaving behind both the rules of hierarchical elites that sought to bind them and the solitude that would leave them impotent. In this sense what SDS sought to offer was what Nancy Rosenblum has called the experience of democracy as the "sublime," where individuals previously distanced from each other feel that they can come together through the sheer aesthetic excitement of the collective experience.[90] "There is no man, no law, no government that can substitute for this creative movement of the people," SDS's Carl Oglesby suggested. The power elite would be swept away, just as an individual's emotions were, by the sensational experience of mass protest and collective action.[91]

For SDS, therefore, the politics of confrontation offered to unleash a spirit of unbounded creative and communal excitement into a nation otherwise

---

[86] Hannah Arendt, "On Violence," in Arendt, *Crises of the Republic*, 163.

[87] See Stefan Brecht. *The Bread and Puppet Theatre*. 2 vols. (New York: Methuen, 1988).

[88] Steve Wiessman, "Civil Disobedience in Action," *SDS Bulletin* 4, no. 1 (1965): 6.

[89] Good discussion of the general theme is found in James J. Farrell, *The Spirit of the Sixties: Making Postwar Radicalism* (New York: Routledge, 1997).

[90] Nancy Rosenblum, "Strange Attractors: How Individualists Connect to Form Democratic Unity," *Political Theory* 18, no. 4 (1990): 585. See, too, the discussion of "democratic aestheticism" in George Kateb, *Patriotism, and Other Mistakes* (New Haven: Yale University Press, 2006), 142–47.

[91] Carl Oglesby, "An Open Letter: Dear McCarthy Supporters," *New Left Notes* 3, no. 26 (1968): 6.

characterized by solitude and sloth. "The democratic moment, the political moment *par excellence*" was unsettling, boundary-denying, exciting, and provocative.[92] This was an experience that SDS thought could be gained in other ways as well. Alternative lifestyles—social and personal experimentation in a broader sense—were encouraged because they could have the same impact on individuals' lives. Of particular importance in this regard was the widespread use of drugs, and especially psychedelic drugs. Although most in SDS were always keen to distance the organization from the self-indulgence of the hippie movement, many nonetheless believed that marijuana and LSD enabled the world to be seen anew.[93] Just like democratic confrontation, drugs freed individuals from the illusions perpetuated by the power elite, giving them a new perspective on their social environment. As Todd Gitlin summarized, if you "go to class stoned; shop for food stoned; go to the movies stoned," you will see "all is transformed, the world just started again!"[94]

Like participation on the democratic front line, the experience of taking drugs was also intended to be intensely positive, uplifting, rule-breaking, and solidarity-inspiring. Drugs were thus celebrated for providing sensations of "peace, love, joy, sensuality, unity and spiritual truth": the kind of emotions that alienated Americans "have only previously heard about," given their humdrum, bureaucratically structured lives.[95] After years of theorists and politicians denying that it was possible to dream of a better future, "drugs planted utopia in your own mind," Todd Gitlin memorably recalled, leaving the experimenters with an experience of a passionate universe that "could not be denied, or forgotten, or assimilated."[96]

As the activist John Pennington suggested, SDS offered a whole package. It incorporated radical confrontational politics, lifestyle experimentation, and psychedelic mind-enhancing chemicals, all of which together could release the American people from the stupor engendered by the power elite. It was SDS's task, Pennington concluded in the idiom of the day, to get the people "grooving again."[97]

---

[92] Nicholas Xenos, "Momentary Democracy," in Aryeh Botwinick and William Connolly, eds., *Democracy and Vision: Sheldon Wolin and the Vicissitudes of the Political* (Princeton: Princeton University Press, 2001), 34.

[93] On tense relationships with the hippies, see Bennett Berger, *The Survival of a Counterculture* (Berkeley: University of California Press, 1981), and Stuart Hall, "The Hippies," in Julia Nagel, ed., *Student Power* (New York: Merlin, 1969).

[94] Gitlin, *The Sixties*, 202.

[95] See Calvert, *Democracy from the Heart*, 224.

[96] Gitlin, *The Sixties*, 202, 209.

[97] Pennington, "RYM Walks Out," 7.

The Unraveling of the Movement

This celebration of free-wheeling creativity, experimentation, and the breakdown of traditional assumptions was, of course, far from restricted to political organizations like SDS or even to the New Left in general in the sixties. Similar developments infused almost all aspects of American life and culture, from the rejection of "form" in the postminimalist art movement of Richard Serra and Bruce Nauman to the hostility to narrative structure characteristic of the writing of Thomas Pynchon and Kurt Vonnegut in their prime. All of this was designed not only to stimulate the creativity of artists themselves but to empower and to energize the previously passive viewer.[98] Hans Haacke's "institutional critique" movement in the visual arts even went one step further still, designed as it was both to draw out new sensations from the viewer and to reveal the "true" interconnections between different elements of the power elite.[99]

But even if it was not unique to politics, SDS's vision had profound implications for the ideal of democracy, especially as it explained anew what it was that the ideal demanded of individual citizens living in a non-ideal age. "What we don't need," Christian Bay insisted, "is the cheerful, loyal, pliable law-abiding, basically privatist type of citizen extolled not only in our high school civics texts but in our professional civic culture and end of ideology literature as well."[100] What was required instead, were citizens willing to explore their own lifestyles, to experiment with new ways of being, to take the risks necessary to engage in dramatic confrontations, and to be swept away in the resulting excitement. Some activists should live, therefore, as agents provocateurs, continually probing social situations, seeking out potential confrontations, and recruiting potential comrades. There was to be no rest in the movement—everyone was to do their part in initiating the process of democratic change, and outside of the movement almost all citizens, especially those who had demonstrated an unwillingness to open up their minds, were suitable targets for provocation.

For all its ubiquity, this was all too much for some critics. SDS's celebration of the unorthodox and the dramatic was chastised as more mindless than mind-expanding, more nihilistic than creative. Two objections in particular were most frequently raised. The first suggested that the politics

---

[98] See, for examples, Kurt Vonnegut, *God Bless You, Mr. Rosewater* (1965), and Thomas Pynchon, *The Crying of Lot 49* (1966). For commentary, see John Krafft, "Thomas Pynchon," *Social Text* 10 (1984): 283–86.

[99] See Carl Andre, Hans Haacke, John Parreault, and Cindy Nemser, "The Role of the Artist in Today's Society," *Art Journal* 34 (1975): 327–31.

[100] Bay, "Civil Disobedience," 181–82.

of transformation through confrontation was essentially ephemeral. This critique, as Hannah Arendt voiced it, suggested that "the strong fraternal sentiments" that the New Left's dramatic form of politics engenders "have misled many good people into the hope that a new community together with a new man will rise out of it." In fact, however, such a "hope is an illusion for the simple reason that no human relationship is more transitory than this kind of brotherhood," built as it is out of momentary excitement rather than out of sustained deliberative engagement.[101]

The second objection contended that the celebration of confrontation and experimentalism was dangerously insensitive to the interests and preferences of those who did not want to confront or experiment—to those, that is, who were genuinely happy with their lot and who had no interest in unsettling the prevailing American consensus. For all of their libertarian talk, these critics held, SDS activists actually advanced a form of "punitive moralism," which described some forms of life (the dramatic, experimental, lively) as "good," and other forms (the contemplative, the obedient, the traditional) as necessarily "bad."[102]

Michael Walzer seized on this latter argument in *Dissent* in 1968. Walzer and most of the rest of the editorial staff of *Dissent* had always been skeptical of SDS, believing that the organization was both soft on Communism and excessively and dangerously utopian in its belief in the possibility of a transformation of the American democratic order. Now, Walzer believed he had a chance to make a searing critique of the whole project. Life within the New Left, Walzer insisted, would leave citizens infused not with the joys of rebellion but with "a suffocating sense of responsibility," suggesting that if they did not rebel they were collaborators in injustice. "Sometimes young radicals sound very much like old Christians," Walzer concluded, not because they were tolerant and full of compassion, but because they were so certain of their lifestyles, so full of dangerous dogmatism, possessed of an unquestioning zeal that condemned the lives of most of their fellow citizens as undeserving of respect and irredeemably unjust.[103]

There was, undoubtedly, much in both of these challenges. SDS activists did not think very much about the long-term implications of the

---

[101] Arendt, "On Violence," 166.

[102] See Oscar Glantz "New Left Radicalism and Punitive Moralism," *Polity* 7, no. 3 (1975): 281–303. Accusations of moralism haunt the scholarly literature on the New Left as well. See Richard J. Ellis, "Romancing the Oppressed: The New Left and the Left Out," *Review of Politics* 58 (1996): 109–54 and John McMillan, "You Didn't Have to Be There: Revisiting the New Left Consensus," in John McMillan and Paul Buhle, ed., *The New Left Revisited* (Philadelphia: Temple University Press, 2003).

[103] Michael Walzer, "A Day in the Life of the Socialist Citizen: Two Cheers for Participatory Democracy," *Dissent* 15 (1968): 246.

confrontational nature of the politics of transformation, nor did they give much weight to the desire of those whom Walzer described as "non-participants" to live a quiet life. But it is nonetheless a mistake to think that SDS's strategy was ever one of "anything goes" or to argue that they lacked any concern about the treatment of rivals. Most importantly, for all of their critics' dismissals, SDS did not offer a form of "snotty nosed Bolshevism," as I. F. Stone once charged, and they certainly did not think that it was always legitimate to impose a new way of life on the vast majority of citizens, whether or not those citizens endorsed it.[104]

There was, in particular, a continual and distinct rejection of any notion of the "vanguard of the proletariat" within SDS circles. C. Wright Mills himself had written powerfully against the idea of "false consciousness" in the late 1950s. It was crucial, Mills insisted, to distance the Left from any arguments that could be used to excuse the blatant coercion of one group to behave simply as another wished. SDS's activists generally agreed, insisting that only "democratic" forms of some admittedly indeterminate sort should be employed, even in the fiercest of battles with the power elite.[105] It was for this reason that the work of the Frankfurt School in general, and Herbert Marcuse in particular, never found a particularly receptive audience in SDS, although it did elsewhere in the more Communistically inspired parts of the New Left. Marcuse's 1964 book *One Dimensional Man* might have echoed many of Mills's themes but it was grounded in a more thoroughgoing rejection of American expectations that chimed ill with SDS.[106]

Part of the reason for the insistence on the use of "democratic" means of some sort was the age-old realization that the means employed in the transition from one political order to the next could have a profound effect on the sort of order that emerged: the same concern that had restrained many civil rights activists and some of the trade unionists of the Depression Era.[107] But activists in SDS were also often concerned not to brutalize the experience of confrontation.[108] It was crucial to their understanding of the role of confrontation, after all, that the practice of battling injustice had to be an uplifting one. It had both to release participants from the illusions

---

[104] See Gitlin, *The Sixties*, 183.

[105] See Mills, *Sociological Imagination*, 192–93.

[106] See Gordon Peterson, "Changing Consciousness," *New Left Notes* 2, no. 5 (1967): 7. For commentary, see Stephen Eric Bronner, "Reconstructing the Experiment: Politics, Ideology, and the American New Left," *Social Text* 8 (1984): 127–41; Paul Brienes, *Critical Interpretations: New Left Perspectives on Herbert Marcuse* (New York: Herder and Herder, 1971); and Alasdair MacIntyre, *Herbert Marcuse* (New York: Viking, 1970).

[107] See chapters 3 and 5 for similar arguments in earlier eras.

[108] See John Rawls, "Justification of Civil Disobedience," in Hugo Bedau, ed., *Civil Disobedience: Theory and Practice* (New York: Pegasus, 1968), 247.

perpetuated by the power elite and to reconfirm the essential values that lay at the movement's core, and those values, of course, included norms of democratic respect. Simple violence, therefore, was ruled out by the hope that confrontational politics would help engender a particular set of political virtues, a set that included some kind of empathy and respect for opponents.

Putting all of that another way, SDS activists were often to be found insisting that there had to be what was called an "insane generosity" to the "generosity of rebellion": "[i]t is love and fecundity or it is nothing at all."[109] Even if the forms of action taken were confrontational or otherwise "nondeliberative," they had to employ "a different set of spiritual values" to those employed in normal coercive politics. Only then would it be possible to "build the new world in the shell of the old."[110]

This was yet another commitment that was in part derived from Camus. He had argued in *The Rebel* that "[i]mmediately rebellion, forgetful of its generous origins, allows itself to be contaminated by resentment, it denies life, dashes toward destruction, and raises up the grimacing cohorts of petty rebels, embryo slaves all of them, who end by offering themselves for sale." In those contexts, action is no longer really "rebellion" but instead descends into "rancour, malice, and tyranny."[111] The injunction of democratic confrontation, therefore, was for individual participants and onlookers to learn to become "men," capable of standing up against political evil, but always "refuse to be a god."[112]

The End of Utopia

Despite these injunctions against violence, there was an undeniably coercive element in SDS and the greater New Left's approach to democratic transformation, and they did not hide from it. That element did not lie in the invocation to experimentation as much as it did in the campaigns in favor of particular, and very concrete, policy outcomes. For all the embrace of countercultural experience, then, SDS was not at one with the hippies.[113] The politics of confrontation were adopted not only because they would enable participants and onlookers to lead new lives but also because all the

[109] Albert Camus, *The Rebel* (London: Penguin, 1951), 268. For commentary, see Fred H. Willhoite Jr., "Albert Camus' Politics of Rebellion," *Western Political Quarterly* 14 (1961): 400–414.

[110] Calvert, *Democracy from the Heart*, 276. See, too, Oppenheimer, "Alienation or Participation," 5.

[111] Camus, *The Rebel*, 268.

[112] Ibid., 269.

[113] Calvert, *Democracy from the Heart*, 11.

other approaches to political action "did not appear to permit significant social change."[114] As well as engendering a new spirit of experimental living, the activists of SDS were also thus convinced that their activities could achieve actual, concrete, political improvements in the present. "We support a program of direct action and political organization which strikes at the economic and power base of the present institutions," the organization explained in its 1962 introductory pamphlet, *What is SDS?*[115] "Power, after all, is what politics is about."[116]

This meant that, at least in certain individual instances, SDS believed that it was acceptable for the movement to achieve its political goals directly, without debate, and with some sort of nonviolent force if necessary. With regard to American intervention in Vietnam, for example, Tom Hayden believed that confrontational tactics could be employed not only to change minds but also to change the actual cost-benefit calculations of American political decision makers. Withdrawal from Vietnam could, that is, be enforced by conducting confrontational action—breaking windows, avoiding the draft, demonstrating on the streets, occupying buildings—that, when taken collectively, would make it too costly for the military of the United States to stay the course.[117] Efforts to expel military-recruitment officers from campus thus became a central campaign strategy, not only because it highlighted the nexus of power relations connecting university, military, and political elites, but also because it could be achieved directly through the use of threat and direct action.[118] As Staughton Lynd summarized, although the movement was convinced that "participatory democracy" was the most desirable political order, both for the movement itself and for the eventual "good society," it was also convinced that political action in the non-ideal present "require[d] tools suited to the age of blood and iron."[119]

It was a relatively short step from here to the acceptance of low-level violence, especially as the political challenges grew more severe in the later part of the 1960s and the early 1970s. Tellingly, in the last two years of its existence, SDS changed its slogan from "let the people speak" to "less talk, more action." The argument would, in time, become the bedrock of the Weather Underground and other even more extremist offshoots, all of which emerged in the late 1960s as a result of the deep despondency that

[114] Breines, *Community and Organization*, 3.
[115] SDS, *What is SDS?* (1962); TS in SDS Papers.
[116] Cited in Breines, *Community and Organization*, 94.
[117] See Gitlin, *The Sixties*, 289.
[118] See Todd Gitlin, "Resistance and the Movement," *New Left Notes* 2, no. 11 (1967): 3–4.
[119] Lynd, "New Left," 71.

gripped the movement in the aftermath of the siege of Chicago in 1968.[120] To the movement's critics all of this was an expected deterioration of an already undesirable set of commitments. It was a "policy of insanity," as Michael Walzer put it.[121]

The relationship between democracy and drugs followed a similar trajectory at the end of the 1960s. For although both democratic rebellion and the taking of drugs were justified by SDS on grounds of engendering profound sensations of communal attachment, they also brought forth the development of strong "us/them" dichotomies, especially after LSD was illegalized in 1966. As Greg Calvert recalls, the "forced criminalization" of people who took drugs "fostered an anti-state mentality on the part of young people and made the police their automatic enemy," thus fostering greater and greater distance from the mechanisms of mainstream politics. It was a short step from that to a real fear of the authorities, exacerbating deep concerns already encouraged by the power elite analysis.[122]

This paranoia undoubtedly played a part in the movement's downward spiral into violence. The sense of the power elite increasing their stranglehold on American society was reinforced by the intensification of the draft, the worsening of the war in Vietnam, the arrest of Tom Hayden and his colleagues in Chicago, and the subsequent election of Richard Nixon in 1968. All of this enhanced the sense of desperation in SDS, such that more action of an increasingly confrontational sort was demanded, until by 1969, the injunctions against violence had all but been forgotten. By then, the primary imperative was to loosen the power elite's hold on political decision making and to do so immediately. Emotional transformation could come later.[123] The politics of democratic transformation through confrontation had taken a decidedly nondemocratic turn. Almost all sense of balance, of limits on what was achievable, and sense of the need to transform the political order in a "virtuous" way had been lost entirely.

The radical journalist Hunter S. Thompson perfectly captured the mood. Although "love was [still] the password," he announced, "paranoia was the style" of student politics in the late 1960s.[124] This paranoia—induced both chemically and by deepening political fear—eventually captured the

---

[120] See Motherfuckers, "Respect for Lawlessness," *New Left Notes* 3, no. 28 (1968): 4–5, and Tom Rose, "Reflections on Violence," *New Left Notes* 3, no. 7 (1968): 6–7. For commentary, see Ron Jacobs, *The Way the Wind Blew: A History of the Weather Underground* (London: Verso, 1997).

[121] Michael Walzer, "Violence: The Police, the Militants, and the Rest of Us," *Dissent* 18 (1971): 127.

[122] See Gitlin, *The Sixties*, 202, and Glantz, "New Left Radicalism," 281–303.

[123] See, for example, Mike Rudd, "Chicago 1969: Demonstration!," in SDS Papers.

[124] Hunter S. Thompson, *The Great Shark Hunt: Strange Tales from a Strange Time* (London: Picador, 1979), 406.

very heart of the movement. Thomas Pynchon described it perfectly in *The Crying of Lot 49*. There the hero, Oedipa Maas, is left entirely unsure as to whether she has uncovered a transhistorical conspiracy of exclusion or whether she is subject simply to ever deepening emotional insecurity.[125] Francis Ford Coppola caught a similar feeling in *The Conversation*, probably the greatest of all of the conspiracy movies to emerge in the last few years of the 1960s and the first years of the 1970s, where the focus again was on the ambiguous relationship between real danger and mental malaise.[126] By the early 1970s Hunter S. Thompson was living the experience himself. Whilst he followed Richard Nixon's presidential campaign around America he became convinced that he was being followed himself by the secret service. Terrified, he began to suspect that he was suffering a drug-induced negative fantasy, only eventually to be relieved to discover that he really *was* under surveillance.[127]

Radicalism Postponed

Despondency and paranoia gripped the New Left at the end of the 1960s and the beginning of the 1970s, detaching the spirit of excitement, creativity, and emotional warmth from the movement's activities and replacing it was an almost unhinged sense of despair. But as Thompson's secret service tale tells us, it was not *just* paranoia that led to this change. The war in Vietnam really was worsening, Lyndon Johnson's Great Society programs were unraveling, social and economic inequalities were deepening, and the four students killed at Kent State really were gunned down by the National Guard, two of them as they simply walked to the library. The violent response of SDS breakaways like the Weather Underground was misguided but the power elite analysis upon which they were based was never entirely without foundation. Their return to adversarialism was at least partially driven by the appalling circumstances of their time, just as it had been in during the Depression.

This qualified critique captures the very essence of SDS's contribution to radical democratic theory. Theirs was a vision of democracy that longed for a world in which deliberation between citizens could take place in an environment of equality, respect, and nonmanipulation—a democracy where citizens overcame their individualism and their self-referentiality

---

[125] See Pynchon, *The Crying of Lot 49*.
[126] Francis Ford Coppolla, *The Conversation* (Los Angeles: Zoetrope Films, 1974).
[127] Thompson, *Great Shark Hunt*, 302–3.

and worked together to discover a common good. In that way, it laid the groundwork for what would become the deliberative democratic movement of the 1990s. But it was also a movement that possessed a deep and abiding skepticism as to the possibility of living and acting by such an ideal under prevailing conditions. The grasp of the power elite would have to be loosened and the psychology of alienated isolation transformed before meaningful deliberation could begin, and it was that end that shaped SDS's entire political strategy. It drew them out of an egalitarian conversation within the movement itself—a conversation that emphasized norms of friendship and consensual exchange—and placed them instead in direct confrontation with forces of authority, both on the campus and on the national political stage.

There is no doubt that such confrontations transformed the lives of those who participated in them: many experienced democratic highs that had eluded previous generations and would elude those who came after them. But as always with highs, there were reciprocal lows. Although the troops did eventually come home from Vietnam, American political life was not rendered dramatically more egalitarian through New Left pressure. Conservative forces eventually rallied against SDS in ever more numbers, paradoxically often employing the very political tactics that the student New Left itself had pioneered.[128] Before too long the era of radical democracy had come to a close, and a conservative reaction had well and truly taken hold. But that, of course, is another story.

In later life, SDS activist Greg Calvert complained that the eventual decline of SDS was due to its failure to keep in touch with the tradition of Abraham J. Muste and his "radical pacifism" of the late 1940s and early 1950s. They had forgotten that radicals should avoid utopianism and steer clear of adversarial forms of political action.[129] But that is to misidentify the cause of the movement's difficulties. Instead, it is largely because SDS *did* keep touch with an alternative tradition—the radical democratic tradition—that it took the course that it did. Through the Progressive Era, the Depression, and the civil rights movement, that tradition had emphasized the difference between the ideal and the non-ideal political order and insisted that democracy places different demands on citizens in the one rather than the other. SDS was wedded to the idea that the United States was not yet an acceptably democratic order. Insofar as it existed at all, the "American creed"

---

[128] See Loren Belker, *Organizing for Political Victory* (Chicago: Nelson Hall, 1982), and Richard Viguerie, *The New Right: We're Ready to Lead* (Falls Church, Va.: Viguerie, 1981). For excellent commentary, see Paul Lyons, *New Left, New Right and the Legacy of the Sixties* (Philadelphia: Temple University Press, 1996).

[129] See Calvert, *Democracy Is from the Heart*, 39.

was a promise as yet unfulfilled. The movement's activists did not want to "mimic" or "prefigure" ideal democratic behaviors in the present, therefore. Instead, they wanted to employ a broad range of political actions, all of which they hoped would bring the democratic ideal closer to realization. The movement descended further and further into drama, and eventually into chaos, only because it viewed that goal as moving father and farther away and they adjusted their strategies accordingly. That was, no doubt, a strategic mistake. But it was not an entirely morally unjustifiable response to the horrors of Vietnam and the continuing inequalities and exclusions of American democratic life.

CONCLUSION

Renewing the American Radical Tradition

To be right, or conservative, "means celebrating society as it is," C. Wright Mills once wrote, whilst to be left, or radical, "means, or ought to mean, just the opposite."[1] This was the conviction that coursed through the veins of all the theorists and practitioners of the radical democratic tradition in the twentieth-century United States. In direct contradiction to celebratory accounts that emphasized the already-established and exceptional liberal democratic character of American political life, these radical democrats insisted that the inequalities, exclusions, injustices, and simple unfairnesses of U.S. society meant that it could not properly be described as a democratic political order. The task that fell to all true American democrats, therefore, was to engage in political life in ways that would further the democratic cause: overcoming injustices, helping the politically excluded to find their voice, seeking constantly to fulfill what Herbert Croly had pointedly called "the *promise* of American life."[2] The political action that such engagement called for was often discordant, dynamic, and unsettling in character. It was also constantly focused on questions of political power, identifying sources of domination and exclusion in contemporary society and imagining ways by which to subvert them. Radical democrats did not, therefore, often call for reasoned dialogue or the pursuit of consensus, at least not in the present. They wished to build American political life anew, and that required means of political struggle that were far removed from the norms of political exchange so beloved of the moderates of the 1950s and the deliberative democrats of today.

The question of whether the methods they employed were successful remains, of course, hugely controversial. Some contemporary scholars have celebrated the "revolutionary struggles" of the radical democrats, arguing as Alasdair MacIntyre has that without these efforts Americans would never have been able to break down "the barriers to achieving modern

---

[1] See C. Wright Mills, "Letter to the New Left," in Irving Horowitz, ed., *Power, Politics, and People: The Collected Essays of C. Wright Mills* (New York: Ballantine, 1964 [1960]), 253.

[2] Herbert Croly, *The Promise of American Life* (New York: MacMillan, 1909).

citizenship." Efforts "to extend the suffrage" and "to secure for the labor movement defenses against capitalist exploitation and victimization," on this account, demanded "degrees and kinds of effective political participation" that seem "alien" to those who cleave to norms of deliberation today but that were essential to the construction a more truly democratic polity.[3] Others, however, are not so sure. They contend, instead, that although nondeliberative means might have been required in the nineteenth-century campaigns—especially in the campagin against slavery—they were inappropriate and ultimately self-defeating for much of the twentieth century. On this perspective, radical political action often alienated potential support, pushing moderate Americans into the embrace of ideologies of reaction and even political exclusion. It is no surprise for these critics that the story of American radical democracy in the twentieth century effectively ended in the early 1970s with Richard Nixon having won the presidential election by mobilizing the country against the excesses of the New Left. Each student radical, Nixon had insisted, should look "in a mirror and finally realize that the problem is . . . not my teachers, not the war, not the environment, but me."[4] It was a message that found widespread support, opening up the so-called culture wars and leading not just to the election of one Republican president but to a whole new era in American electoral politics, an era that brought forth a fully fledged conservative response in the form of the "Reagan revolution."[5]

Crucial though this historical dispute undoubtedly is, it is not the sort of argument that is ever likely to be resolved through analysis of empirical data alone. The variables are too complex and interleaved to be clearly distinguishable, even if the most sophisticated techniques are employed.[6] Moreover, the interpretations themselves are always dependent on underlying normative and conceptual disagreements. We cannot answer questions such as whether Lyndon Johnson or Martin Luther King Jr. played the "most

---

[3] Alasdair MacIntyre, *Dependent Rational Animals: Why Human Beings Need the Virtues* (Chicago and La Salle, Ill.: Open Court, 2006), 142. See, too, John A. Guidry and Mark Q. Sawyer, "Contentious Pluralism: The Public Sphere and Democracy," *Perspectives on Politics* 1 (2003): 273–89.

[4] Richard Nixon, cited in Robert Mason, *Richard Nixon and the Quest for a New Majority* (Chapel Hill: University of North Carolina Press, 2004), 142.

[5] See Eric Foner, *The Story of American Freedom* (New York: W. W. Norton, 1999), 307–32, and Byron Shafer, *The Two Majorities and the Puzzle of Modern American Politics* (Lawrence: University Press of Kansas, 2003).

[6] This is not to say, of course, that the extraordinarily rich empirical work now produced does not aid our understanding. For classic examples, see Doug McAdam, Sidney Tarrow, and Charles Tilly, *Dynamics of Contention* (Cambridge: Cambridge University Press, 2001), and Sidney Tarrow, *Power in Movement: Social Movements and Contentious Politics* (Cambridge: Cambridge University Press, 1998). For a diametrically opposed analysis, however, see Robert Weissberg, "Politicized Pseudo Science," *PS: Political Science and Politics* 39 (2004): 33–37.

important" role in the civil rights campaign, or whether Franklin Roosevelt's New Deal programs would have been more or less ambitious without the pressures of the League for Independent Political Action and the League for Industrial Democracy, without previously resolving the deep and underlying problems of where power really lies in the United States: whether citizens are motivated to act more by coercion, interest, or moral suasion, and whether political change is best secured by elites or by mass mobilization.[7]

What we must do instead, therefore, is return to the central normative questions that have shaped this whole study. The central question is, were the radical democrats justified in considering employing nondeliberative, perhaps even coercive, forms of political action in their struggles for a better democracy? Put another way, it remains for us to return to the current-day dispute between deliberative democrats and their realist rivals, as sketched in the introduction, and to see what, if anything, the tradition described in the remainder of this book has to say to these rival conceptions of democracy and whether it can help us discern the kinds of citizen behaviors that should rightfully be employed in the United States today.

Deliberative and Realist Challenges

Three general arguments distance the radical democratic tradition from both deliberative democrats and democratic realists. The first concerns the radical democrats' faith in the future. With the exception of those writing in the immediate aftermath of the Second World War, all of the individual movements analyzed in this book were certain that they knew, at least in rough outline, what sort of political order they desired to build and they were equally certain that history was, to a greater or lesser extent, on their side. Such contentions were probably at their clearest in the first period considered in the present study. The language and iconography of both Progressivism and of the CIO constantly suggested that it was only the antiquated obstacles of reaction that were preventing the realization of a perfect political order. Sonner or later, the future would be realized and the democratic promise of the United States fulfillled. Such ideas struggled to find adherents in the immediate aftermath of the Second World War, inflected as they appeared to be by the taint of Nazism and Soviet Communism. They were resurrected, though, in the campaigns for civil rights and by the New Left. Neither of these movements of radical democrats disputed the claim that the destiny of the United States was inclusive and democratic, although

---

[7] See the discussions in chapters 3 and 5.

they thought that the path toward that goal was longer and more treacherous than their prewar predecessors had believed.

By the end of the twentieth century, however, democratic theorists of almost all stripes were far more wary of such optimistic expectations. The final collapse of the Soviet Union, the increasing focus on the politics of identity, multiculturalism, and cultural diversity, and the concomitant rise of postmodern social theory all rendered singular, teleological political visions suspect. For many, then, the temporal understandings that were characteristic of the radical democratic approach began to seem both naive and dangerous. Theorists of democratic progress in such an atmosphere were increasingly charged with being locked in a unilinear imaginary, incapable of seeing that the future might involve political retreats as well as advances, new beginnings as well as old continuities, and are also said to be obsessed with a commonality of vision that said little to the interests of many excluded groups, especially those wary of the liberal democratic values that radical democrats espoused.[8] Seen in this way, it appears that most twentieth-century radical democrats were capable of offering only a "single, universal *telos*" that "when examined in its implications for the character of human social and political life is repressive."[9]

Realists, of course, have become especially skeptical of this view, with many insisting that openness, diversity, uniqueness, and difference should be the watchwords of a radical politics, and further arguing that all of these run counter to the essentially unilinear temporal understanding implicit in a story of democratic "progress."[10] Failure to grasp this point introduces a dangerously destabilizing tendency into contemporary politics, a tendency that often fails to see the good in the prevailing order because of a myopic focus on unobtainable idealized goals for the future. No one has better assimilated and enunciated these concerns than has Judith Shklar. "The pursuit of the perfect city is an insult to the actual town," she once remarked, "and that is a very questionable political action."[11]

Many deliberative democrats appear to share these concerns. An overbearing confidence in some idealized future, they contend, might engender an overly harsh rejection of the aspects of political life that actually existing citizens already value. It is crucial for idealists to persuade citizens of their visions rather than to cajole them into accepting them. Failure to

[8] For a survey of these themes, see John Gray, *Enlightenment's Wake: Politics and Culture at the Close of the Modern Age* (New York: Routledge, 1995).

[9] Stephen Schneck, "Connolly's Postmodern Liberalism," *Review of Politics* 51 (1989): 283.

[10] See William Connolly, *Pluralism* (Durham: Duke University Press, 2005), 97–130, and Judith Shklar, *Ordinary Vices* (Cambridge, Mass.: Harvard University Press, 1984).

[11] Judith Shklar, "Emerson and the Inhibitions of Democracy," *Political Theory* 18 (1990): 612.

do so merely goes to demonstrate an unwillingness to justify the putative ideal to citizens in terms that those citizens themselves could reasonably be expected to accept, and that in itself opens the door to the worst sort of political coercion.[12]

Widely shared though this view is, however, it is hard to accept that it is the fact of holding optimistic expectations or ideals itself that is the problem here. After all, very few democratic theorists today are entirely satisfied with the prevailing political order. Whilst realists and deliberative democrats might believe that short-term improvement in the political order is difficult, most of them nonetheless aspire to an improved future of some sort. Just as the radical democrats do, they desire to create a political order that better meets the demands of their political values. Deliberative democrats have spent much of the last decade producing whole lists of ways in which democratic life could be improved, ranging from more effective use of new information technologies to the redesign of partisan election campaigns.[13] Realists, too, despite their commitment to open-endeness and diversity, express an almost constant wish to move beyond the confines of the political present. Even though they insist that many of the competitive characteristics that deliberative democrats reject cannot be removed from democratic politics, they do not simply to accept the status quo. Instead, most of them suggest that it is somehow possible to generate a better order. Even those most deeply committed to the notion that social conflict is unavoidable in all modern societies have argued for a more tolerant and more "generous ethos of engagement between multiple constituencies."[14] Chantal Mouffe and William Connolly have both written often about the need to "tame" prevailing political passions and to "transform potential antagonism into agonism."[15]

The second potential critique moves from a generalized unease with the commitment to improvement per se to a more specific concern with the radical democrats' specific vision of the future order or, more accurately, to

[12] See Amy Gutmann and Dennis Thompson, "Democratic Disagreement" in Stephen Macedo, ed., *Deliberative Politics: Essays on* Democracy and Disagreement (Oxford: Oxford University Press, 1999), esp. 278–79.

[13] For examples, see Bruce Ackerman and James Fishkin, *Deliberation Day* (New Haven: Yale University Press, 2004); Benjamin Barber, *A Passion for Democracy: American Essays* (Princeton: Princeton University Press, 2001); John Gastil and Peter Levine, eds., *The Deliberative Democracy Handbook: Strategies for Effective Civic Engagement in the Twenty-First Century* (San Francisco: Jossey-Bass, 2005).

[14] William Connoly, "Politics and Vision," in Aryeh Botwinik and William Connolly, eds., *Democracy and Vision: Sheldon Wolin and the Vicissitudes of the Political* (Princeton: Princeton University Press, 2001), 17.

[15] Chantal Mouffe, *Politics and Passions: The Stakes of Democracy* (London: Centre for the Study of Democracy, 2002), 8–9. See, too, Connolly, *Pluralism*, 123.

the concern that the account of the future that they offered was worryingly underspecified. Whilst deliberative democrats have thus spent a great deal of time and intellectual energy in giving specific content to their "ideal of public reason," specifying often in numbing detail the precise behavioral commitments citizens of such an ideal society should have, the vast majority of the twentieth century's radical democrats did no such thing. Rather, their ideals were often frustratingly vague. Most Progressives shared some commitment to engendering a common good across the nation. Theorists in the years of the CIO were convinced of the need for economic equality in a democracy. Civil rights activists aspired to a form of racial inclusiveness. And most student radicals demanded a more participatory political order. But beyond that, little time was spent in describing the future order precisely and even less was dedicated to presenting the intellectual case as to why one particular vision of the democratic ideal was preferable to all of its alternatives. For all of their many strengths, then, the democratic theories of John L. Lewis, Bob Moses, or even Tom Hayden would not pass muster in the editorial offices of *Political Theory* or *Philosophy and Public Affairs* today.

This critique can also be overstated, however. For although it is true that the radical democrats discussed in this study did not outline their vision with the same degree of rigor and precision that is demanded of professional political theorists today, the targets of their critical ire actually shared much in common with more recent democrats, of both the deliberative and agonistic strains. All of them shared the assumption that an ideal democracy was a "network of giving and receiving where all are able to participate in the making of decisions which shape their lives and none are solely the object of arbitrary power," as MacIntyre has recently put it, and all of them campaigned vigorously against characteristics of the real political world that stood in the way of the realization of such an ideal.[16] Each generation demanded an end to political exclusion on grounds of class or of race. They condemned corruption in the political parties and in the established hierarchies of American politics; they insisted that political power should be effectively distributed to all citizens and not concentrated in a self-serving, self-perpetuating political elite. And they argued powerfully that money should cease to play such a crucial role in the American political process today. Not one of these notions is seriously contested by more "sophisticated" democrats today.

The key difference between the radical democrats of previous generations and more recent thinkers in this regard, then, is the degree of precision

[16] MacIntyre, *Dependent Rational Animals*, 102.

with which a vision of the ideal state is articulated. There might, however, be reasons for thinking that the decision of the radical democrats to spend less time on articulating a detailed vision for the future was a wise one. As Bernard Williams and others have argued, there is a cost to overprecision in the crafting of political visions, just as there is to underprecision. "Philosophers often say that the point of their efforts is to make the unclear clearer," Williams once wrote, but in their obsession with the fine detail of their political visions "they may make the clear unclear: they may cause plain truths to disappear into difficult cases, sensible concepts to dissolve into complex definitions, and so on."[17] There was no chance of that in the radical democratic tradition. These thinkers and practitioners were campaigning for an improved democracy, and they knew, even if only roughly, what such a democracy would look like. To their mind the task of outlining its precise features fell to the writers of utopian fiction, or of campaign poetry and songs, rather than to the political theorists themselves. That, in other words, was the work of inspirational visionaries and not of hardheaded activists.[18]

The third, and final, critique can accept that it was reasonable for radical democrats to have kept their theorizing at an advanced level of generality and agree that it was legitimate of them to have hoped for an improved political future but argues vigorously that it was wrong to have encouraged citizens with potentially extreme and certainly unpopular views to attempt to foist those views upon their fellows, rather than to persuade them of their merits through reasoned, and reasonable, argument. It further contends that radical democrats were excessively incautious as to the perils of political conflict in the modern world, failing to understand that conflict is dangerous not only in its short-term consequences but in its long-term effects too.[19]

Such an argument can again be made by both deliberative democrats and realists. For deliberative democrats, it emerges from a twofold concern.

[17] Bernard Williams, "Human Rights and Relativism," in Geoffrey Hawthorn, ed., *Bernard Williams: In the Beginning Was the Deed: Realism and Moralism in Political Argument* (Princeton: Princeton University Press, 2005), 64.

[18] Those visions remained important, of course, in mobilizing, inspiring, and informing. See the discussions in Robert Cantwell, *When We Were Good: The Folk Revival* (Cambridge: Harvard University Press, 1996); Michael Denning, *The Cultural Front* (London: Verso, 1997); Gary Gerstle, *Working-Class Americanism: The Politics of Labor in a Textile City, 1914–1960* (New York: Cambridge University Press, 1989); Morris Dickstein, *Gates of Eden: American Culture in the Sixties* (New York: Basic, 1977); and Julia Micklenberg, *Learning from the Left: Children's Literature, the Cold War, and Radical Politics in the United States* (New York: Oxford University Press, 2006).

[19] See Gopal Balakrishnan, *The Enemy: An Intellectual Portait of Carl Schmitt* (London: Verso, 2000).

First, there is rejection of the radical democrats' willingness to endorse the use of coercion by some citizens to impose their will on others. Second, there is a worry that the dramatic political action that radical democrats demanded—incorporating strikes, sit-ins, mass demonstrations, and carnivalesque protest—could undermine the social harmony essential to the protection and identification of a common good. As Cass Sunstein puts it, for deliberative democrats "a central democratic goal is to ensure a large measure of social integration . . . across multiple lines, in a way that broadens sympathies" and thus makes common agreement more rather than less likely in a diverse society. [20] Many contemporary realists share precisely these anxieties. For them, after all, political peace is a hard-won good, "unnatural" in a world more likely to be characterized by deep disagreement than pre-political harmony. Scholars who have spent time with Hobbes, as most realists have, are thus unlikely to welcome an upsurge in political excess and political enthusiasm, which is more likely to be characterized by distressing "antagonism" than by open-minded and tolerant "agonism." [21] As George Kateb explains, such thinkers will always worry about a democratic theory that seems to require a "demotic rage" stoked by "the idiocies" of fanaticism. [22]

It is clear once again that there is something of value in this critique. Democratic action for change has to offer more than just a "delirious holiday" for the enthusiast and the extremist. [23] But although this line of attack might be powerfully persuasive in individual instances, it is once again far from compelling as a universal rule. Any democrat, after all, must be compelled to agree that there are *some* circumstances within which more radical, less deliberative, less socially inclusive, and less stabilizing political actions will be required. It is unquestionable that the Revolutionary War, the Civil War, and the war against Fascism were all essential to the maintenance of democratic rule and it is also clear that all had to be fought, at least in part, by "zealots": that is, by those prepared to overlook the obstacles in their path, to sacrifice everything if necessary, and to cause "commotion" in the name of a democratic future. [24] As Sheldon Wolin perceptively summarizes, "democracy was born in transgressive acts," for "the demos could not

---

[20] Cass Sunstein, *Republic.Com* (Princeton: Princeton University Press, 2001), 196.

[21] For a detailed survey, see Marc Stears, "Liberalism and the Politics of Compulsion," *British Journal of Political Science* 37 (2007): 533–53.

[22] George Kateb, "Wolin as a Critic of Democracy," in Botwinik and Connolly, *Democracy and Vision*, 45.

[23] Kateb, "Wolin as a Critic," 49.

[24] See Joel Olson, "The Freshness of Fanaticism: The Abolitionist Defense of Zealotry," *Perspectives on Politics* 5 (2007): 685–702.

participate in power without shattering the class, status, and value systems by which it is excluded."[25]

In their more reflective moments, even the most peaceable of deliberative democrats concede this point. Indeed, John Rawls himself made the same argument in explaining the need for occasional recourse to coercive, even violent, politics in the name of preserving or constructing democratic government. In *Political Liberalism*, for example, he openly argued that the "political agitation" of the radical abolitionists was "a necessary political force leading to the Civil War and so to the destruction of the great evil and curse of slavery." Both agitation and eventual violence were, therefore, essential to the task of bringing "about a well-ordered and just society in which the ideal of public reason could eventually be honored."[26] At the very philosophic heart of the deliberative project, there is no absolute injunction against dramatic, coercive political action. And neither should there be.

What this means, of course, is that all democrats—whether deliberative or realist—must accept that it is at least occasionally legitimate to employ dramatic political strategies in order to pursue fundamental democratic goals against a backdrop of extreme injustice or exclusion. Thus there can be no sweeping rules in democratic theory as to the acceptability of particular political strategies at all times and in all places. Indeed there cannot even be such rules as to the status of violence. What is needed, instead, is an assessment of particular recommendations for political action at particular times and in particular places. Once described in this way, such a position might, of course, seem obvious; as the conditions of the real world stray away from the democratic ideal then behavioral prescriptions intended for the ideal state surely become less pertinent to real-world situations. It is, nonetheless, all too rarely noted in early twenty-first-century political theory, where there is a far too frequent tendency to blur the distinction between the deliberative expectations of an ideal state and the non-ideal conditions of the existing political order.[27] It is also a position that has far-reaching implications for any normative evaluation of the previous century's tradition of radical democracy.

---

[25] Sheldon Wolin, "Fugitive Democracy," in Seyla Benhabib, ed., *Democracy and Difference: Contesting the Boundaries of the Political* (Princeton: Princeton University Press, 1998), 37.

[26] See John Rawls, *Political Liberalism* (New York: Columbia University Press, 1993), 251. See, too, Andrew Sabl, "Looking Forward to Justice: Rawlsian Civil Disobedience and its Non-Rawlsian Lessons," *Journal of Political Philosophy* 9, no. 3 (2001): 307–30.

[27] See chapter 1.

Virtue and Democratic Transformation

All of the radical democrats discussed in this study were committed to the notion that the effort to build an ideal democratic future out of a non-ideal political present required the use of political behaviors that would be deemed inappropriate, even unacceptable, in that future ideal state. There was no point in simply "mimicking" ideal citizen behaviors in a non-ideal context. They were also, however, generally convinced that the sort of political campaign waged in the non-ideal present could have a crucial role to play in shaping the nature of the democratic future. Generation after generation, therefore, opposed violent insurrection because it would be likely to cause irreparable damage to the social order of the United States, just as Tocqueville had argued the revolution in France had done.[28] Beyond this, many also contended that the campaigns of the present had to provide their participants with an opportunity to enjoy some of the advantages of the democratic future even in the non-ideal here-and-now. The trade union campaigns of the Progressive and Depression eras provided alienated industrial workers a taste of social solidarity. The struggle for civil rights offered activist African Americans the chance to enjoy "freedom now," even if only in their own communities. And the New Left's efforts to build an open-minded, creative, and experimental participatory democracy in the United States at large provided student radicals with the chance to "expand their minds" on the campus picket-lines.

All of this, of course, meant that those who shaped the radical democratic tradition were in no way committed to a doctrine of "anything goes" in political struggle. They were neither anarchists nor revolutionaries in the traditional sense. This leaves analysts, however, in something of a quandary as the radical democrats seem to inhabit the largely uncharted terrain between the detailed and determinate behavioral prescriptions that we now associate with deliberative democracy and the more open-ended political strategizing associated with the advocates of realism.[29] Such lack of clarity is exacerbated still further when it is recognized that almost all theorists of radical democracy were convinced that it was impossible to provide much more in the way of detailed guidance as to which forms of political conduct were acceptable and which were not in the campaign for democracy—that is, they were all convinced that contingency and indeterminacy were crucial features of all political campaigns. Radical democrats were certain that participants in the struggle for a better democratic order always had to keep

---

[28] See the discussions in chapters 3, 5, and 6.
[29] On realism, see chapter 3.

"their eyes on the prize," as the civil rights campaign's most famous ballad went, but beyond that they believed that campaigners would have to judge the appropriateness or lack of same of each particular strategy according to the precise circumstances that they faced. Even within the most moralizing elements of the civil rights movement, such as the early CORE and SNCC, there were no straightforwardly hard-and-fast rules capable of telling activists which particular sit-in was acceptable or which mass demonstration should be led.[30] As the song itself continued, there was only one definite "thing we did right," and that "was the day we started to fight."[31]

This is not to say, however, that there was nothing at all to guide the making of those decisions or to help choose how that fight should be conducted. Most radical democrats, especially those who emerged in the decades after the Second World War, suggested that activists would make the right decisions more often if they were able to develop the requisite political virtues. That is, participants in the campaign for a better democratic order would need to develop the practical wisdom to be able to evaluate political campaigns, events, and responses in ways that were true to the underlying democratic ideals for which they strove but that also recognized the political realities with which they were faced. Activists possessed of such wisdom, displaying such virtues, would make the right decisions when faced with the ever changing choices of a campaign for democracy. An activist who lacked them would not.

The crucial issue thus becomes the identification of the virtues themselves. They have been too often underspecified in radical democratic political thought. At different times in the tradition's development, then, different political virtues were emphasized. For the Progressives, they were often the virtues of national solidarity, including true patriotism and generosity of spirit. For the campaigners of the CIO era, they were the soldierly virtues of loyalty, patience, and obedience. For the civil rights movement, they were the virtues that had come from a history long on disappointment—virtues of courage, steadfastness, and determination—and those that promised an experience of political enjoyment in the present, including togetherness, pride, and compassion. Finally, for the student radicals of the New Left they were the virtues of extreme social and personal transformation, including open-mindedness, a willingness to experiment, and the ability to struggle without hatred in one's heart. Such variety, of course, reflects implicit disagreements as to the nature of the ideal future democratic order and also

---

[30] See chapter 5. See, too, Connolly, "Politics and Vision," 10, and Mark Philp, *Political Conduct* (Cambridge, Mass.: Harvard University Press, 2007), esp. 4–11.

[31] See http://www.springsteenlyrics.com/lyrics/e/eyesontheprize.php

arguments about the nature of the political obstacles that prevented the realization of that order. It is impossible, therefore, fully to articulate the radical democratic account of the sorts of political conduct that should be considered acceptable in the struggle for a better democratic future, if only because that account shifted so dramatically across the generations.

Despite this, the radical democratic tradition does at least direct our attention to the right question. It points out, that is, that what matters most of all in a democratic theory of political action in non-ideal circumstances is an account of the political virtues needed to shape the right response to those circumstances, a response that has the prospect of improving the democratic order, of bringing the ideal closer to realization. Few contemporary democratic theorists have moved in this direction, but one who has, as briefly mentioned in the introduction, is Archon Fung.

Fung accepts the argument (also made throughout this book) that the non-ideal circumstances of current political life ensure that it is wrong to expect citizens to adhere to strict rules of deliberation in the here-and-now. Instead, he outlines four virtues, each of which is derived from the commitment to enhancing the prospects for cross-community deliberation in a diverse society, but which recognize that such deliberation requires background conditions that are far from met in the present. He calls his four virtues "fidelity," "charity," "exhaustion," and "proportionality." Fidelity requires citizens' authentic dedication to the deliberative ideal; they must truly dedicate themselves to the advance of deliberative democracy even when they behave in nondeliberative ways. "Charity" insists that each citizen do her utmost to understand the position of her rivals and not presuppose that their actions are undergirded by irretrievably bad intent. "Exhaustion" demands that deliberative strategies are always attempted before recourse is made to nondeliberative political approaches. And "proportionality" insists that nondeliberative action must always be limited to the precise task at hand rather than employed in a manner that is more far-ranging.[32]

Fung's list of virtues faces two objections. The first, and most obvious, relates to his underlying democratic ideal. His virtues, after all, directly serve only the deliberative ideal itself and thus one would have to be a fully signed-up deliberative democrat before one could accept that they were the right virtues for present action. The vast majority of the radical democrats of the twentieth century would have forthrightly disagreed with Fung's list, just as they rejected the view, widespread amongst many deliberative

[32] Archon Fung, "Deliberation before the Revolution: Toward an Ethics of Deliberative Democracy in an Unjust World," *Political Theory* 33 (2005): 402.

democrats, that "patience and humility" are the "chief democratic virtues" required by those trying to change the political world.[33]

The second objection is more troubling with regard to the present. It begins by asking where these virtuous citizens are supposed to come from. Like CORE and SNCC before him, therefore, Fung requires a remarkable amount of dedication, integrity, and self-control in his citizens. They are to adhere strictly to the bases of the deliberative ideal, despite all of the temptations and provocations that they face, and always engage in political life in a way that reinforces the likelihood of deliberative practices taking wider hold in the long term. The behavioral standard that his virtues demand is thus very high. And this, of course, is precisely what has concerned critics of the radical democratic tradition from the Progressive Era to the present. For as Reinhold Niebhur argued in between the wars , it might well be too much to expect citizens, especially citizens faced with grave injustice, to hold back so much in their political struggles. Such citizens might not have the will, the know-how, or the desire to act in the virtuous spirit that Fung or others recommend, and all democratic theorists must surely be willing to face that possibility, and be able to respond accordingly.

This objection thus returns us to the paradox of politics that has haunted this entire study. Radical democrats constantly have to move backward and forward in time. They are committed to building a better democratic order, in part so as to foster better citizens who are possessed of a full-range of citizen virtues. They are also dedicated, however, to creating that order through the actions of citizens themselves, and they require citizens living in the far-from-ideal present to exhibit many of those future virtues in the present struggle. The paradox is a constant in the struggle for a better political future, and it always threatens to shake democratic theory to its core because whilst faith in democracy generally demands taking citizens as they are, the struggle to create a democracy means being skeptical of those self-same citizens' qualities and aspirations.[34]

Two partial responses emerge to this paradox from the history of the radical democratic tradition and it behooves us to take both of them seriously. The first emphasizes the potential difference between the virtues required for struggle and the virtues required for the operation of a peaceful, stable, and just political order. It is plausible that the virtues of struggle are easier to tease out in consequences of injustice, spawned by the direct experiences of democratic exclusion. Few would dispute that courage, solidarity, hope, and unstinting commitment were witnessed in the motor plants of Flint in

---

[33] Barber, *Passion for Democracy*, 40.
[34] See the discussion in chapter 6.

1937, on the streets of Montgomery in 1955, and on the campus at Berkeley in 1964 and Columbia in 1968. Indeed the hardest task facing radical democrats might not lie in developing these virtues but in knowing when to tame them. The moment of transition—the timing of the move from one set of virtues to another—might well provide a more difficult challenge for radical democrats than eliciting the virtues of struggle in the first place.[35]

The second response emphasizes the importance of guidance from above. It is possible, after all, that some in our prevailing political order are possessed of the knowledge, expertise, and practical wisdom required to help the rest of us develop the necessary virtues and learn to live as democratic citizens. Leadership is thus crucial to the virtuous creation of a new democratic order. Leaders need to inspire the enthusiasm of followers, to develop the talents of newcomers, to know when to make decisions for the benefit of the group, and when to acquiesce to the demands and expectations of their memberships and constituencies.[36] It thus falls to people like Bob Moses, Ella Baker, Martin Luther King, even John L. Lewis and Tom Hayden to forge the way: building institutions for the rest of us to live and work in and helping to engender a new spirit of democracy as they do.

This second kind of argument might, of course, look elitist to some; it might even seem to violate the very democratic ethos that the radical democrats were committed to engendering. But it is not quite as simple as that. For as Bonnie Honig has argued, all moments of political construction need their "lawgivers" and even the most ambitious of them faces a democratic constraint: "The lawgiver may offer to found a people, he may even attempt to shape them," Honig thus suggests, "but in the end it is up to the people themselves to accept or reject his advances."[37]

The Democratic Future

One key question remains after all of this has been considered: what should the radical democratic tradition mean to us today? In trying to answer that, it should be apparent that the obstacles to the realization of an ideal democratic order in the United States remain severe today, almost as severe as they have been at any point in the twentieth century. There have, unquestionably,

[35] See Jack A. Gladstone, "Bridging Institutionalized and Noninstitutionalized Politics," in Gladstone, ed., *States, Parties, and Social Movements* (Cambridge: Cambridge University Press, 2003), 1–26.

[36] For an inspired discussion, see Polletta, *Freedom Is an Endless Meeting.*

[37] Bonnie Honig, "Between Decision and Deliberation: Political Paradox in Democratic Theory," *American Political Science Review* 101 (2007): 6.

been advances across the last one hundred years. The franchise is now extended to all adults, formal racial exclusions from democratic practice have been effectively outlawed, and the remnants of New Deal and Great Society programs offer some form of protection to those excluded by economic inequalities. To some, then, the difficult days of American democratization are now in the past. The United States stands established as a democratic order, and the virtues that its citizens need now display stand closer to those of the deliberative ideal than the revolutionary battleground.

Few who take their political theory seriously, however, can surely be as sanguine as that. For whatever the advances of recent years, American democracy is now blighted by new difficulties and many of those that remain from before are of a magnitude far greater than is usually acknowledged. Since the beginning of the twenty-first century, Americans have become subject to a vastly expanded bureaucratic machine, impervious to the preferences of many citizens. Beyond that, they have seen effective power increasingly dispersed to global decision-making bodies only partially responsive, if at all, to localized demands, and witnessed an expansion of economic inequalities such that the discrepancies between citizens are now wider than at any point since the beginning of the twentieth century.

Reflecting on these trends, the political scientists Larry Bartels and Martin Gilens have recently contended that senior politicians pay less and less attention to the concerns of their poorest countrymen, and more and more to those of the wealthiest. "Senators are consistently responsive to the views of affluent constituents," Bartels writes, "but entirely *unresponsive* to those with low incomes."[38] So shocking does Gilens find the magnitude of this "representational bias" that he believes it "calls into question the very democratic chatacter of our society" as it exists today.[39] One does not need to share the searing pessimism of Sheldon Wolin, therefore, to recognize that American democracy is in poor health, despite the excitement that a new generation rightly felt as the United States inaugurated its first African American President.[40] As in the past, the ideal of democracy demands political action in the contemporary United States.

Within the world of professional political theory today, however, there are shockingly few attempts to consider how to respond to these demands. The amount of writing on social protest, mass movements, revolution, and

[38] Larry Bartels, *Unequal Democracy: The Political Economy of the New Guilded Age* (Princeton: Princeton University Press, 2008), 275.

[39] Martin Gilens, "Inequality and Democratic Responsiveness," *Public Opinion Quarterly* 69 (2005): 796.

[40] See Sheldon Wolin, *Democracy Inc.: Managed Democracy and the Specter of Inverted Totalitarianism* (Princeton: Princeton University Press, 2008).

civil disobedience in political theory pales into insignificance when compared to that on deliberative democracy or the ideal of social justice. It is true that the academy has not been entirely silent: John Dryzek and Mark Warren have recently emphasized the need to make the most of the opportunities of "civil society" and Jane Mansbridge has powerfully argued for the need to foster "enclaves of resistance" or safe havens for the exploration of democratic alternatives.[41] But it is nonetheless striking that each of these suggestions is characterized by a notable modesty, especially in comparison to the arguments of the past. Few political theorists today appear to possess the moral outrage at existing conditions that filled the pages of earlier generations' radical democratic writings. There is a tendency, therefore, to call for slow, incremental change, to accept that the basic outlines of our political system are set, shaped as they are by forces beyond our control and against which it is futile to struggle. The fall of the Soviet Union no doubt resonates here, just as the onset of the Cold War blighted crusading optimism in the aftermath of the Second World War.[42] This is just the opposite of what is required, however. For what is needed to redress these shortcomings is authentic democratic passion, a clear sense of the urgency of the task, and a desire always to relate democratic political ideals in the future to practical suggestions for strategic action in the present.

There is a limit, of course, to the role that political theory can play in that regard. But one thing it definitely can do is ask the right questions. In 1972 Clyde Frazier did just that when he identified what he called "the dilemma" that faced "citizens in the United States today." Citizens, Frazier insisted, "are keenly aware of the value of the system under which they live," but "at the same time they see that system committing what they feel are immoral acts both at home and abroad." "Unable to justify revolution, many citizens have been convinced that the only remaining alternatives are obedience and ineffectual protest," he continued. "Many others have become revolutionaries by default, because they feel that the evils are intolerable," whilst still others seek out "a wide range of possible actions short of revolution."[43] The key question in all of political theory, Frazier concluded, is, which of these responses is right?

---

[41] See John Dryzek, "Deliberative Democracy in Divided Societies: Alternatives to Agonism and Analgesia," *Political Theory* 33 (2005): 218–42; Mark Warren, "What Can Democratic Participation Mean Today?," *Political Theory* 30 (2002): 677–701; and Jane Mansbridge, "Using Power/Fighting Power: The Polity," in Benhabib, *Democra   cy and Difference*, 46–66.

[42] See chapter 5.

[43] Clyde Frazier, "Between Obedience and Revolution," *Philosophy and Public Affairs* 1 (1972): 334.

The question remains today. Along with the citizens of other non-ideal democracies, Americans ought constantly to be struggling to decide between political actions that seek to preserve the best aspects of the prevailing order and those that, even if riskier, might help to construct a better, fairer, more inclusive alternative. At present, the full moral force of that decision is all too rarely felt. If the radical democratic tradition is to be renewed, it is this challenge that must once again become central to all of our political lives.

BIBLIOGRAPHY

Note: This bibliography contains only signed works cited in the text. Editorial and anonymous works are as referenced in the footnotes.

Manuscripts and Personal Papers

The Congress of Racial Equality Papers, Wisconsin State Historical Society, Madison, Wisconsin.

The Felix Frankfurter Papers, Law School Library, Harvard University, Cambridge, Massachusetts.

The Paul Kellogg Papers, Social Welfare History Archive, University of Minnesota, Minneapolis, Minnesota.

The League for Industrial Democracy Records, The Tamiment Institute, New York University, New York, New York.

The Learned Hand Papers, Law School Library, Harvard University, Cambridge, Massachusetts.

The Staughton Lynd Papers, Wisconsin State Historical Society, Madison, Wisconsin.

The Abraham J. Muste Papers, Labor-Management Document Center, Cornell University, Ithaca, New York.

The James Peck Papers, Wisconsin State Historical Society, Madison, Wisconsin.

The Students for a Democratic Society (SDS) Papers, The Tamiment Institute, New York University, New York, New York.

The Walter Weyl Papers, Rutgers University Library Special Collections, Rutgers University, New Brunswick, New Jersey.

Books, Pamphlets, Articles, and Motion Pictures

Ackerman, Bruce, and James Fishkin. *Deliberation Day.* New Haven: Yale University Press, 2004.

Adamic, Louis. "The Crisis is an Opportunity," *Common Ground* 1 (1940): 6273.

Addams, Jane et al., *Woman and the Larger Citizenship.* Chicago: Chicago Civics Society, 1914.

Adorno, Theodor W., Else Frenkel-Brunswik, Daniel J. Levinson, and R. Nevitt Sanford. *The Authoritarian Personality.* New York: Harper and Row, 1950.

Alexander, Franz. *Our Age of Unreason: A Study of Irrational Forces in Social Life.* Philadelphia: Lippincott, 1951.

Alinsky, Saul D. *Rules for Radicals: A Pragmatic Primer for Realistic Radicals.* New York: Vintage, 1971.

Allen, Barbara. "Martin Luther King's Civil Disobedience and the American Covenant Tradition," *Publius* 30 (2000): 71–113.

Allen, Danielle. *Talking to Strangers: Anxieties of Citizenship since* Brown versus Board of Education. Chicago: University of Chicago Press, 2004.

Altenbaugh, Richard J. *Education for Struggle: The American Labor Colleges of the 1920s and 1930s.* Phladelphia: Temple University Press, 1990.

Andre, Carl, Hans Haacke, John Parreault, and Cindy Nemser. "The Role of the Artist in Today's Society," *Art Journal* 34 (1975): 327–31.

Appleby, Joyce. *Liberalism and Republicanism in the Historical Imagination.* Cambridge, Mass.: Harvard University Press, 1992.

Arendt, Hannah. *Crises of the Republic.* New York: Harcourt, Brace, and Co., 1972.

Baker, Ray Stannard. *Following the Color Line.* New York: MacMillan, 1908.

Balakrishnan, Gopal. *The Enemy: An Intellectual Portrait of Carl Schmitt.* London: Verso, 2000.

Barber, Benjamin. *A Passion for Democracy: American Essays.* Princeton: Princeton University Press, 2001.

Barbour, Floyd D., ed. *The Black Power Revolt.* New York: Porter Sargent, 1968.

Barclay, Hartley. "We Sat Down with the Strikers and General Motors," *Mill and Factory* 2 (1937): 33–40.

Bartels, Larry. *Unequal Democracy: The Political Economy of the New Gilded Age.* Princeton: Princeton University Press, 2008.

Barton, Allen. "The Columbia Crisis," *Public Opinion Quarterly* 32 (1968): 333–51.

Baskin, Darryl. "Pluralism: Theory, Practice, and Ideology," *Journal of Politics* 32 (1970): 71–95.

Bassett, William R. *When the Workmen Help You Manage.* New York: Century, 1919.

Baylin, Bernard. *The Ideological Origins of the American Revolution.* Cambridge, Mass.: Harvard University Press, 1967.

Beard, Charles. "The Promise of American Life," *New Republic*, February 6, 1935, 350–53.

Bedau, Hugo, ed. *Civil Disobedience.* New York: Pegasus, 1968.

Belker, Loren. *Organizing for Political Victory.* Chicago: Nelson Hall, 1982.

Bell, Daniel. "The Power Elite Reconsidered," *American Journal of Sociology* 64 (1958): 238–50.

——. *The End of Ideology: On the Exhaustion of Political Ideas in the Fifties.* Glencoe, Ill.: Free Press, 1960.

Bellamy, Edward. *Looking Backward.* Toronto: G. N. Morang, 1897.

Bemis, Edward. "Tom L. Johnson's Achievements as Major of Cleveland," *Review of Reviews* (May 1911): 558–60.

Benhabib, Seyla, ed. *Democracy and Difference: Contesting the Boundaries of the Political.* Princeton: Princeton University Press, 1996.

Bensel, Richard F. *The Political Economy of American Industrialization, 1877–1920.* Cambridge: Cambridge University Press, 2000.

Berger, Bennett. *The Survival of a Counterculture.* Berkeley: University of California Press, 1981.

Berman, Ronald. "America in Fitzgerald," *Journal of Aesthetic Education* 36 (2002): 38–51.

Berman, William. *The Politics of Civil Rights in the Truman Administration.* Columbus: Ohio State University Press, 1970.

Bernstein, Irving. *Turbulent Years: A History of the American Worker, 1933–1941* Boston: Houghton Mifflin, 1970.

Bingham, Arthur. "Liberalism and Social Action," *Common Sense* 4 (1935): 28.

——."The State in Theory and Practice," *Common Sense* 4 (1935): 27–28.

——. "What Does American Mean?," *Common Sense* 4 (1935): 24–25.

Blake, Casey. "Public Intellectuals Without a Public," *American Quarterly* 41 (1989): 577–82.

Bliven, Bruce. "Franklin D. Roosevelt: Patron of Politics," *New Republic*, June 1, 1932, 62–64.

Bogardus, Ralph, and Fred Schroeder. "Andrew Wyeth and the Transcendental Tradition," *American Quarterly* 17 (1965): 559–67.

Bohman, James, and William Rehg. *Deliberative Democracy: Essays on Reason and Politics.* Cambridge, Mass.: The MIT Press, 1997.

Booth, Paul. "Facing the American Leviathan," *New Left Notes* 1 (1966): 1–8.

Bordeau, Edward J. "John Dewey's Ideas about the Great Depression," *Journal of the History of Ideas* 32 (1971): 67–84.

Botwinick, Aryeh, and William E. Connolly, eds. *Democracy and Vision: Sheldon Wolin and the Vicissitudes of the Political.* Princeton: Princeton University Press, 2001.

Bourne, Randolph. "American Uses for German Ideals," *New Republic*, July 1, 1916, 117–19.

Bradford, Carole. "Nonviolence on a New Orleans Picket Line," *CORE-lator* 88 (1961): 1–2.

Brandeis, Louis. "On Industrial Relations," in Brandeis, *The Curse of Bigness.* New York: Kennikat, 1962 [1914].

Brecht, Stefan. *The Bread and Puppet Theatre.* New York: Methuen, 1988.

Breines, Wini. *Community and Organization in the New Left, 1962–1968: The Great Refusal.* New York: Praeger, 1982.

Brennan, Mary C. *Turning Right: The Conservative Capture of the GOP* (Chapel Hill: University of North Carolina Press, 1995).

Brick, Harold. *Daniel Bell and the Decline of Intellectual Radicalism: Social Theory and Reconciliation in the 1940s.* Madison: University of Wisconsin Press, 1986.

Brienes, Paul. *Critical Interpretations: New Left Perspectives on Herbert Marcuse.* New York: Herder and Herder, 1971.

Brinkley, Alan. *Voices of Protest: Huey Long, Father Coughlin and the Great Depression.* New York: Vintage, 1983.

——. *The End of Reform: New Deal Liberalism in Depression and War.* New York: Alfred Knopf, 1995.

——. *Liberalism and its Discontents.* Cambridge, Mass.: Harvard University Press, 1998.

Bronner, Stephen Eric. "Reconstructing the Experiment: Politics, Ideology, and the American New Left," *Social Text* 8 (1984): 127–41.

Burke, Kenneth. "Liberalism's Family Tree," *New Republic*, March 4, 1936, 115–16.

Calhoun, Charles, ed. *Sociology in America.* Chicago: University of Chicago Press, 2007.

Calkins, Fay. *The CIO and the Democratic Party.* Chicago: University of Chicago Press, 1952.

Callahan, John F., ed. *The Collected Essays of Ralph Ellison*. New York: Random House, 2003.

Calvert, Greg. "Participatory Democracy, Collective Leadership and Political Responsibility," *New Left Notes* 2, no. 45 (1967): 1–7.

———. *Democracy from the Heart: Spiritual Values, Decentralism, and Democratic Idealism in the Movement of the 1960s*. Eugene, Ore.: Communitas, 1991.

Camus, Albert. *The Rebel*. London: Penguin, 2000 [1961].

———. *The Plague*. London: Penguin, 2002 [1947].

Cantwell, Robert. *When We Were Good: The Folk Revival*. Cambridge, Mass.: Harvard University Press, 1996.

Carey, Gordon. "New Freedom Task Force in the South," *CORE-lator* 99 (1963): 1–2.

Carmichael, Stokely. *Power and Racism*. Nashville: Southern Student Organising Committee, 1966.

Carson, Claybourne. *In Struggle: SNCC and the Black Awakening of the 1960s*. Cambridge, Mass.: Harvard University Press, 1981.

Case, Clarence. *Non-Violent Coercion: A Study in Methods of Social Pressure*. London: George Allen and Unwin, 1923.

Chamberlain, John. "A Planned Society," *Modern Quarterly* 6 (1932): 116–18.

———. *Farewell to Reform: The Rise, Life, and Decay of the Progressive Mind in America*. New York: John Day and Co., 1933.

Chambers, Simone. "Deliberative Democratic Theory," *Annual Review of Political Science* 6 (2003): 307–26.

Chase, Stuart. *A New Deal*. New York: MacMillan, 1932.

———. "A New Deal for America: The Road to Revolution," *New Republic*, July 6, 1932, 199–201.

———. "On the Paradox of Plenty," *New Republic*, January 18, 1933, 258–60.

———. *Roads to Agreement*. New York: Harpers, 1951.

Ciepley, David. *Liberalism in the Shadow of Totalitarianism*. Cambridge, Mass.: Harvard University Press, 2006.

Cohen, Lizabeth. *Making a New Deal: Industrial Workers in Chicago, 1919–1939*. New York: Oxford University Press, 1999.

Commons, John R. *Myself*. Madison: University of Wisconsin, Press, 1964 [1934].

Connolly, William E. *Pluralism*. Durham, N.C.: Duke University Press, 2005.

Cooley, Charles. *Social Organization*. New York: Charles Scribner's Sons, 1902.

Croly, Herbert. *The Promise of American Life*. New York: MacMillan, 1909.

———. "State Political Reorganization," *Proceedings of the American Political Science Association* 8 (1911): 122–35.

———. *Progressive Democracy*. New York: MacMillan, 1914.

———. "The Obligation of the Vote," *New Republic*, October 9, 1915, 5–10.

———. "The Future of the State," *New Republic*, September 15, 1917, 179–83.

Cywar, Alan. "John Dewey in World War One," *American Quarterly* 21 (1969): 578–94.

Daalder, Hans, ed. *Comparative European Politics: The Story of a Profession*. London: Pinter, 1997.

Dahl, Robert. *A Preface to Democratic Theory*. Chicago: University of Chicago Press, 1956.

———. *Who Governs? Democracy and Power in an American City*. New Haven: Yale University Press, 1961.

Davis, Harry R., and Robert C. Good, eds. *Reinhold Niebuhr on Politics*. New York; Charles Scribner's Sons, 1960.

Davis, Jerome. "Moral Man and Immoral Society," *Annals of the American Academy of Political and Social Science* 166 (1933): 231.

Dawley, Alan. *Struggles for Justice: Social Responsibility and the Liberal State.* Cambridge, Mass.: Belknap, 1991.

Denning, Michael. *The Cultural Front.* London: Verso, 1997.

Derber, Milton. *The American Idea of Industrial Democracy, 1865–1965.* Chicago and Urbana: University of Illinois Press, 1970.

Dewey, John. "A New Social Science," *New Republic,* April 6, 1918, 292–94.

———. *Reconstruction in Philosophy.* London: University of London Press, 1921.

———. *Human Nature and Conduct.* New York: Modern Library, 1922.

———. "Public Opinion," *New Republic,* May 3, 1922, 286–88.

———. "Social Change and its Human Direction," *Modern Quarterly* 5 (1930): 422–25.

———. "Prospects for a Third Party," *New Republic,* July 27, 1932, 278–79.

———. "The Imperative Need for a New Radical Political Party," *Common Sense* 2 (1933): 6–7.

———. "Why I am Not a Communist," *Modern Monthly* 8 (1934), 135–37.

———. "The Future of Liberalism," *Journal of Philosophy* 22 (1935): 225–30.

———. "Democracy is Radical," *Common Sense* 6 (1937): 10–11.

———. *The Public and its Problems.* Chicago: Gateway, 1946 [1927].

———. *Lectures in China.* Honolulu: University of Hawaii Press, 1973 [1920].

———. *Liberalism and Social Action.* Amherst, Mass.: Prometheus, 2000 [1935].

Dewey, John and John H. Tufts. *Ethics.* New York: MacMillan, 1908.

Dickstein, Morris. *Gates of Eden: American Culture in the Sixties.* New York: Basic, 1977.

———, ed. *The Revival of Pragmatism: New Essays on Social, Thought, Law and Culture.* Durham: University of North Carolina Press, 1997.

Diggins, John Patrick. "Knowledge and Sorrow: Louis Hartz's Quarrel with American History," *Political Theory* 16 (1988): 355–76.

———. "From Pragmatism to Natural Law: Walter Lippmann's Quest for the Foundations of Legitimacy," *Political Theory* 19 (1991): 519–38.

———. "Power and Suspicion: The Perspectives of Reinhold Niebuhr," *Ethics and International Affairs* 6 (1992): 141–61.

———. "Philosophy Without Foundations, Politics With Illusions," *Reviews in American History* 12 (1993): 116–20.

DiNunzio, Maurice, ed. *Theodore Roosevelt: An American Mind.* New York: Penguin, 1995.

Divine, Robert. *The Reluctant Belligerent: American Entry into World War II.* New York: John Wiley, 1979.

Dryzek, John. *Deliberative Democracy and Beyond: Liberals, Critics, Contestations.* Oxford: Oxford University Press, 2000.

———. "Deliberative Democracy in Divided Societies: Alternatives to Agonism and Analgesia," *Political Theory* 33 (2005): 218–42.

Dubofsky, Melvyn. *When Workers Organize: New York City in the Progressive Era.* Amherst: University of Massachusetts Press, 1968.

DuBois, W. E. B. *The Philadelphia Negro: A Social Study.* Philadelphia: Published for the University, 1899.

———. "Close Ranks," *Crisis* 8 (1918): 111.

Dunn, John. *The Cunning of Unreason: Making Sense of Politics.* London: HarperCollins, 2000.

Eisen, Jonathan, and David Steinberg. "The Student Revolt Against Liberalism," *Annals of the American Academy of Political and Social Science* 382 (1969): 83–94.

Ekrich, Arthur. *Progressivism in America: A Study from Theodore Roosevelt to Woodrow Wilson.* New York: New Viewpoints, 1974.

Eliot, Charles W. *The Future of Trade-Unionism and Capitalism in a Democracy.* New York: Putnam, 1910.

Elliot, William Y. *The Pragmatic Revolt in Politics: Syndicalism, Fascism and the Constitutional State.* New York: MacMillan, 1928.

Ellis, Mark. " 'Closing Ranks' and 'Seeking Honors': W. E. B. Du Bois in World War I," *Journal of American History* 79 (1992): 96–124.

Ellis, Richard J. "Romancing the Oppressed: The New Left and the Left Out," *Review of Politics* 58 (1996): 109–54.

Ellison, Ralph W. *Essays: Second Series.* London: Geoffrey Chapman, 1949.

———. *Invisible Man.* New York: Vintage, 1995 [1952].

von Eschen, Donald, Jerome Kirk, and Maurice Pinard. "The Disintegration of the Negro Non-Violent Movement," *Journal of Peace Research* 6 (1969): 215–34.

Estlund, David. *Democratic Authority: A Philosophical Framework.* Princeton: Princeton University Press, 2008.

Fairclough, Adam. "Martin Luther King Jr. and the Quest for Nonviolent Social Change," *Phylon* 47 (1986): 1–15.

Fanon, Frantz. *The Wretched of the Earth.* London: Penguin, 2001 [1965].

Farber, David. *Chicago '68.* Chicago: University of Chicago Press, 1988.

Farmer, James. *Freedom — When?* New York: Random House, 1965.

———. *Lay Bare the Heart: An Autobiography of the Civil Rights Movement.* Austin: Texas Christian University Press, 1985.

Farrell, James J. *The Spirit of the Sixties: Making Postwar Radicalism.* New York: Routledge, 1997.

Feffer, Andrew. "The Presence of Democracy: Deweyan Exceptionalism and Communist Teachers in the 1930s," *Journal of the History of Ideas* (2005): 79–97.

Feinman, Ronald. *Twilight of Progressivism: The Western Republican Senators and the New Deal.* Baltimore: The Johns Hopkins University Press, 1981.

Feldman, Paul. "The Pathos of Black Power," *Dissent* 14 (1967): 69–79.

Fine, Nathan. *Labor and Farmer Parties in the United States, 1828–1928.* New York: Russell and Russell, 1961.

Fine, Sidney. *Sit-Down: The General Motors Strike of 1936–1937.* Ann Arbor: University of Michigan Press, 1969.

Fink, Leon. *Progressive Intellectuals and the Dilemmas of Democratic Commitment.* Cambridge, Mass.: Harvard University Press, 1997.

Finkelstein, Leon, ed., *Thirteen Americans: Their Spiritual Biographies.* New York: Institute for Religious and Social Studies, 1950.

Fishkin, James. *Democracy and Deliberation: New Directions for Democratic Reform.* New Haven: Yale University Press, 1991.

Fitzgerald, F. Scott. *Tales of the Jazz Age.* New York: Charles Scribner's Sons, 1923.

Flacks, Richard. "On the Uses of Participatory Democracy," *Dissent* 8 (1966): 701–9.

Fleischman, Harry. *Norman Thomas: A Biography.* New York: W. W. Norton, 1967.

Foley, Barbara. "The Rhetoric of Anti-Communism in *Invisible Man*," *College English* 59 (1997): 530–47.

Foner, Eric. *The Story of American Freedom.* New York: W. W. Norton, 1998.

Forcey, Charles. *The Crossroads of Liberalism: Croly, Weyl, Lippmann, and the Progressive Era 1900–1925*. New York: Oxford University Press, 1965.

Forcey, James. *United States 1967: High Tide of Black Resistance*. New York: Students for a Democratic Society, 1967.

Fowler, Robert Booth. *Believing Skeptics: American Political Intellectuals, 1945–1964*. Westport: Greenwood, 1978.

Fox, Richard. "Reinhold Niebuhr and the Emergence of the Liberal Realist Faith, 1930–1945," *Review of Politics* 38 (1976): 244–65.

Frank, Waldo. *The Re-discovery of America*. New York: Charles Scribner's Sons, 1929.

———. "Will Fascism Come to America?," *Modern Monthly* 8 (1934): 464–66.

Fraser, Steve, and Gary Gerstle, eds. *The Fall of the New Deal Order, 1930–1960*. Princeton: Princeton University Press, 1989.

Frazier, Clyde. "Between Obedience and Revolution," *Philosophy and Public Affairs* 1 (1972): 315–34.

Fuller, Helen. "Southern Students Take Over: The Creation of the Beloved Community," *New Republic*, May 2, 1960, 14–16.

Fung, Archon. "Deliberation Before the Revolution," *Political Theory* 33 (2005): 397–419.

———. *Empowered Participation: Reinventing Urban Democracy*. Princeton: Princeton University Press, 2006.

Fung, Archon, and Erik Olin Wright, eds. *Deepening Democracy: Institutional Innovations in Empowered Participatory Governance*. London: Verso, 2003.

Gastil, John, and Peter Levine, eds. *The Deliberative Democracy Handbook: Strategies for Effective Civic Engagement in the Twenty-First Century*. San Francisco: Jossey-Bass, 2005.

Gaus, Gerald F. *Contemporary Theories of Liberalism*. London: Sage, 2003.

Gerstle, Gary. "The Politics of Patriotism: Americanization and the Formation of the CIO," *Dissent* 33 (1986): 84–92.

———. *Working-Class Americanism: The Politics of Labor in a Textile City, 1914–1960*. New York: Cambridge University Press, 1989.

———. "The Protean Character of American Liberalism," *American Historical Review* 99 (1994): 1043–73.

———. "Liberty, Coercion, and the Making of Americans," *Journal of American History* 84 (1997): 524–58.

———. *American Crucible: Race and Nation in the Twentieth Century*. Princeton: Princeton University Press, 2002.

Gilens, Martin, "Inequality and Democratic Responsiveness," *Public Opinion Quarterly* 69 (2005): 778–96.

Gitlin, Todd. "Resistance and the Movement," *New Left Notes* 2, no. 11 (1967): 3–4.

———. *The Sixties: Years of Hope, Days of Rage*. New York: Bantam, 1987.

Gladstone, Jack A., ed. *States, Parties, and Social Movements*. Cambridge: Cambridge University Press, 2003.

Glantz, Oscar, "New Left Radicalism and Punitive Moralism," *Polity* 7, no. 3 (1975): 281–303.

Gleason, Arthur. "The Discovery," *Survey*, May 19, 1917, 151–59.

———. *Inside the British Isles*. New York: Century, 1917.

———. *What the Workers Want*. London: George Allen and Unwin, 1920.

Goebel, Thomas. "Becoming American: Ethnic Workers and the Rise of the CIO," *Labour History* 29 (1988): 173–98.

Goebel, Thomas. "A Case of Democratic Contagion: Direct Democracy in the American West, 1890–1920," *Pacific Historical Review* 66 (1997): 213–30.

Goldberg, Arthur J. *AFL-CIO Labor United.* New York: McGraw-Hill, 1957.

Goldberg, David J. *Discontented America: The United States in the 1920s.* Baltimore: The Johns Hopkins University Press, 1999.

Goldfield, Mike. "What is a Radical Perspective?," *New Left Notes* 2, no. 5 (1967): 3–6.

Goldwin, Robert A., ed. *Civil Disobedience: Five Essays.* Kenyon, Ohio: Public Affairs Conference Center, 1968.

Good, Tom. "Ideology and SDS," *New Left Notes* 1, no. 29 (1966): 5.

Goodman, Walter. *The Committee: The Extraordinary Career of the House Committee on Un-American Activities.* New York: Farrar, Straus, and Giroux, 1968.

Gordon, Max. "Radicalism: Old and New," *New Left Notes* 1, no. 29 (1966): 1–10.

Gorer, Geoffrey. *The American People.* New York: W. W. Norton, 1948.

Graham, Otis. *Encore for Reform: Old Progressives and the New Deal.* New York: Oxford University Press, 1967.

Gray, John. *Enlightenment's Wake: Politics and Culture at the Close of the Modern Age* New York: Routledge, 1995.

Greene, Julie. *Pure and Simple Politics: The American Federation of Labor and Political Mobilization.* New York: Cambridge University Press, 1998.

Gregg, Richard B. *Non-Violent Resistance.* New York: MacMillan, 1935.

Griffith, Robert. "The Selling of America: The Advertising Council and American Politics, 1942–1960," *Business History Review* 57 (1986): 388–412.

Gruening, Martha. "Non-Violent Resistance," *New Republic*, May 22, 1935, 55.

Guess, Raymond. *Philosophy and Real Politics.* Princeton: Princeton University Press, 2008.

Guidry, John A., and Mark Q. Sawyer. "Contentious Pluralism: The Public Sphere and Democracy," *Perspectives on Politics* 1 (2003): 273–89.

Gutmann, Amy, and Dennis Thompson, *Democracy and Disagreement.* Cambridge, Mass.: Harvard University Press, 1996.

———. *Why Deliberative Democracy?* Princeton: Princeton University Press, 2004.

Haber, Al. "Radical Education Project," *New Left Notes* 1, no. 10 (1964): 2.

Habermas, Jürgen. *Communication and the Evolution of Society.* Boston: Beacon, 1979.

Halliwell, Steve. "Personal Liberation and Social Change," *New Left Notes* 2, no. 30 (1967), 1.

Hampshire, Stuart. "In Defence of Radicalism," *Dissent* 3 (1956): 170–76.

Harlam, Louis R., and Raymond W. Smock, eds. *The Booker T. Washington Papers.* Chicago: University of Chicago Press, 1979.

Harland, H. Gordon. *The Thought of Reinhold Niebuhr.* New York: Oxford University Press, 1960.

Harrington, Michael. *The Other America: Poverty in the United States.* New York: MacMillan, 1962.

Hartz, Louis. "American Political Thought and the American Revolution," *American Political Science Review* 46 (1952): 321–42.

———. *The Liberal Tradition in America: An Interpretation of American Political Thought since the Revolution.* New York: Harcourt, Brace, and Co., 1955.

Hartz, Louis et al. "Goals for Political Science: A Discussion," *American Political Science Review* 45 (1951): 1001–15.

Haslach, Henry. "Thoughts on Leadership," *New Left Notes* 2, no. 24 (1967): 4–5.

Hawley, Ellis. *The Great War and the Search for a Modern Order*. New York: St Martin's, 1979.

Hawthorn, Geoffrey, ed. *Bernard Williams: In the Beginning Was the Deed—Realism and Moralism in Political Argument*. Princeton: Princeton University Press, 2005.

Hayden, Casey. "Notes on Organizing Poor Southern Whites," *ERAP Newsletter*, August 27, 1965, 7–11.

Hayden, Tom. *Revolution in Mississippi: A Special Report*. New York: Students for a Democratic Society, 1960.

———. *Reunion: A Memoir*. New York: Random House, 1988.

———. *Radical Nomad: C. Wright Mills and his Times*. Boulder, Colo.: Paradigm, 2006.

Hayden, Tom et al. *The Port Huron Statement*. New York: Thunder's Mouth Press, 2005 [1962].

Hensen, Pat, and Ken McEldowney. "A Statement of Values," *New Left Notes* 1, no. 42 (1966): 5.

Heseltine, William. "Coercion in American Life," *Liberation* 2 (1957), 12–19.

Hilton, Oscar A. "Public Opinion and Civil Liberties in Wartime, 1917–1919," *Southwestern Social Science Quarterly* 28 (1947): 201–24.

Hofstadter, Richard. *The Age of Reform: From Byran to FDR*. New York: Alfred A. Knopf, 1955.

Holland, Catherine. "Democracy Beside Itself," *Political Theory* 34 (2006): 488–98.

Holmes, Stephen. *Passions and Constraint: On the Theory of Liberal Democracy*. Chicago: University of Chicago Press, 1995.

Homan, Paul. "Economic Planning: The Proposals and the Literature," *Quarterly Review of Economics* 47 (1932): 102–22.

Honig, Bonnie. *Political Theory and the Displacement of Politics*. Ithaca: Cornell University Press, 1993.

———. "Between Deliberation and Decision: Political Paradox in Democratic Theory," *American Political Science Review* 101 (2007): 1–17.

Hook, Sidney. "The Nonsense of the Whole," *Modern Quarterly* 5 (1930): 506–9.

———. "On Workers' Democracy," *Modern Monthly* 8 (1934): 529–44.

Hoopes, James. *Community Denied: The Wrong Turn of Pragmatic Liberalism*. Ithaca: Cornell University Press, 1998.

Horowitz, Irving, ed. *Power, Politics, and People: The Collected Essays of C. Wright Mills*. New York: Ballantine, 1964.

Horton, Carol. *Race and the Making of American Liberalism*. Oxford: Oxford University Press, 2005.

Howe, Frederic. *The City: Hope of Democracy*. New York: Charles Scribner's Sons, 1905.

Howe, Irving. "The Negro Revolution," *Dissent* 10 (1963): 205–14.

———. *A Margin of Hope: An Intellectual Autobiography* (San Diego: Harcourt, Brace, and Co., 1993).

Hughan, Jessie. "Guildsmen and American Socialism," *Intercollegiate Socialist* 7 (1920): 165–68.

Jacobs, Ron. *The Way the Wind Blew: A History of the Weather Underground*. London: Verso, 1997.

James, William. *Some Problems in Philosophy*. London: Longmans, 1911.

Johnpoll, Bernard, and Mark Yenburgh, eds. *The League for Industrial Democracy: A Documentary History*. Westport, Conn.: Greenwood, 1980.

Johnson, Alvin. "Revolutionary Reconstruction," *New Republic*, December 15, 1920, 80.

Johnson, Gerald. *This American People*. New York: Harper and Row, 1951.

Jones, Richard. "Social Centers and Hymns for Democracy," *Common Good* (December 1913): 3–5.

Jordan, John. *Machine-Age Ideology: Social Engineering and American Liberalism, 1911–1939*. Chapel Hill: University of North Carolina Press, 1994.

Jordan, William. " 'The Damnable Dilemma': African-American Accommodation and Protest during World War I," *Journal of American History* 81 (1995): 1562–83.

Kaplan, Sidney. "Social Engineers as Saviors: Effects of World War I on Some American Liberals," *Journal of the History of Ideas* 17 (1956): 347–69.

Kateb, George. *Patriotism, and Other Mistakes*. New Haven: Yale University Press, 2006.

Katznelson, Ira. "At the Court of Chaos: Political Science in an Age of Perpetual Fear," *Perspectives on Politics* 5 (2007): 3–15.

Kefley, Charles, and Robert W. Bertall, eds. *Reinhold Niebuhr: His Religious, Social, and Political Thought*. New York: MacMillan, 1956.

Kennedy, David. *Over Here: The First World War and American Society*. New York: Oxford University Press, 1980.

———. *Freedom from Fear: The American People in Depression and War*. New York: Oxford University Press, 1999.

Keyssar, Alexander. *The Right to Vote: The Contested History of Democracy in the United States*. New York: Basic, 2000.

King, Desmond. *In the Name of Liberalism: Illiberal Social Policy in the USA and Britain*. Oxford: Oxford University Press, 1998.

———. *Making Americans: Immigration, Race, and the Origins of the Diverse Democracy*. Cambridge, Mass., and London: Harvard University Press, 2000.

King, Martin Luther, Jr. "The Social Organization of Nonviolence," *Liberation* 4 (1959): 5–6.

King, Richard H. *Civil Rights and the Idea of Freedom*. Oxford: Oxford University Press, 1992.

Kitchell, Mark. *Berkeley in the Sixties*. Berkeley: Kitchell Films, 1990.

Klarman, Michael. *From Jim Crow to Civil Rights: The Supreme Court and the Struggle for Racial Equality*. New York: Oxford University Press, 2004.

Kloppenberg, James T. *Uncertain Victory: Social Democracy and Progressivism in European and American Thought, 1870–1920*. New York: Oxford University Press, 1986.

———. "Deliberative Democracy and Judicial Supremacy," *Law and History Review* 13 (1995): 393–411.

Kornbluh, Joyce L. *Rebel Voices: An IWW Anthology*. Ann Arbor: University of Michigan Press, 1968.

Kornweibel, Theodore. "Apathy and Dissent: Black America's Negative Responses to World War I," *South Atlantic Quarterly* 80 (1981): 322–38.

Korstad, Robert, and Nelson Lichtenstein. "Opportunities Found and Lost: Labor, Radicals, and the Early Civil Rights Movement," *Journal of American History* 75 (1988): 786–811.

Krafft, John. "Thomas Pynchon," *Social Text* 10 (1984): 283–86.

Kurtz, Paul. "Misuses of Civil Disobedience," *Dissent* 17 (1970): 66 -67.

Lamont, Margaret. "The Negro Unionist," *Modern Quarterly* 10 (1937): 15.

Larmore, Charles. "Political Liberalism," *Political Theory* 18 (1990): 339–60.

Lasch-Quinn, Elizabeth. *Black Neighbors: Race and the Limits of Reform in the American Settlement House Movement, 1890–1945.* Chapel Hill: University of North Carolina Press, 1993.

Laue, James. "The Changing Character of Negro Protest," *Annals of American Academy of Political and Social Science* 357 (1965): 119–26.

Lens, Sidney. "Participatory Democracy," *New Left Notes* 1, no. 3 (1966): 3.

Leopold, David, and Marc Stears, eds. *Political Theory: Methods and Approaches* Oxford: Oxford University Press, 2008.

Levin, Murray. *Political Hysteria in America: The Democratic Capacity for Repression* New York: Basic, 1971.

Levy, David. *Herbert Croly of the New Republic: The Life and Thought of an American Progressive.* Princeton: Princeton University Press, 1985.

Lewis, John L. "The Struggle for Industrial Democracy," *Common Sense* 6 (1937): 8–11.

Lichtenstein, Nelson. *State of the Union: A Century of American Labor.* Princeton: Princeton University Press, 2002.

Lichtenstein, Nelson, and Howell Harris, eds. *Industrial Democracy in America: The Ambiguous Promise.* Cambridge: Cambridge University Press, 1996.

Lilla, Mark. *The Reckless Mind: Intellectuals in Politics.* London: Granta, 2001.

Ling, Peter. *Martin Luther King, Jr.* London: Routledge, 2002.

Link. Arthur S. "What Happened to the Progressive Movement in the 1920s?," *American Historical Review* 64 (1959): 833–51.

Lippmann, Walter. *Preface to Politics.* New York: Michael Kennerley, 1913.

———. *Drift and Mastery: An Attempt to Diagnose the Current Unrest.* New York: Michael Kennerley, 1914.

———. "A Clue," *New Republic,* April 14, 1917, 316–17.

———. "Unrest," *New Republic,* November 12, 1919, 315–22.

———. *Public Opinion.* New York: MacMillan, 1922.

———. *The Phantom Public: A Sequel to Public Opinion.* New York: MacMillan, 1925.

———. "Planning in an Economy of Abundance," *Atlantic Monthly* 159 (1937): 46.

Lovett, Robert Morss. "The Farmer-Labor Fiasco," *New Republic,* July 18, 1923, 198–200.

———. "Liberalism and the Class War," *Modern Quarterly* 4 (1928): 191–94.

———. "The Coming of a New Party," *New Republic,* August 31, 1932, 77–78.

———. "Politics and Ethics," *New Republic,* January 18, 1933, 273.

Lupia, Arthur, and John Matsusaka. "Direct Democracy: New Approaches to Old Questions," *Annual Review of Political Science* 7 (2004): 463–82.

Lustig, R. Jeffrey. *Corporate Liberalism: The Origins of Modern American Political Theory.* Berkeley: University of California Press, 1982.

Lynd, Staughton. "SNCC: Beginning of an Ideology," *Activist* 5 (1965): 12.

———. "The New Radicals and Participatory Democracy," *Dissent* 12 (1965): 324–33.

———. ed., *Non-Violence in America: A Documentary History.* New York: Bobbs-Merrill, 1966.

———. "The New Left," *Annals of the American Academy of Political and Social Science* 382 (1969): 64–72.

———. "We Are All Leaders": *The Alternative Unionism of the Early 1930s.* Urbana and Chicago: University of Illinois Press, 1996.

Lyons, Paul. *New Left, New Right and the Legacy of the Sixties.* Philadelphia: Temple University Press, 1996.

MacDonald, David. "Why I am No Longer a Socialist," *Liberation* 3 (1957): 4–6.

Macedo, Stephen, ed. *Deliberative Politics: Essays on Democracy and Disagreement.* New York: Oxford University Press, 1999.

MacGilvary, Eric. *Reconstructing Public Reason.* Cambridge, Mass.: Harvard University Press, 2004.

MacIntyre, Alasdair. *Herbert Marcuse.* New York: Viking, 1970.

———. *Dependent Rational Animals: Why Human Beings Need the Virtues.* Chicago and La Salle, Ill.: Open Court, 2006.

Magrath, C. Peter. "Democracy in Overalls: The Futile Quest for Union Democracy," *Industrial and Labor Relations Review* 12 (1959): 503–25.

Manin, Barnard. "On Legitimacy and Political Deliberation," *Political Theory* 15 (1987): 338–68.

Mansbridge, Jane. "The Limits of Friendship," *Nomos* 16 (1975): 48–51.

———, ed. *Beyond Self-Interest.* Chicago: University of Chicago Press, 1990.

Mason, Robert. *Richard Nixon and the Quest for a New Majority.* Chapel Hill: University of North Carolina Press, 2004.

Mattson, Kevin. *Creating a Democratic Public: The Struggle for Urban Participatory Democracy during the Progressive Era.* University Park: University of Pennsylvania Press, 1998.

McAdam, Doug, Sidney Tarrow, and Charles Tilly, *Dynamics of Contention.* Cambridge: Cambridge University Press, 2001.

McCormick, Richard L. *The Party Period and Public Policy: American Politics from the Age of Jackson to the Progressive Era.* New York: Oxford University Press, 1986.

McDonagh, Eileen L. "The "Welfare Rights State" and the "Civil Rights State": Policy Paradox and State Building in the Progressive Era," *Studies in American Political Development* 7 (1993): 225–74.

McGerr, Michael. *The Decline of Popular Politics: The American North, 1865–1928.* New York: Oxford University Press, 1986.

———. *A Fierce Discontent: The Rise and Fall of the Progressive Movement in America, 1870–1920.* Oxford: Oxford University Press, 2003.

McMillan John, and Paul Buhle, eds. *The New Left Revisited.* Philadelphia: Temple University Press, 2003.

McWilliams, Wilson Carey. "Reinhold Niebuhr: New Orthodoxy for Old Liberalism," *American Political Science Review* 56 (1962): 874–85.

Mead, Margaret. *And Keep Your Powder Dry.* New York: William Morrow, 1942.

Medearis, John. "Social Movements and Deliberative Democratic Theory," *British Journal of Political Science* 35 (2004): 53–75.

Meier, August, and Elliott Rudwick. *CORE: A Study in the Civil Rights Movement, 1942–1968.* New York: Oxford University Press, 1973.

Metz, Harold, and Charles Thompson. *Authoritarianism and the Individual.* Washington, D.C.: Brookings Institution, 1950.

Micklenberg, Julia. *Learning from the Left: Children's Literature, the Cold War, and Radical Politics in the United States.* New York: Oxford University Press, 2006.

Milkis, Sidney, and James Mileur, eds. *Progressivism and the New Democracy.* Amherst: University of Massachusetts Press, 1999.

Miller, Arthur. *A View from the Bridge*. New York: Viking, 1955.

Miller, David. *Citizenship and National Identity*. Cambridge: Polity, 1997.

Miller, James. *Democracy Is in the Streets: From Port Huron to the Siege of Chicago*. Cambridge, Mass.: Harvard University Press, 1987.

Mills, Charles. "Ideal Theory as Ideology," *Hypatia* 20 (2005): 165–84.

Mills, C. Wright. *The New Men of Power: America's Labor Leaders*. New York: Harcourt, Brace, and Co., 1948.

———. *The Power Elite*. New York: Oxford University Press, 1956.

———. *The Sociological Imagination*. Oxford: Oxford University Press, 1959.

Molotch, Harvey. "Radicals in Urban Politics," *Contemporary Sociology* 4 (1974): 434–35.

Morgenthau, Hans. *Scientific Man versus Power Politics*. Chicago: University of Chicago Press, 1946.

Morone, James. *The Democratic Wish: Popular Participation and the Limits of American Government*. New Haven: Yale University Press, 1998.

Morris, Aldon. "Black Southern Student Sit-In Movement," *American Sociological Review* 46 (1981): 744–67.

———. "A Retrospective on the Civil Rights Movement," *Annual Review of Sociology* 25 (1999).

Mouffe, Chantal. *The Return of the Political*. London: Verso, 1993.

———. *Politics and Passions: The Stakes of Democracy*. London: Centre for the Study of Democracy, 2002.

Murphy, John. "The IWW: An American Export," *Socialist Review* 11 (1920): 196–200.

Murray, Paul. "An American Credo," *Common Ground* 5 (1945): 22–24.

Muste, Abraham J. "Militant Progressivism?," *Modern Quarterly* 4 (1928): 332–41.

———. "The Problem of Violence" *Modern Monthly* 10 (1937): 7–9.

———. *Where Are We Now?* New York: Liberation, 1956.

Myrdal, Gunnar. "The Negro Problem: A Prognosis," *New Republic*, July 9, 1962: 43–5.

Myrdal, Gunnar, with the assistance of Richard Sterner and Arnold Rose. *An American Dilemma: The Negro Problem and Modern Democracy* 1. New York: Harper and Brothers, 1944.

Nagel, Julia, ed. *Student Power*. New York: Merlin, 1969.

Nagel, Thomas. "Moral Conflict and Political Legitimacy," *Philosophy and Public Affairs* 16 (1987): 215–40.

Naveh, Eyal J. *Reinhold Niebuhr and Non-Utopian Liberalism: Beyond Illusion and Despair* (Brighton: Sussex Academic, 2002).

Neufeld, Maurice. "The Persistence of Ideas in the American Labor Movements," *Industrial and Labor Relations Review* 35 (1982): 207–20.

Neumann, Franz. "Anxiety in Politics," *Dissent* 2 (1955): 133–43.

Niebuhr, Reinhold. *Moral Man and Immoral Society*. New York: Continuum, 2005 [1932].

———. "After Capitalism—What?," *World Tomorrow* 16 (1933): 203–21.

———. *The Children of Light and the Children of Darkness: A Vindication of Democracy and A Critique of Its Traditional Defenders*. New York: Charles Scribner's Sons, 1944.

———. ed., *Civil Disobedience: Is it the Answer to Jim Crow?* New York: Non-Violent Action Committee, 1947.

———. *The Irony of American History*. New York: Charles Scribner's Sons, 1951.

Nuechterlein, James. "Arthur M. Schlesinger Jr. and the Discontents of Postwar American Liberalism," *Review of Politics* 39 (1977): 3–40.

———. "The Dream of Scientific Liberalism: The New Republic and American Progressive Thought, 1914–1920," *Review of Politics* 42 (1980): 167–90.

Oglesby, Carl. "Liberalism and the Corporate State," *New Left Notes* 1, no. 1 (1966): 2–3.

———. "An Open Letter: Dear McCarthy Supporters," *New Left Notes* 3, no. 26 (1968): 2–7.

Olson, Joel. "The Freshness of Fanaticism: The Abolitionist Defense of Zealotry," *Perspectives on Politics* 5 (2007): 685–702.

Oppenheimer, Martin. "Alienation or Participation: The Sociology of Participatory Democracy," *New Left Notes* 1, no. 45 (1966): 4–5.

Pape, L. M. "Moral Man and Immoral Society," *American Political Science Review* 27 (1933): 296–97.

Patrick, G.T.W. "The Play of a Nation," *Scientific Monthly* (October 1921): 350–62.

Patten, Simon Nelson. *The New Basis of Civilization*. New York: MacMillan, 1907.

Peck, Jim. *Cracking the Color Line: Non-Violent Direct Action Methods of Eliminating Racial Discrimination*. New York: CORE, 1962.

Pells, Richard. *Radical Visions and American Dreams: Culture and Social Thought in the Depression Years*. Middletown, Conn.: Wesleyan University Press, 1973.

Pennington, John. "RYM Walks Out," *New Left Notes* 5, no. 1 (1969): 1–2.

Perlstein, Daniel. "Teaching Freedom: SNCC and the Creation of the Mississippi Freedom Schools," *History of Education Quarterly* 30 (1990): 297–324.

———. "Minds Stayed on Freedom: Politics and Pedagogy in the African-American Freedom Struggle," *American Educational Research Journal* 39 (2002): 249–77.

Peterson, Gordon. "Changing Consciousness," *New Left Notes* 2, no. 5 (1967): 7.

Philp, Mark. *Political Conduct*. Cambridge, Mass.: Harvard University Press, 2007.

Pinchot, Amos. *History of the Progressive Party, 1912–1916*. New York: New York University Press, 1958.

Plotke, David. "The Wagner Act, Again: Politics and Labor, 1935–1937," *Studies in American Political Development* 4 (1989): 105–56.

Pocock, John G. A. *The Machiavellian Moment: Florentine Political Thought and the Atlantic Political Tradition*. Princeton: Princeton University Press, 1975.

Polletta, Francesca. *Freedom Is an Endless Meeting: Democracy in American Social Movements*. Chicago: Chicago University Press, 2002.

Pope, Jim. "Worker Lawmaking, Sit-Down Strikes, and the Shaping of American Industrial Relations, 1935–1958," *Law and History Review* 24 (2006): 45–113.

Potter, David M. "The End of Ideology," *New Republic*, May 23, 1960.

Power, Paul. F. "Morphologies of Nonviolent Action," *Journal of Conflict Resolution* 12 (1968): 381–85.

Pynchon, Thomas. *The Crying of Lot 49*. Philadelphia: Lippincott, 1966.

———. *Slow Learner*. London: Vintage, 2000 [1960].

Rabban, David M. *Free Speech in its Forgotten Years*. Cambridge: Cambridge University Press, 1997.

Ranney, Austin. *Curing the Mischiefs of Faction: Party Reform in America*. Berkeley: Unviersity of California Press 1975.

Rawls, John. *A Theory of Justice*. Oxford: Oxford University Press, 1972.

———. *Political Liberalism*. New York: Columbia University Press, 1993.

————. *The Law of Peoples and Other Essays*. Cambridge, Mass.: Harvard University Press, 2002.

Record, Jane, and Wilson Record. "Ideological Forces and the Negro Protest," *Annals of the American Academy of Political and Social Science* 357 (1965): 89–96.

Resek, Carl, ed. *The Progressives*. Indianapolis and New York: Bobbs-Merrill, 1967.

Reuther, Victor. *The Brothers Reuther and the Story of the UAW: A Memoir*. Boston: Houghton Miffin, 1976.

Rice, Daniel F. *Reinhold Niebuhr and John Dewey: An American Odyssey*. Albany: State University of New York Press, 1993.

Rich, Marvin. "The Congress on Racial Quality and its Strategy," *Annals of the American Academy of Political and Social Science* 357 (1965): 113–18.

Riesman, David. "Neighbors in Utopia," *New Republic*, April 30, 1951.

Rochester, Stuart. *American Liberal Disillusionment in the Wake of World War I*. University Park: Pennsylvania State University Press, 1977.

Rodman, Selden. "After Roosevelt, the Kingfish?," *Common Sense* 2 (1933): 15–17.

Rodgers, Daniel T. "In Search of Progressivism," *Reviews in American History* 10 (1982): 112–32.

————. *Atlantic Crossings: Social Politics in a Progressive Age*. Cambridge, Mass.: Belknap, 1998.

Rogers, Bob. "Referendum Democracy: A Proposal," *New Left Notes* 1, no. 29 (1966): 8–9.

Rorabaugh, W. J. *Berkeley at War*. New York: Oxford University Press, 1989.

Rorty, Richard. *Achieving Our Country: Leftist Thought in Twentieth-Century America*. Cambridge, Mass.: Harvard University Press 1998.

Rose, Tom. "Reflections on Violence," *New Left Notes* 3, no. 7 (1968): 6–7.

Rosenblum, Nancy. "Strange Attractors: How Individualists Connect to Form Democratic Unity," *Political Theory* 18, no. 4 (1990): 576–86.

————. *On the Side of the Angels: An Appreciation of Parties and Partisanship*. Princeton: Princeton University Press, 2008.

Royce, Josiah. *The Philosophy of Loyalty*. New York: MacMillan, 1908.

Runciman, David. *The Politics of Good Intentions: History, Fear and Hypocrisy in the New World Order*. Princeton: Princeton University Press, 2006.

————. *Political Hypocrisy: The Mask of Power, From Hobbes to Orwell and Beyond*. Princeton: Princeton University Press, 2008.

Rustin, Bayard. "Jail vs Bail," *Student Voice* 1 (1960): 12.

Ryan, Alan. *John Dewey and the High Tide of American Liberalism*. New York: W. W. Norton, 1995.

Sabl, Andrew. "Looking Forward to Justice: Rawlsian Civil Disobedience and its Non-Rawlsian Lessons," *Journal of Political Philosophy* 9 (2001): 307–30.

————. "Community Organizing as Tocquevillian Politics: The Art, Practices, and Ethos of Association," *American Journal of Political Science* 46 (2002): 1–19.

Sale, Kirkpatrick. *SDS*. New York: Vintage, 1974.

Sandel, Michael. *Democracy's Discontent: America in Search of a Public Philosophy*. Cambridge, Mass.: Harvard University Press, 1996.

Schaeffer, Robert. *America in the Great War: The Rise of the War Welfare State*. New York: Oxford University Press 1991.

Schafer, Axel R. "W. E. B. Du Bois, German Social Thought, and the Racial Divide in American Progressivism, 1892–1909," *Journal of American History* 88 (2001): 925–49.

Schlesinger, Arthur M., Jr. *The Vital Center: The Politics of Freedom.* Boston: Houghton Mifflin, 1949.

———. *The American as Reformer.* Cambridge, Mass.: Harvard University Press, 1950.

Schlesinger, Arthur M., Jr., and Morton White, eds. *Paths of American Thought* Boston: Houghton Muffin, 1963.

Schmalhausen, Samuel. "The Logic of Leninism," *Modern Quarterly* 5 (1930): 454–60.

Schmitt, Carl. *The Concept of the Political.* Chicago: University of Chicago Press, 1995 [1932].

Schneck, Stephen. "Connolly's Postmodern Liberalism," *Review of Politics* 51 (1989): 281–90.

Schrecker, Ellen. *Many Are the Crimes: McCartyhism in America.* Boston: Little, Brown, 1998.

Schwartz, Delmore. "Films," *New Republic,* April 25, 1955.

Schwartz, Joseph M. *The Permanence of the Political.* Princeton: Princeton University Press, 1995.

Scolum, J. David. *Rebel Without a Cause: Approaches to a Maverick Masterwork.* Albany: State University of New York Press, 2005.

Shafer, Byron. *The Two Majorities and the Puzzle of Modern American Politics.* Lawrence: University Press of Kansas, 2003.

Shapiro, Herbert. *White Violence and Black Response: From Reconstruction to Montgomery.* Amherst: University of Massachusetts Press, 1988.

Shapiro, Ian. *The State of Democratic Theory.* Princeton: Princeton University Press, 2003.

Shaw, George Bernard. "The Future of Democracy," *New Republic,* April 14, 1937.

Sheingate, Adam. "Political Entrepreneurship, Institutional Change, and American Political Development," *Studies in American Political Development* 17 (2003): 185–203.

Shelton, Willard. "The CIO's Own Revolution," *New Republic,* January 3, 1949.

Shepard, William. "The Tools for Ethnic Democracy," *Common Ground* 4 (1944): 3–17.

Shklar, Judith. *After Utopia: The Decline of Political Faith.* Princeton: Princeton University Press, 1957.

———. *Ordinary Vices.* Cambridge, Mass.: Harvard University Press, 1984.

———. "Emerson and the Inhibitions of Democracy," *Political Theory* 18 (1990): 601–14.

Simich, J. L., and Rick Tilman, "Radicalism vs. Liberalism: C. Wright Mills' Critique of John Dewey's Ideas," *American Journal of Economics and Sociology* 37 (1978): 413–30.

Sinclair, Upton. *The Jungle.* New York: Doubleday, Page, and Co., 1906.

———. *The Industrial Republic: A Study of the America of Ten Years Hence.* New York: Doubleday, Page, and Co., 1907.

Sklar, Kathryn Kish. *Florence Kelley and the Nation's Work: The Rise of Women's Political Culture, 1830–1900.* New Haven: Yale University Press, 1995.

Sklar, Martin. *The Corporate Reconstruction of American Capitalism, 1880–1916.* Cambridge: Cambridge University Press 1988.

Skocpol, Theda, and Kenneth Feingold. "State Capacity and Economic Intervention in the Early New Deal," *Political Science Quarterly* 97 (1982): 255–78.

Skowronek, Stephen. *The Making of the American State: The Expansion of National Administrative Capacities, 1877–1920.* Cambridge: Cambridge University Press, 1992.

Smith, Allen. "Present at the Creation and Other Myths: The Port Huron Statement and the Origins of the New Left," *Peace and Change* 25 (2000): 339–62.

Smith, Rogers M. "Beyond Tocqeuville, Myrdal, and Hartz: The Multiple Traditions in America," *American Political Science Review* 87 (1993): 549–66.

———. *Civic Ideals: Conflicting Visions of Citizenship in U.S. History.* New Haven: Yale University Press, 1998.

———. *Stories of Peoplehood: The Politics and Morals of Political Membership.* Cambridge: Cambridge University Press, 2003.

Snyder, Robert, Rebecca Zurier, and Virgina Mecklenburg. *Metropolitan Lives: The Ashcan Artists and Their New York.* Washington, D.C.: National Museum of American Art, 1996.

Soule, George. *A Planned Society.* New York: MacMillan, 1932.

———. "Roosevelt Confronts Capitalism," *New Republic,* October 18, 1933, 269–70.

———. *The Coming American Revolution.* London: George Routledge and Sons, 1934.

———. *The Future of Liberty.* New York: MacMillan, 1936.

Sparks, Holloway. "Dissident Citizenship: Democratic Theory, Political Courage, and Activist Women," *Hypatia* 12 (1997): 74–110

Spenser, Gerald. "A New Deal," *Modern Quarterly* 6 (1932): 102–3.

Spinrad, William. "Assessing the 1960s," *Sociological Forum* 5, no. 3 (1990): 511–16.

Spitz, David. "Democracy and the Problem of Civil Disobedience," *American Political Science Review* 48 (1954): 386–403.

———, ed. *Political Theory and Social Change.* New York: Atherton, 1967.

Stears, Marc. *Progressives, Pluralists and the Problems of the State: Ideologies of Reform in the United States and Britain, 1909–1926.* Oxford: Oxford University Press, 2002.

———. "Liberalism and the Politics of Compulsion," *British Journal of Political Science* 37 (2007): 533–53.

———. "The Liberal Tradition and the Politics of Exclusion," *Annual Review of Political Science* 10 (2007): 85–101.

Steel, Ronald. *Walter Lippmann and the American Century.* London: Bodley Head, 1980.

Steppan-Nottis, Judith, and Maurice Zeitlan. "Insurgency, Radicalism and Democracy in America's Industrial Unions," *Social Forces* 75 (1996): 1–32.

Stettner, Edward. *Shaping Modern Liberalism: Herbert Croly and Progressive Thought.* Lawrence: University Press of Kansas, 1994.

Sunstein, Cass R. *The Partial Constitution.* Cambridge, Mass.: Harvard University Press, 1994.

———. *Republic.com.* Princeton: Princeton University Press, 2001.

Tarde, Gabriel. *The Laws of Imitation.* New York: Henry Holt and Co., 1903.

Tarrow, Sidney. *Power in Movement: Social Movements and Contentious Politics.* Cambridge: Cambridge University Press, 1998.

Taylor, A.J.P. "Up From Utopia: How Two Generations Have Survived Their Wars," *New Republic,* October 30, 1950.

Taylor, O. H. "The Economics of a Free Society: Four Essays," *Quarterly Journal of Economics* 62 (1948): 641–70.

Tead, Ordway. "Guilds for America," *Intercollegiate Socialist* 7 (1919): 31–33.

———. *New Adventures in Democracy: Practical Applications of the Democratic Ideal.* New York: McGraw Hill, 1939.

Thelen, David. "Social Tensions and the Origins of Progressivism," *Journal of American History* 56 (1969): 323–41.

Thompson, John, and David Held, eds. *Habermas: Critical Debates.* Cambridge, Mass.: The MIT Press, 1982.

Thompson, John A. *Reformers and War: Progressive Publicists and the First World War.* Cambridge: Cambridge University Press, 1987.

Thompson, Hunter S. *The Great Shark Hunt: Strange Tales from a Strange Time.* London: Picador, 1979.

Tobin, Eugene. *Organize or Perish: America's Independent Progressives, 1913–1933.* Westport, Conn.: Greenwood, 1986.

de Tocqueville, Alexis. *Democracy in America*, vol. 2. London: Everyman Library, 1994 [1840].

Trilling, Lionel. *The Liberal Imagination.* New York: Viking, 1950.

Tugwell, Rexford. "The Design of Government," *Political Science Quarterly* 48 (1933): 321–32.

Tully, James. "The Agonic Freedom of Citizens," *Economy and Society* 28 (1999): 161–82.

———. "Political Philosophy as a Critical Activity," *Political Theory* 30 (2002): 533–55.

Umoja, Akinyele O. "The Ballot and the Bullet: A Comparative Analysis of Armed Resistance in the Civil Rights Movement," *Journal of Black Studies* 29 (1999): 558–78.

Veblen, Thorstein. *The Engineers and the Price System.* New York: B. W. Hubesch, 1921.

Viguerie, Richard. *The New Right: We're Ready to Lead.* Falls Church, Va.: Viguerie, 1981.

Villard, Oswald. "A Letter FDR Ought to Write," *Nation*, June 6, 1937, 218–20.

Vonnegut, Kurt. *God Bless You, Mr. Rosewater.* New York: Dell, 1965.

Waldron, Jeremy. *Law and Disagreement.* Oxford: Oxford University Press, 1999.

Wall, Wendy L. *Inventing the "American Way": The Politics of Consensus From the New Deal to the Civil Rights Movement.* Oxford: Oxford University Press, 2008.

Wallas, Graham. *Human Nature and Politics.* London: Constable and Co., 1910.

Walzer, Michael. "A Cup of Coffee and a Seat," *Dissent* 7 (1960): 111–20.

———. "The Idea of Resistance," *Dissent* 7 (1960): 369–73.

———. "A Day in the Life of the Socialist Citizen: Two Cheers for Participatory Democracy," *Dissent* 15 (1968): 243–47.

———. "Violence: The Police, the Militants, and the Rest of Us," *Dissent* 18 (1971): 119–27.

———. *Politics and Passion: Toward a More Egalitarian Liberalism.* New Haven: Yale University Press, 2004.

Ward, J. A. *Unspeakable Silences: The Realism of James Agee, Walker Evans, and Edward Hopper.* Baton Rouge: Louisiana State University Press, 1985.

Ware, Alan. *The American Direct Primary: Party Institutionalization and Transformation in the North.* Cambridge: Cambridge University Press, 2002

Warren, Mark. "What Can Democratic Participation Mean Today?," *Political Theory* 30 (2002): 677–700.

Weinstein, James. *The Decline of Socialism in America, 1912–1925.* New Brunswick, N.J.: Rutgers University Press, 1984.

Weissberg, Robert. "Politicized Pseudo Science," *PS: Political Science and Politics* 39 (2004): 33–37.

Weissman, Steve. "Civil Disobedience in Action," *SDS Bulletin* 4 (1965): 6–7.

Wells, H. G. Wells. *The Future in America: A Search After Realities*. New York: Harpers, 1906.

West, Cornel. "The Paradox of Afro-American Rebellion," *Social Text* 9 (1984): 44–58.

———. *Democracy Matters: Winning the Fight Against Imperialism*. New York: Penguin, 2005.

Westbrook, Robert. *John Dewey and American Democracy*. Ithaca: Cornell University Press, 1991.

Weyl, Walter. *The New Democracy: An Essay on Certain Political and Economic Tendencies in the United States*. New York: MacMillan, 1912.

———. "The Sovereign Crowd," *New Republic*, October 9, 1915, 266–67.

White, Morton. "Of Moral Predicaments," *New Republic*, May 5, 1952.

White, Willard A. *The Old Order Changeth: A View of American Democracy*. New York: MacMillan, 1910.

Wiebe, Robert H. *The Search for Order, 1877–1920*. New York: Hill and Wang, 1967.

Wilde, Norman. "Plural Sovereignty," *Journal of Philosophy* 16 (1919): 658–65.

———. *The Ethical Basis of the State*. Princeton: Princeton University Press, 1924.

Wiley, Malcolm. "Review: The Phantom Public and Others," *Social Forces* 4 (1926): 854–58.

Willhoite, Fred H., Jr. "Albert Camus' Politics of Rebellion," *Western Political Quarterly* 14 (1961): 400–414.

Wolfe, Jesse. "Ambivalent Man: Ellison's Rejection of Communism," *African American Review* 34 (2000): 621–37.

Wolin, Sheldon. *Politics and Vision: Continuity and Vision in Western Political Thought*. Princeton: Princeton University Press, 1960.

———. *Democracy Incorporated: Managed Democracy and the Specter of Inverted Totalitarianism*. Princeton: Princeton University Press, 2008.

Zieger, Robert H. *The CIO, 1935–1955*. Chapel Hill: University of North Carolina Press, 1995.

Zinn, Howard. *SNCC: The New Abolitionists*. Boston: Beacon, 1964.

Zinn, Howard, ed. *New Deal Thought*. New York: Bobbs-Merrill, 1969.

INDEX